NEW YORK POLITICS AND GOVERNMENT

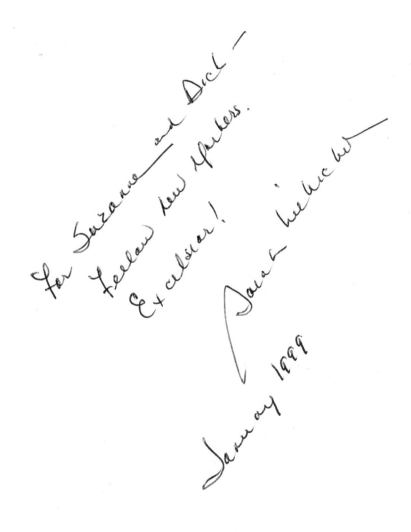

SARAH F. LIEBSCHUTZ
WITH ROBERT W. BAILEY,
JEFFREY M. STONECASH, JANE SHAPIRO ZACEK,
AND JOSEPH F. ZIMMERMAN

New York Politics & Government

COMPETITION AND COMPASSION

UNIVERSITY OF NEBRASKA PRESS
LINCOLN AND LONDON

⊗ The paper in this book
meets the minimum requirements of
American National Standard
for Information Sciences—Permanence of
Paper for Printed Library Materials,
ANSI Z39.48-1984.

Library of Congress
Cataloging-in-Publication Data
Liebschutz, Sarah F.
New York politics and government :
competition and compassion /
Sarah F. Liebschutz ; with
Robert W. Bailey . . . [et al.].
p.   cm.—(Politics and governments
of the American states)
Includes bibliographical
references and index.
ISBN 0-8032-2925-9 (cl : alk. paper). —
ISBN 0-8032-7971-X (pa : alk. paper)
I. New York (State)—Politics and government.
I. Bailey, Robert W., 1957–
II. Title.   III. Series.
JK3416.L48   1998
320.9747—dc21
97-268980 CIP

For Jennifer and Rebecca

CONTENTS

TABLES, MAPS, AND FIGURES

Series Preface

The purpose of this series is to provide information and interesting books on the politics and governments of the fifty American states, books that are of value not only to the student of government but also to the general citizens who want greater insight into the past and present civic life of their own states and of other states in the federal union. The role of the states in governing America is among the least well known of all the 85,006 governments in the United States. The national media focus attention on the federal government in Washington DC, and local media focus attention on local government. Meanwhile, except when there is a scandal or a proposed tax increase, the workings of state government remain something of a mystery to many citizens—out of sight, out of mind.

In many respects, however, the states have been, and continue to be, the most important governments in the American political system. They are the main building blocks and chief organizing governments of the whole system. The states are the constituent governments of the federal union, and it is through the states that citizens gain representation in the national government. The national government is one of limited, delegated powers; all other powers are possessed by the states and their citizens. At the same time, the states are the empowering governments for the nation's 84,955 local governments—counties, municipalities, townships, school districts, and special districts. As such, states provide for one of the most essential and ancient elements of freedom and democracy, the right of local self-government.

Although, for many citizens, the most visible aspects of state government are state universities, some of which are the most prestigious in the world, and state highway patrol officers, with their radar guns and handy ticket books, state governments provide for nearly all domestic public services.

Whether elements of those services are enacted or partly funded by the federal government and actually carried out by local governments, it is state government that has the ultimate responsibility for ensuring that Americans are well served by all their governments. In so doing, all of the American states are most democratic, more prosperous, and better governed than most of the world's nation-states.

This is a particularly timely period in which to publish a series of books on the governments and politics of each of the fifty states. Once viewed as the "fallen arches" of the federal system, states today are increasingly seen as energetic, innovative, and fiscally responsible. Some states, of course, perform better than others, but that is to be expected in a federal system. Each state is unique in its own right. It is our hope that this series will shed light on the public life of each state and that, taken together, the books will contribute to a better, more informed understanding of the states themselves and of their often pivotal roles in the world's first and oldest continental-sized federal democracy.

DANIEL J. ELAZAR

Series Introduction

The American domain is given form and character as a federal union of fifty different states whose institutions order the American landscape. The existence of these states made possible the emergence of a nation where liberty, not despotism, reigns and self-government is the first principle of order. The great American republic was born in its states, as its very name signifies. America's first founding was repeated on thirteen separate occasions over 125 years, from Virginia in 1607 to Georgia in 1732. Each colony became a self-governing commonwealth. Its revolution and second founding was made by those commonwealths, now states, acting in congress, and its constitution was written together and adopted separately. As the American tide rolled westward from the Atlantic coast, it absorbed new territories by organizing thirty-seven more states over the next 169 years.

Most of the American states are larger and better developed than most of the world's nations. Territorially, New York is a medium-sized state, but in terms of its population and its gross domestic product it ranks with the larger nations of the world and is a power in its own right.

From its earliest settlement, New York was a major gateway into the North American continent, whose importance increased over the years. While the state is no longer the largest of the fifty (both California and Texas are now larger), New York City is still the center of immigration into the United States, not only from Europe but from Asia and Latin America as well. Wave after wave of immigrants have come to the Big Apple and have periodically reshaped the character of its diversity. New York surpassed Pennsylvania in this respect at the very beginning of the nineteenth century, and while the peak years of immigration came at the end of that century, throughout the twentieth century New York has continued to play the major role.

Because of the particular character of its diversity, New York has become the quintessential Eastern state in the minds of most Americans, although in fact that image is most appropriate to the New York City metropolitan area, while the rest of the state is quite different in most respects.

The American states exist because each is a unique civil society within their common American culture. First given political form, they then acquired their other characteristics. Each has its own constitution and laws, its own political culture and history, its own relationship to the federal union.

It is in and through the states, no less than the nation, that the great themes of American life play themselves out. The advancing frontier and the continuing experience of Americans as a frontier people, the drama of American ethnic blending, the tragedy of slavery and racial discrimination, all have found their expression in the states.

Some states began as commonwealths devoted to establishing model societies based on a religiously informed vision (Massachusetts, Connecticut, Rhode Island). At the other end of the spectrum, Hawaii is a transformed pagan monarchy. At least three states were independent for a significant period of time (Hawaii, Texas, and Vermont). Others were created from nothing by hardly more than a stroke of the pen (the Dakotas, Idaho, Nevada). Several are permanently bilingual (California, Louisiana, and New Mexico). Each has its own landscape and geographic configuration, which time and history transform into a specific geo-historical location. In short, the diversity of the American people is expressed in no small measure through their states, each of whose politics and government have their own fascination.

New York Politics and Government is the seventeenth book in the Politics and Governments of the American States series of the Center for the Study of Federalism and University of Nebraska Press. The aim of the series is to provide books on the politics and government of the individual states of the United States that will appeal to three audiences: political scientists, their students, and the wider public in each state. Each volume in the series examines the specific character of one state, looking at the state as a polity—its political culture, traditions and practices, constituencies and interest groups, constitutional and institutional frameworks.

Each book in the series reviews the political development of the state to demonstrate how the state's political institutions and characteristics have evolved from the first settlement to the present, presenting the state in the context of the nation and its particular section of the country and reviewing the roles and relations of the state vis-à-vis its sister states and the federal government. The state's constitutional history, its traditions of constitution-making and constitutional change, are examined and related to the workings of the state's political institutions and processes. State–local relations, local government, and community politics are examined. Finally, each volume reviews the state's policy concerns and their implementation, from the budgetary process to particular substantive policies. Each book concludes by summarizing the principal themes and findings to draw conclusions about the current state of the state, its continuing traditions, and emerging issues. Each volume also contains a bibliographic survey of the existing literature on the state and a guide to the use of that literature and state government documents in learning more about the state and political system. Although the books in the series are not expected to be uniform, all focus on the common themes of federalism, constitutionalism, political culture, and the continuing American frontier, to provide a framework within which to consider the institutions, routines, and processes of state government and politics.

FEDERALISM

Both the greatest conflicts of American history and the most prosaic day-to-day operations of American government are closely intertwined with American federalism—the form of American government (in the eighteenth-century sense of the term, which includes both structure and process). American federalism has been characterized by two basic tensions. One is between state sovereignty—the view that in a proper federal system, authority and power over most domestic affairs should be in the hands of the states—and national supremacy—the view that the federal government has a significant role to play in domestic matters affecting the national interest. The other tension is between dual federalism—the idea that a federal system functions best when the federal government and the states function as separately as possible, each in its own sphere—and cooperative federalism—the view that federalism works best when the federal government and the states, while preserving their own institutions, cooperate closely on the implementation of joint or shared programs.

CONSTITUTIONALISM

The American constitutional tradition grows out of the Whig understanding that civil societies are founded by political covenant, entered into by the first founders, and reaffirmed by subsequent generations, through which the powers of government are delineated and limited and the rights of the constituting members clearly proclaimed in such a way as to provide moral and practical restraints on governmental institutions. That constitutional tradition was modified by the federalists, who accepted its fundamental principals but strengthened the institutional framework designed to provide energy in government while maintaining the checks and balances they saw as needed to preserve liberty and republican government. At the same time, they turned nonbinding declarations of rights into enforceable constitutional articles.

American state constitutions reflect a melding of these two traditions. Under the U.S. Constitution, each state is free to adopt its own constitution, provided that it establishes a republican form of government. Some states have adopted highly succinct constitutions, such as the 6,600-word Vermont Constitution of 1793 that is still in effect with only fifty-two amendments. Others are just the opposite—for example, Georgia's Ninth Constitution, adopted in 1976, has 583,000 words. State constitutions are potentially far more comprehensive than the federal constitution, which is one of limited, delegated powers. Because states are plenary governments, they automatically possess all powers not specifically denied them by the U.S. Constitution or their citizens. Consequently, a state constitution must be explicit about limiting and defining the scope of governmental powers, especially on behalf of individual liberty. So state constitutions normally include an explicit declaration of rights, almost invariably broader than the first ten amendments to the U.S. Constitution.

The detailed specificity of state constitutions affects the way they shape each state's governmental system and patterns of political behavior. Unlike the open-endedness and ambiguity of many portions of the U.S. Constitution, which allow for considerable interpretative development, state organs, including state supreme courts, generally hew closely to the letter of their constitutions because they must. This means that formal change of the constitutional document occurs more frequently through constitutional amendment, whether initiated by the legislature, special constitutional commissions, constitutional conventions, or direct action by the voters, and, in a number of states, the periodic writing of new constitutions. As a result, state constitutions have come to reflect quite explicitly the changing conceptions of government that have developed over the course of American history.

Overall, six different state constitutional patterns have developed. One is the commonwealth pattern, developed in New England, which emphasizes Whig ideas of the constitution as a philosophic document designed first and foremost to set a direction for civil society and to express and institutionalize a theory of republican government. A second is the constitutional pattern of the commercial republic. The constitutions fitting this pattern reflect a series of compromises required by the conflict of many strong ethnic groups and commercial interests generated by the flow of heterogeneous streams of migrants into particular states and the early development of large commercial and industrial cities in those states.

The third constitutional pattern is found in the South and can be described as the southern contractual pattern. Southern state constitutions are used as instruments to set explicit terms governing the relationship between polity and society, such as those that protected slavery or racial segregation, or those that sought to diffuse the formal allocation of authority in order to accommodate the swings between oligarchy and factionalism characteristic of southern state politics. Of all the southern states, only Louisiana stands somewhat outside this pattern, since its legal system was founded on the French civil code. Its constitutions have been codes—long, highly explicit documents that form a pattern in and of themselves.

A fifth constitutional pattern is that found frequently in the states of the Far West, where the state constitution is first and foremost a frame of government explicitly reflecting the republican and democratic principles dominant in the nation in the late nineteenth century, but emphasizing the structure of state government and the distribution of powers within that structure in a direct, businesslike manner. Finally, the two newest states, Alaska and Hawaii, have adopted constitutions following the managerial pattern developed and promoted by twentieth-century constitutional reform movements in the United States. Their constitutions are characterized by conciseness, broad grants of power to the executive branch, and relatively few structural restrictions on the legislature. They emphasize natural resource conservation and social legislation.

New York's constitutions have been of the second pattern since New York seems to have been destined to be a commercial republic from the first. While its original Dutch charter made some effort to build a communitarian society, even before the Dutch were replaced by the English the commercial interests of the colony's settlers had made most of the communitarian dimensions of its basic law a dead letter and in subsequent constitutions eliminated them. What emerged instead out of those Dutch and later influences was a liberal democratic political design of a commercial republic, not incompatible with its commercial goals, to insure a liberal political order grounded in certain humanitarian expectations. Those two principles have walked hand in hand throughout New York's constitutional and political history.

THE CONTINUING AMERICAN FRONTIER

For Americans, the very word *frontier* conjures up the images of the rural-land frontier of yesteryear—of explorers and mountain men, of cowboys and Indians, of brave pioneers pushing their way west in the face of natural obstacles. Later, Americans' picture of the frontier was expanded to include the inventors, the railroad builders, and the captains of industry who created the urban-industrial frontier. Recently television has begun to celebrate the entrepreneurial ventures of the automobile and oil industries, portraying the magnates of those industries and their families in the same larger-than-life frame as once was done for the heroes of that first frontier.

As is so often the case, the media responsible for determining and catering to popular taste tell us a great deal about ourselves. The United States was founded with a rural-land frontier that persisted until World War I, more or less, spreading farms, ranches, mines, and towns across the land. Early in the nineteenth century, the rural-land frontier generated the urban frontier based on industrial development. The generation of new wealth through industrialization transformed cities from mere regional service centers into generators of wealth in their own right. That frontier persisted for more than a hundred years as a major force in American society as a whole and perhaps another sixty years as a major force in various parts of the country. The population movements and attendant growth on the urban-industrial frontier brought about the effective settlement of the United States in freestanding cities from coast to coast.

Between the world wars, the urban-industrial frontier gave birth in turn to a third frontier stage, one based on the new technologies of electronic communication, the internal combustion engine, the airplane, synthetics, and petrochemicals. These new technologies transformed every aspect of life and turned urbanization into metropolitanization. This third frontier stage generated a third settlement of the United States, this time in metropolitan regions from coast to coast, involving a mass migration of tens of millions of Americans in search of opportunity on the suburban frontier.

In the 1970s, despite the widespread "limits of growth" rhetoric, a fourth frontier stage was opened in the form of the rurban, or citybelt-cybernetic, frontier generated by the metropolitan-technological frontier just as the latter had been generated by its predecessor.

The rurban-cybernetic frontier first emerged in the Northeast, as did its predecessors, as the Atlantic Coast metropolitan regions merged into one another to form a six-hundred-mile-long megalopolis—a matrix of urban and suburban settlements in which the older central cities yielded importance if not prominence to smaller ones. It was a sign of the times that the computer was conceived at MIT in Cambridge, first built at the University of Illinois in Urbana, and developed at IBM in White Plains, three medium-sized cities that have become special centers in their own right. This in itself is a reflection of the two primary characteristics of the new frontier. The new loci of settlement are in medium-sized and small cities and in the rural interstices of the megalopolis.

The spreading use of computer technology is the most direct manifestation of the cybernetic tools that make such citybelts possible. Both the revival of small cities and the shifting of population growth into rural areas are as much a product of long-distance direct dialing, the fax, and the Internet as they are of the continued American longing for small-town or country living.

The new rurban-cybernetic frontier is finding its true form in the South and West, where these citybelt matrices are not being built on the collapse of earlier forms but are developing as an original form. The present Sunbelt frontier—strung out along the Gulf Coast, the southwestern desert, and the fringes of the California mountains—is classically megalopolitan in citybelt form and cybernetic with its aerospace-related industries and Sunbelt living made possible by air conditioning and the new telecommunications.

The continuing American frontier has all the characteristics of a chain reaction. In a land of great opportunity, each frontier, once opened, has generated its successor and, in turn, has been replaced by it. Each frontier has created a new America with new opportunities, new patterns of settlement, new occupations, new challenges, and new problems. As a result, the central political problem of growth is not simply how to handle the physical changes brought by each frontier, real as they are. It is how to accommodate newness, population turnover, and transience as a way of life. That is the American frontier situation.

New York, located in the mainstream of American life since it was settled, has passed through or entered each of the four frontier stages when they first appeared, has capitalized on each in turn, and has developed accordingly. Indeed, the history of New York is exemplary of each of the four stages, and New York has been a pioneer in all of them.

THE PERSISTENCE OF SECTIONALISM

Sectionalism—the expression of social, economic, and especially political differences along geographic lines—is part and parcel of American political life. The more or less permanent political ties that link groups of contiguous states together as sections reflect the ways in which local conditions and differences in political culture modify the impact of the frontier. This overall sectional pattern reflects the interaction of the three basic factors. The original sections were produced by the variations in the impact of the rural-land frontier on different geographic segments of the country. They, in turn, have been modified by the pressures generated by the various frontier stages. As a result, sectionalism is not the same as regionalism. The latter is essentially a phenomenon—often transient—that brings adjacent state, substate, or interstate areas together because of immediate and specific common interests. The sections are not homogeneous socioeconomic units sharing a common character across state lines but are complex entities combining highly diverse states and communities with common political interests that generally complement one another socially and economically.

Intrasectional conflicts often exist, but they do not detract from the long-term sectional community of interest. More important for our purposes, certain common sectional bonds give the states of each section a special relationship to national politics. This is particularly true in connection with those specific political issues that are of sectional importance, such as the race issue in the South, the problems of the megalopolis in the Northeast, and the problems of agriculture and agribusiness in the West.

The nation's sectional alignments are rooted in the three great historical, cultural, and economic spheres into which the country is divided. The greater Northeast includes all those states north of the Ohio and Potomac rivers and east of Lake Michigan gathered in these sections: New England, Middle Atlantic, and the Near West. The greater South includes the states below that line but east of the Mississippi—the Upper and Lower South plus Missouri, Arkansas, Louisiana, Oklahoma, and Texas. All the rest of the states compose the greater West, further divided into the Northwest and Far West.

As already mentioned, New York is the quintessential "East" and, since seizing the lead from Pennsylvania, has long dominated its section, the entire greater Northeast, and for a long time the country as a whole, at least economically and culturally. Indeed, its economic dominance extended over much of the country until after World War II. New York gained economic wealth and political power through its sectional position but also made enemies among those who viewed the state and especially New York City as examples of internal American colonialism from which they sought to emancipate themselves as soon as it became possible to do so. New York today is more a first among equals than a colonialist power. This change has led to shifts in the balance of power within the state as well as in the Union as a whole.

From the New Deal years through the 1960s, Americans' understanding of sectionalism was submerged by their concern with urban-oriented socio-economic categories, such as the struggle between labor and management or between the haves and have-nots in the big cities. Even the racial issue, once the hallmark of the greater South, began to be perceived in nonsectional terms as a result of black immigration northward. This is not to say that sectionalism ceased to exist as a vital force, only that it was little noted in those years.

Beginning in the 1970s, however, there was a resurgence of sectional feeling as economic social cleavages increasingly came to follow sectional lines. The sunbelt–frost belt division is the prime example of this new sectionalism. *Sunbelt* is the new code word for the Lower South, Western South, and Far West; *Frostbelt*, later replaced by *Rust belt*, is the code word for the New England, Middle Atlantic, and Great Lakes (Near Western) states. Not only is New York part of the frost belt, but it has been affected by its rust belt characteristics; the economy of its large and medium-sized cities has been badly hit by obsolescence as the successes of the urban-industrial frontier receded into history. Still, New York's favored east coast location has given it the opportunity to adapt to the changes in economic development and the political conflicts that flow from them.

THE VITAL ROLE OF POLITICAL CULTURE

The United States as a whole shares a general political culture that is rooted in two contrasting conceptions of the American polity order that can be traced back to the earliest settlement of the country. In the first, the polity is conceived as a marketplace in which the primary public relationships are products of bargaining among individuals and groups acting primarily out of self-interest. In the second, the polity is conceived to be a commonwealth, in which the whole people have an undivided interest, and the citizens cooperate in an effort to create and maintain the best government in order to implement certain shared moral principles. The influence of these two conceptions can be felt through American political history, sometimes in conflict and sometimes complementing each other.

This general political culture is a synthesis of three major political subcultures—individualistic, moralistic, and traditionalistic. Each reflects its own particular synthesis of the marketplace and the commonwealth. All three are of nationwide proportions, having spread, in the course of time, from coast to coast. At the same time, each subculture is strongly tied to specific sections of the country, reflecting the streams and currents of migration that have carried people of different origins and backgrounds across the continent in more or less orderly patterns.

New York, while predominantly individualistic in its political culture—indeed, almost in many parts of the state quintessentially so—has also had an infusion of the moralistic political culture as a result of the in-migration of New England Yankees, Dutch, Jews, and others. Since these in-migrants from moralistic political cultural backgrounds rather quickly established themselves as people of influence, they were able to introduce a moralistic leaven into what otherwise would have been a purely individualistic political culture. On the other hand, the quantitative majority of migrants into the state came from traditional or traditionalistic political cultures, whether from the Old World, from the American South, or from Latin America and the Caribbean. In their case, settlement in New York led to a transformation of their political cultures into individualistic ones, thus reenforcing the state's commercially grounded predilections for the marketplace.

THE EMPIRE STATE FACES A NEW MILLENNIUM

New York today is less an Empire State for the United States and more an Empire State for the world. Curiously enough, that shift has also made it more self-contained and self-aware as a state and perhaps even more greatly aware of its unity as a political community, competing and cooperating with the rest of the world. Since World War II when the United Nations headquarters was established in New York City, the state's international position, strong economically even earlier, became politically strong as well. For most of the state's inhabitants, New York's international position is a matter of pride but not of obvious personal impact, except when VIPs tie up Manhattan traffic. In fact, changes, particularly after the 1960s, have reduced the conflict between "New York City," meaning the metropolitan area, and "upstate," meaning everything from Putnam County north and westward. The impact of the metropolitan-technological and the rurban-cybernetic frontiers has blurred the differences between regions and given them common interests by forcing them to confront common problems. In a certain sense, New York is at present reconstituting itself accordingly, giving it a new sense of itself as a state.

Acknowledgments

New York's size and complexity are the characteristics that make it an intriguing state; they are also the qualities that make New York a challenging subject to "get one's arms around." I am grateful to Daniel J. Elazar and John Kincaid for inviting me to take on the challenge, and for their close reading and constructive, insightful comments on earlier versions of the manuscript. John Kincaid played a particularly key role in encouraging and helping me to shape the book's theme of competition and compassion.

I thank especially my collaborators, Bob Bailey, Jeff Stonecash, Jane Zacek, and Joe Zimmerman. They extended the breadth and depth of analysis with their contributions; their enthusiasm for the project and responsiveness to deadlines made for a pleasurable partnership.

My student research assistants Mary Hussong-Kallen, Jeffrey D. Cook, Kathleen A. Frank, and Sean Rickert all contributed in important ways. The comments of Justin L. Vigdor and Stephen L. Schechter on selected chapters were especially useful, as was the ongoing willingness of Gerald Benjamin to share his knowledge about New York politics.

Hundreds of New Yorkers—elected and appointed public, private, and nonprofit-sector officials—were interviewed for this book. We are indebted to them for their observations about and insights into various aspects of the history, politics, government, and public policy of the Empire State. Their contributions are specifically referenced throughout the book.

Finally, I am especially grateful for the support and encouragement of four generations of New Yorkers: Goldye K. Fisher, Sanford J. Liebschutz, Jane M. Liebschutz, David S. and Elizabeth H. Liebschutz, and the newest New Yorkers, Jennifer and Rebecca.

NEW YORK POLITICS AND GOVERNMENT

CHAPTER ONE

The Character of New York: Competition and Compassion

Sarah F. Liebschutz

"After living a dozen years in New York, I don't pretend to comprehend their politics," observed Oliver Wolcott, an early governor of Connecticut. "It is a labyrinth of wheels within wheels."[1] Two centuries later, New York's politics are still labyrinthine. They continue to reflect the ethnic, regional, and cultural diversity that has characterized the state since pre-Revolutionary times. Such diversity has shaped the character of New York, a character dominated by two values often at odds with each other: competition and compassion. For much of its history, when New York was America's most populous and powerful state, the two values coexisted more or less compatibly. Since the 1970s, and New York's fall from undisputed preeminence of size and economy, the coexistence between competiton and compassion has been sorely tested. As the twentieth century comes to a close, the tension between them is strong and played out overtly in the political arena.

NEW YORK: MANY NATIONS

New York is many nations. Its geography and its people are remarkable for their diversity. With nearly 18 million people and 47.7 thousand square miles of land, New York is the largest state in the northeastern United States. The New York landscape contains much more than Manhattan's concrete canyons and asphalt jungles. This fact seems to amaze many people— Americans and foreign visitors alike—who think New York and New York City are one and the same.

New York's geography is among the most beautiful and varied of all the fifty states. Its elevations range from Mt. Marcy in the Adirondack Mountains, at five thousand feet, to the Atlantic Ocean at sea level. New York is

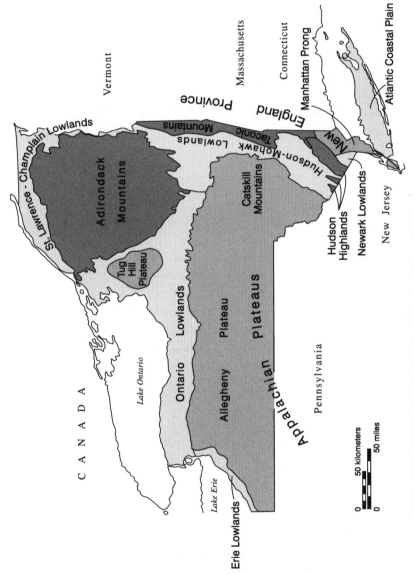

Map 1: The Geography of New York

Source: University of The State of New York, State Education Department, *Geology of New York*, 1991.

Table 1: Population Change in New York State, 1790–1990

Year	Population	Percent Change
1790	340,100	
1800	589,100	+75
1810	959,000	+62
1820	1,372,800	+43
1830	1,918,600	+39
1840	2,428,900	+27
1850	3,097,400	+27
1860	3,880,700	+25
1870	4,382,400	+13
1880	5,082,900	+16
1890	5,997,900	+18
1900	7,268,900	+21
1910	9,113,600	+25
1920	10,385,200	+14
1930	12,588,100	+21
1940	13,479,100	+ 7
1950	14,830,200	+10
1960	16,782,300	+13
1970	18,241,400	+ 9
1980	17,558,100	− 4
1990	17,990,455	+ 2

Source: Statistical Abstract of the United States.

bordered by Atlantic Ocean waters, the Great Lakes of Ontario and Erie, and the St. Lawrence Seaway; its land boundaries touch New Jersey, Pennsylvania, Connecticut, Massachusetts, Vermont, and the Canadian provinces of Ontario and Quebec. Within New York's borders are the mountainous Adirondack and Catskill parks and forests, the wine-growing terraces of the Finger Lakes and Long Island, the farms of the rural "North Country," the affluent suburbs of Westchester, and the urban centers of Albany, Binghamton, Buffalo, Rochester, Syracuse, Yonkers, and Utica, as well as New York City (see map 1).

New York was the most populous state in the nation from 1810 to 1970, when that distinction passed to California. During the 1970s, as shown in table 1, New York's longtime pattern of population growth was reversed dramatically. The state lost nearly 700,000 residents between 1970 and 1980; the decline was driven almost entirely by the loss of 10 percent of New York City's population. Thereafter, the state resumed its pattern of growth. But the rate of growth during the 1980s, 2.5 percent, was well below the national rate of nearly 10 percent. In 1990, the total population residing within New

York's boundaries was slightly under 18 million; it was still the second largest state, with Texas and Florida close on its heels. In 1994, the U.S. Bureau of the Census announced that Texas had overtaken New York; projections for the year 2000 showed Florida as challenger to New York as the nation's third largest state.

Ethnic Diversity

New York, originally settled by Algonkian Indians, has long been noteworthy for the diversity of its people. The five nations that would become the Iroquois Confederacy (Mohawk, Oneida, Onondaga, Cayuga, and Seneca tribes) arrived in the early 1300s, claiming the land from the Mohawk River to the Genesee River and moving the Algonkians south and east to the Hudson River Valley, Long Island, western New England, and eastern Pennsylvania.

In the early 1600s, the Dutch established the colony of New Netherland with trading posts on Manhattan Island and at Albany. The Dutch brought African slaves to New Amsterdam as early as 1626, in numbers large enough to comprise 10 percent of the population at that time, excluding the Indians.[2] The French and the British explored the North Country during this time, and Henry Hudson estimated the Indian population at approximately 30,000. The British conquered New Netherland in 1664 and named it New York in honor of its new proprietor—James, duke of York. New York City became an important port for supplying the British Empire with goods from the Western Hemisphere. The province of New York, however, did not become a large population and economic center until the early 1800s, with the construction of the Erie Canal linking the Great Lakes to the Hudson River and New York City.

By the early 1800s, the following groups had placed their cultural stamps on the areas in which they lived: the Poles in Buffalo; Swedes in Jamestown; Italians in Utica and Rochester, as well as on farms around Rome and Canastota; Irish and Dutch in Albany; Czechs in Binghamton; German Mennonites on farms in the Black River Valley; New Englanders ("Yankees") on Long Island; Palatine Germans in the Schoharie and Mohawk Valleys; Scots in the northern Mohawk Valley (although most had fled to Canada at the start of the Revolutionary War); Protestant Irish in Cherry Valley along the Hudson; and French Canadians in the North Country. While slaves and free black people did not, by and large, come to characterize regions, their numbers grew steadily throughout the state during the eighteenth century. The second federal census of 1800 counted 20,663 slaves and 8,439 slave owners, the largest number of whom were in Albany County.

"Give me your tired, your poor, your huddled masses yearning to breathe free," Emma Lazarus wrote in 1886 in poetry inscribed on the base of the Statue of Liberty.[3] And come they did! New York City, the welcoming gateway for the Dutch, English-Huguenots, and other Europeans in the eighteenth and nineteenth centuries, opened its arms wide to Irish, Italians, and Jews in the early twentieth century. While some immigrants dispersed to cities and towns upstate, most remained for a generation or more in New York City. "In the period between 1930 and 1960, for instance, one out of every six foreign-born Americans lived in New York City."[4]

Nearly a century later, David N. Dinkins, the first African-American mayor of New York City, eloquently declared: "I see New York as a gorgeous mosaic of race and religious faith, of national origin and sexual orientation, of individuals whose families arrived yesterday and generations ago, coming through Ellis Island or Kennedy Airport or on buses bound for the Port Authority."[5]

Immigration, Suburbanization, Interregional Shifts

Immigration, suburbanization, and interregional shifts have had profound impacts on the size and the character of New York's population. Of these, immigration was the key factor in the state's growth and diversity for most of its history. From the first national census in 1790 until 1930, New York State's population growth was fueled by immigration from abroad. The impact of the foreign-born population was particularly dramatic between 1900 and 1910, when the number of foreign-born persons grew from 1.2 million to nearly 2 million in New York City alone. Immigrants from abroad composed more than 30 percent of the state's population in 1910.

During the 1930s, 1940s, and 1950s, New York's foreign-born population declined, a result almost entirely due to the United States Immigration Act of 1924. Had it not been for this restrictive federal legislation, events in Europe—especially the Great Depression, the Spanish Civil War, the rise of fascism in Spain, Portugal, Germany, and Italy, and the Nazi invasion and occupation of most of Europe—would have produced a tidal wave of immigration. Unfortunately, unlike the Cubans and Haitians who came later, Europeans could not get on rafts and small boats and float across the Atlantic Ocean to seek refuge in the United States.

In 1965, when Nathan Glazer and Daniel Patrick Moynihan described the diversity of New York City's residents in *Beyond the Melting Pot*, they were portraying a city still dominated—numerically, geographically, and in other ways—by the children and grandchildren of Irish, Italian, and Jewish immigrants of the early 1900s.[6] The other two groups about whom Glazer and Moynihan wrote, African Americans, large numbers of whom had migrated from the South since the 1930s, and Puerto Ricans, were very recent migrants, struggling to establish themselves.

Beginning in 1965, changes to national immigration laws, deliberately intended to be less discriminatory toward non-Europeans, set new waves of immigration in motion. Unprecedented levels of immigration from Asia, the Caribbean, and South America, as well as Europe, were obvious in the significantly increased diversity and multiethnic character of New York City.[7] By 1980, nonnative persons had attained nearly 24 percent of New York City's population, the same percentage as in 1950; the same was true of their percentage of New York State's population, almost 14 percent.

Suburbanization and interregional shifts have also contributed importantly to New York's demographic diversity, especially since World War II. Suburbanization—the movement of city residents to areas surrounding older cities—resulted in population decline after 1950 in New York's largest cities—Albany, Binghamton, Buffalo, New York City, Rochester, Syracuse, Utica, and Yonkers. Interregional movements, primarily of blacks from the South to the North between 1900 and 1960 and of non-Hispanic whites moving from Snowbelt states to Sunbelt states since 1960, were also important. New York's black population increased over 400 percent from 1940 to 1990—from 571,000 (less than 4 percent of the state's population) to 2.9 million (16 percent). The white population declined slightly during those fifty years in absolute terms, from 12.9 million to 12.5 million, but dramatically in relative terms, from 95 percent of all New York state residents to 74 percent.

The combined effects of immigration, suburbanization, and interregional shifts were most dramatically visible in New York City. Between 1985 and 1990, nearly 900,000 New York City residents seeking better jobs or more satisfying living moved to the suburbs or left the New York City region entirely. However, because the magnetism of New York's largest city continued undiminished for immigrants from Hispanic America and from Asia during the same period, the net loss in New York City's population in 1990 was only about 45,000. During the 1990–95 period, out-migration accelerated and immigration slowed; a 1996 study estimated that about 300,000 more people left the city than moved in. Nonetheless, as a New York City

Table 2: Population Characteristics of Selected New York Metropolitan Cities and
Counties, 1990

Jurisdiction	Total Population	Percent White	Percent Black	Percent Hispanic*
Albany City	101,082	75	21	3
Albany County	292,594	89	8	2
Binghamton City	53,008	92	5	2
Broome County	212,160	96	2	1
Buffalo City	328,123	65	31	2
Erie County	968,532	86	11	2
Elmira City	33,724	85	12	3
Chemung County	95,195	93	6	2
New York City	7,332,564	52	29	24
Rochester City	231,636	61	32	9
Monroe County	713,968	84	12	4
Syracuse City	163,860	75	20	3
Onondaga County	468,963	89	8	2
Utica City	68,637	87	11	3
Oneida County	250,836	93	5	2

Source: 1990 U.S. Bureau of the Census, Census of Population and Housing.
*Hispanic persons are of any race.

official observed, it was still the case that "the native-born population is
moving out and the foreign-born population is moving in. Relative to their
country of origin, New York City still offers far more opportunity."[8]

The net result of immigration, suburbanization, and interregional shifts is
an astonishing melange of languages, cuisines, arts, and literature in New
York. Such ethnic pluralism generates continuing vitality and excitement for
all New Yorkers. New York, therefore, is still "not a finished culture, [but]
one continually coming into being."[9]

Demography and Politics

New York's demographic diversity is politically potent because groups,
whether divided by race, income, or family type, are unevenly distributed
within the state's metropolitan areas. For example, nonwhites were 11 percent of the state's total population in 1980; the proportion increased to 16 percent in 1990.[10] However, nonwhite New Yorkers are disproportionately, and
increasingly, concentrated in the state's central cities. The 1980 census, for
example, showed New York City to be 39 percent nonwhite, while its six
suburban ring counties were 10 percent nonwhite.[11] In 1990, nonwhites composed 48 percent of the city's population; the proportion of nonwhite persons

in the suburban ring counties was 14 percent. Similar distributions are found in the state's other central cities and their suburbs. For example, Rochester's nonwhite population increased by 30 percent between 1980 and 1990, from 30 to 39 percent. For Monroe County, which overlies Rochester, the comparable increase was less than half, from 14 percent in 1980 to 16 percent in 1990. (For other central cities in New York and their overlying counties, see table 2.)

The distribution of Hispanic New Yorkers, who may be either white or nonwhite, follows a similar pattern. The differential is particularly dramatic for New York City: Hispanics were 15 percent of the city's population in 1980, but only 4 percent of the population of the city's suburban ring. In 1990, Hispanics had increased to 24 percent of the city's population, but only to 7 percent of the suburban ring counties. Hispanics constituted much smaller proportions of other New York metropolitan cities and counties in 1990, but the general pattern held.

Deep cleavages in education and income separate non-Hispanic whites from blacks and Hispanics. Twenty-eight percent of adult non-Hispanic whites living in New York's cities in 1990 had completed at least four years of college compared to only 11 percent for blacks and 7 percent for Hispanics. There were, as well, substantial inequalities in the income available to support households and families. In 1990, the median income for a New York family headed by a non-Hispanic white was $43,072; for a family headed by an African American, median income was 37 percent lower, at $27,923; and for a Hispanic-headed family, nearly 50 percent lower, at $23,198.

Finally, nonwhite households are more likely to be headed by single-female parents than are non-Hispanic white households. In 1990 in New York City, nearly one in every two black families with children under eighteen and two in every five Hispanic families were headed by a woman—in contrast with one in every seven white families. This is one reason why 28 percent of New York City's Hispanic families and 22 percent of the city's black families—in contrast with less than 6 percent of white non-Hispanic families— were living in poverty in 1990.

Such disparities directly affect local and state politics and policymaking. New York's central cities are home to more poor, uneducated, young, elderly, unemployed American-born persons, as well as immigrants, than are their suburbs. These dependent populations, and the politicians who represent them, make demands for health, transportation, education, and social

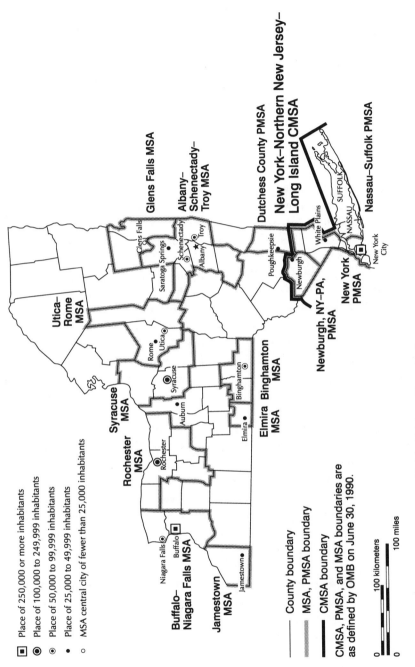

Map 2: Metropolitan Areas of New York

Place of 250,000 or more inhabitants

Place of 100,000 to 249,999 inhabitants

Place of 50,000 to 99,999 inhabitants

Place of 25,000 to 49,999 inhabitants

MSA central city of fewer than 25,000 inhabitants

County boundary

MSA, PMSA boundary

CMSA boundary

CMSA, PMSA, and MSA boundaries are
as defined by OMB on June 30, 1990.

Glens Falls MSA

Albany–
Schenectady–
Troy MSA

Dutchess County PMSA

New York–Northern New Jersey–
Long Island CMSA

Nassau–Suffolk PMSA

Utica–
Rome
MSA

Newburgh, NY–PA,
PMSA

New York
PMSA

Syracuse
MSA

Binghamton
MSA

Elmira
MSA

Rochester
MSA

Buffalo–
Niagara Falls MSA

Jamestown
MSA

Glens Falls

Schenectady

Saratoga Springs

Troy

Albany

Poughkeepsie

White Plains

Newburgh

New York
City

SUFFOLK

NASSAU

Rome

Utica

Syracuse

Binghamton

Auburn

Elmira

Rochester

Niagara Falls

Buffalo

Jamestown

100 kilometers

100 miles

0

0

Source: U.S. Department of Commerce, Economics and Statistics Administration, Bureau of the Census.

services that strain the resources of city governments. Elected city officials look to the state government for assistance. Many individual taxpayers and businesses throughout the state resist the imposition of higher taxes and, in fact, call for lowering taxes to keep New York economically competitive. The challenge to politicians to balance these points of view within an ethnically diverse context has been compared to "walking a tightrope during a hurricane."[12]

NEW YORK: MANY STATES

Demographically and geographically, New York is not one but many states. Differences between metropolitan and nonmetropolitan areas are among several important factors of demarcation. The vast majority of New Yorkers, more than 92 percent in 1990, live in the state's thirteen metropolitan areas, generally identified by their central cities: Albany-Schenectady-Troy; Binghamton; Buffalo–Niagara Falls; Elmira; Glens Falls; Jamestown; Nassau-Suffolk; New York City; Newburgh; Poughkeepsie; Rochester; Syracuse; and Utica-Rome.[13] In 1990, about half of all New Yorkers lived in central cities, typically with populations greater than 50,000. About one-third lived in the suburbs, and 9 percent lived in more rural places within metropolitan areas. Finally, 8 percent of New Yorkers lived outside of metropolitan boundaries in rural areas or very small communities (see map 2).

This overall distribution of New York's central-city, suburban, and rural populations, however, is not typical for all its metropolitan areas. It is skewed by the fact that New York City, with 7.3 million residents in 1990, accounts for the lion's share of all the state's central-city residents. Outside the New York City metropolitan area, central cities have constituted smaller and smaller proportions of their metropolitan-area populations since 1960. For example, in 1990, the city of Buffalo accounted for only 27 percent of its metropolitan-area population, down from 41 percent in 1960; for Rochester, the comparable figures were 22 percent in 1990 and 43 percent in 1960; and for Syracuse, 22 percent in 1990 and 38 percent in 1960. At the same time, the suburban portions of these metropolitan areas were growing.

Geographers, demographers, political scientists, and state agencies all draw the state's subregions differently. Even agencies of the state government serve different regional areas. Depending on their mission, agencies draw different regional districts based on social services, economic development patterns, labor force characteristics, or other factors.

Regardless of individual perspective, however, most analysts of New York State agree, more or less, that historical, demographic, geographic,

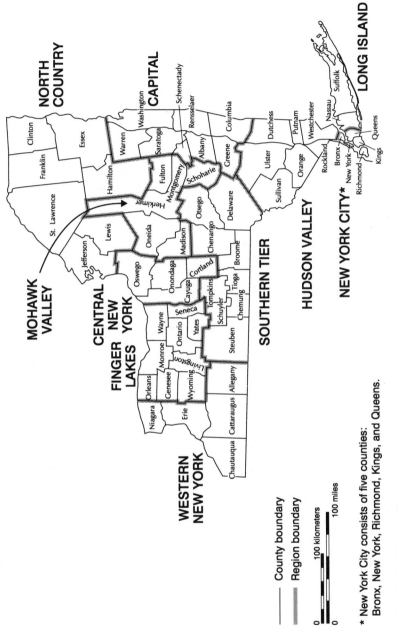

NORTH COUNTRY

Clinton
Franklin
Essex
St. Lawrence

CAPITAL

Washington
Schenectady
Rensselaer
Warren
Saratoga
Albany
Columbia
Greene
Dutchess
Fulton
Schoharie
Hamilton
Montgomery
Herkimer
Lewis
Oneida
Otsego
Delaware

MOHAWK VALLEY

Jefferson
Oswego
Onondaga
Madison
Chenango
Cortland
Broome

CENTRAL NEW YORK

Wayne
Seneca
Cayuga
Tompkins
Tioga
Schuyler
Chemung

FINGER LAKES

Niagara
Orleans
Genesee
Monroe
Ontario
Yates
Livingston
Wyoming
Erie
Allegany
Steuben
Cattaraugus
Chautauqua

WESTERN NEW YORK

SOUTHERN TIER

HUDSON VALLEY

Ulster
Sullivan
Orange
Putnam
Westchester
Rockland

NEW YORK CITY*

Bronx
New York
Richmond
Kings
Queens

LONG ISLAND

Nassau
Suffolk

——— County boundary
▨▨▨ Region boundary

0   100 kilometers
0   100 miles

* New York City consists of five counties: Bronx, New York, Richmond, Kings, and Queens.

Source: New York Department of Labor.

Map 3: Ten Subregions of New York

and cultural factors can be combined to yield distinctive subregions. The ten regions of the New York State Department of Labor (DOL) capture well the many separate "New Yorks": Long Island, New York City, Hudson Valley, Capital District, North Country, Mohawk Valley, Central New York, Finger Lakes, Southern Tier, and Western New York (see map 3). Each "little New York state" has separate and unusual traits that trace back to the early history of the state.

Regional Folklore

New York's regional diversity has long been celebrated and embellished in its folktales of life in the remote North Country, the Long Island seacoast, the mist-laden Catskill Mountains, and the faster paced, commercially oriented New York City.

The North Country, like most wilderness regions in North America, produced legends of a Paul Bunyan character, John Cheney, who lived near Ticonderoga in the early 1800s. Once, when he was telling of his encounter with a crouching panther, someone asked how he had felt. The fearless Cheney is said to have responded, "I felt as if I should kill him." [14]

Pirates became a part of the marine vista off Long Island, along with whalers and trade ships. The infamous Captain Kidd's exploits are preserved in Washington Irving's *Tales of a Traveler*, which he based on folk stories. [15] The account is of a romantic character, more a victim of circumstance than an evil man. But, however good a citizen and sympathetic a figure Kidd was in the New World, he was hanged for murder and piracy in England ten years later. Although an original map of his buried treasure was used as barter for many years after his death, no treasure was ever found. [16]

Central New York's leatherstocking country produced its own mythical characters. Natty Bumppo, a rough-hewn scout and quintessential Yankee-Yorker, was the creation of James Fenimore Cooper in *The Leatherstocking Saga*. [17] Bumppo stands as a protest on behalf of simplicity and perfect freedom against encroaching law and order. Escaping deeper and deeper into the Adirondack woods, Bumppo finally loses the battle to advancing civilization. He is everyman's Paul Bunyan, not larger than life but somehow more concerned with principles and the order of nature.

Catskills characters were typically more refined than those of the leatherstocking region. Living closer to New York City, so never as removed from civilization, these Knickerbockers, as Washington Irving called them, were romantic figures. The landscape was less treacherous and demanding, less opposing of civilization. In describing the Catskills, "these fairy mountains," Irving wrote: "When the weather is fair and settled, they are clothed in blue and purple, and print their bold outlines on the clear evening sky; but sometimes when the rest of the landscape is cloudless they will gather a hood of gray vapors about their summits, which, in the last rays of the setting sun, will glow and light up like a crown of glory."[18] The Catskill Mountains and Hudson Valley were reputedly populated by mischievous, impish spirits, which the residents incorporated into folklore. Rip Van Winkle and Ichabod Crane, for example, represent ordinary villagers—henpecked, unhandsome—chosen for salvation and fame by the mountain spirits.

The Dutch, especially those in what is now the Capital District, were much more interested in commerce and government than in the supernatural. This is most apparent in the absence of witch trials during Dutch rule in New York. Yet, however averse to the occult, the folklore of the Albany area did involve encounters with the spirits. One such encounter concerned a baker named Volckert Jan Pietersen Van Amsterdam, known as "Baas." Late on New Year's Eve in 1655, an old, ugly beggar appeared, demanding a dozen St. Nicholas cookies. Baas gave the woman her cookies, but she protested that there were only twelve cookies, while "One more than twelve makes a dozen." Baas pushed her into the street with her twelve cookies. The woman reappeared each New Year's Eve, the scene was repeated, and the baker encountered more mysterious bad luck. Finally, after three years, St. Nicholas himself appeared to Baas, instructing him to serve the old woman with the spirit demanded by the holidays. The next year, Baas gave the woman her thirteen cookies, cheerfully wishing her a Happy New Year. With that, the witch broke the spell. Baas swore on the likeness of St. Nick that in all of the patronship of Van Rensselaer, thirteen would make a baker's dozen.[19]

In the area that would become the five boroughs of New York City, the many ethnic groups were smaller and closer to one another than in upstate. Preservation of traditions was more difficult in the confines of bustling neighborhoods and in the unavoidable interaction of growing numbers of residents. Religious, cultural, and economic tolerance evolved in New York City. The prevailing doctrine of mercantilism laid the foundation for the city's emergence as a leader in commerce.[20] Its location, local tolerance, and British protection allowed its advantage to flourish. But along with growth and progress came problems. The city government clearly directed the greater part of its attention to business and commerce; its approach to sanitation, public health, fire, and crime was somewhat disorganized. Filthy streets and unreliable trash removal, an unsafe water supply, absence of fire enforcement codes, prostitution, and assault were all common problems.

Baron Axel Klinckowstrom of Sweden described New York City in 1818: "[It] is not as clean as cities of the same rank and population in Europe; in spite of the fact that the police regulations are good, they are not enforced and one finds in the streets dead cats and dogs, which make the air very bad; dust and ashes are thrown out into the streets, which are swept every fortnight in the summer; only, however, in the largest and most frequented streets, otherwise they are cleaned only once a month. . . . The drinking water in New York is very bad and salty. Even the so-called Manhattan water . . . is not good."[21]

The center of community life often became the local tavern, where citizens could negotiate business, recruit employees, auction goods and services, and collect and send mail. It is said that New York City supported one tavern for every twelve adult males.[22]

Upstate versus Downstate

Although various regional differences derived from historic settlement patterns and geographic characteristics continue to exert influence, the most basic regional distinction is "upstate" and "downstate." Downstate can mean New York City, or it can refer to New York City and suburbs (including Nassau, Suffolk, Westchester, and, perhaps, Rockland and Putnam Counties). However downstate is defined, the rest of the state is upstate. Regardless of how the geographic lines are drawn, attitudinal and stylistic differences are evident to New Yorkers. Downstaters view upstate as "apple-knocker territory" and often regard its inhabitants with a certain condescension.[23] Upstaters think that downstaters are strident and pushy, "fast-talking, fast-thinking, and fast-spending."

Examples abound of the upstate/downstate split in the political arena. The "in-your-face" style of politics described and practiced by U.S. Senator Alfonse (Al) D'Amato is associated in the public mind with downstate. In D'Amato's words: "New York isn't for the faint of heart. Most New Yorkers have come to expect aggressive, in your face campaigns, and the media loves them too, but it's more than just a left [hook] for a political street fight. New Yorkers demand a frank, no nonsense, tell-it-like-it-is approach from their political candidates. They see through empty rhetoric and publicity stunts. You've got to stand up for what you believe in. It may not always be pretty, but it is what the people want. Hey, it's New York!"[24]

Edward I. (Ed) Koch, seeking the Democratic nomination for governor in the 1982 primary election, characterized upstaters in a *Playboy* interview as "wasting time in a pickup truck when you have to drive 20 miles to buy a gingham dress or a Sears Roebuck suit."[25] Those remarks, even in jest, may well have cost Koch, the popular mayor of New York City from 1977 to 1990, the nomination.

Barber Conable, member of the U.S. House of Representatives from the upstate Rochester area from 1965 through 1984, purposely hung paintings and photos of pastoral scenes on the walls of his congressional office to disassociate himself from New York City representatives.

These rival perspectives are reflected in campaign strategies, candidate preferences by upstate and downstate voters, and the policy choices of their representatives in the state legislature—all elaborated in later chapters.

NEW YORK: PARADOXICAL POLITICAL CULTURE

New York's diverse regions and people are often cited as its most outstanding feature, the feature that makes it seem more like a "country" than a state.[26] Historians, from Frederick Jackson Turner to David Maldwyn Ellis, have described New York as America in microcosm. Turner, in the late eighteenth century, noted New York's "composite nationality . . . [its] wide mixture of nationalities, varied society, mixed town and county system of government, varied economic life, [and] many religious sects."[27] Ellis, in the twentieth century, observed the state's "pluralistic political system, diversified economy, and heterogeneous society."[28]

Yet New York's character is unique. Shaped by the state's economic leadership for much of American history and its role as a magnet for immigrants, the New York character contains two dominant values: individual entrepreneurship and collective benevolence. New Yorkers generally believe that government should facilitate individual endeavors. At the same time, they "have generally shown a spirit of tolerance even though they have not necessarily loved each other."[29] These values, separately and in combination, have generated a distinctive political culture in the Empire State.

Entrepreneurial Capitalism

New York has long personified entrepreneurial capitalism. "As early as 1794 Talleyrand stated that New York was the best place in the world to make money fast."[30] New York's official nickname, the Empire State, reflects its role as a major center of industry and commerce for the nation and the world for much of American history. At the end of the twentieth century, however, the nickname may signify New York's aspirations more than its reality.

The notion of successive frontiers, developed by Daniel J. Elazar, is quite relevant to New York. "The continuing frontier," Elazar writes, "has been the crucial if not the decisive factor in the progression of generations and centuries" in American history.[31] Elazar delineates America's continuing frontier in four successive, overlapping, stages:

- the rural-land frontier—lasting roughly from the seventeenth through the nineteenth centuries, characterized by the westward movement of a basically rural population and "development of a socioeconomic system based on agricultural and extractive pursuits in both its urban and rural components"[32]

- the urban-industrial frontier—overlapping the rural-land frontier in the early nineteenth century and extending through the mid-twentieth century, dominated by the transformation of cities into "centers of opportunity, producers of new wealth, and social innovators"[33]

- the metropolitan-technological frontier—generated by the urban-industrial frontier in the mid-twentieth century and continuing until the mid-1970s, "characterized by the radical reordering of an industrial society through rapidly changing technologies and a settlement pattern that encourage[d] the diffusion of an urbanized population within large metropolitan regions"[34]

- the rurban-cybernetic frontier—emerging in the late 1970s and based on cybernetic technologies such as "minicomputers, satellite-transmitted communications facilities, cable television, and new data-processing devices" and "urbanites engaged in traditionally urban pursuits, but living lives that mixed city and small town or rural elements"[35]

New York, after faltering during the first half of the first frontier, did well through the second, encountered problems on the third, and has fallen behind on the rurban-cybernetic frontier.

During the rural-land and urban-industrial frontiers, the work ethic and "materialism, more vulgarly the pursuit of the almighty dollar, characterized the mind-set and life-styles of New Yorkers."[36] As David Ellis has written, "Persons of New England stock, comprising over half the [state's] population [in 1825], exemplified the Protestant ethic. In this respect, immigrants differed but slightly, if at all, because most had sailed west to better themselves. Hard-working and frugal, many were quick to show enterprise in starting small businesses. Persons of every ethnic background and nationality—Italians, Scots, Jews, Germans, Greeks, Armenians, Lebanese, Chinese—enthusiastically joined the race for riches."[37]

Completion of the Erie Canal in 1825 was an important turning point in the history of New York's commercial leadership. Until the canal was built, transportation within New York was difficult. Not all of the upstate rivers were navigable, and they did not form a usable network. More important, the roads were rough and dangerous, due to poor construction and upkeep and to the state's harsh weather, especially in winter.

The canal marked the beginning of the modern age for the Empire State. Commerce flourished across the state and inland across the Great Lakes. New York City became a more important trade and financial center than ever before. Perhaps most significantly for its people, New Yorkers were no longer isolated from one another. The "melting pot" began to heat up after the canal linked the Atlantic Ocean with the Great Lakes, linking towns, villages, and cities across the state and beyond. The canal fostered rapid growth in towns like Rochester and Syracuse, which eventually became the heart of the "urban corridor" extending from Albany to Buffalo.

The Erie Canal's importance extended beyond the state to the nation. In the words of David Ellis, "New York's transportation revolution galvanized America's economy far beyond the borders of the Empire State. Its greatest achievement, the Erie Canal, became the linchpin of national unity, a tribute to free institutions, and a demonstration of American ingenuity and enterprise."[38]

What the canal began in 1825, the railroads accelerated in the 1840s. In fact, by 1870, the canal was permanently eclipsed by the railroads in passenger and freight services. Like the canal, the railroads were built primarily by the Irish. With the exception of the most remote areas of the Adirondack Mountains, the entire state was covered by a remarkable commercial network of railways and waterways by 1859.

Through the nineteenth century and well into the twentieth, when "the Northeast was the heart of America's industrial might, New York dominated the Northeast."[39] Manufacturing—of iron and steel, textiles, apparel, radios and television sets, engines and turbines—provided substantial and consistent employment across the state. Wall Street symbolized New York's leadership in banking and finance. In agriculture, the state's single largest industry, New York was a national leader in the production of fruits, vegetables, and dairy products.

By the mid-1970s, however, as the metropolitan-technological frontier was coming to a close and the rurban-cybernetic frontier was getting underway, "the colossus of the Northeast was showing unmistakable signs of decay. Advanced decay."[40] New York's share of the nation's jobs slipped from 11 percent in 1963 to 7.7 percent in 1978. New York was the only state to experience a net loss of 146,000 jobs in the private sector during the 1970s. Although employment in the service sector increased, the loss of more than 370,000 manufacturing jobs could not be overcome. The decline in manufacturing jobs was most precipitous in New York City (which accounts for about half of the state's jobs), but the shift toward service jobs was also true for Buffalo, Rochester, Syracuse, Albany, Binghamton, and Utica. "There is little doubt," economists associated with *New York State Project 2000* concluded in 1988, "that New York has undergone deindustrialization."[41]

By the mid-1980s, the popular perception had shifted away from a "permanently stagnant" to a "selectively booming" northeastern economy.[42] Key indicators of the state's economic health showed a "marked turnaround" between 1976 and 1986.[43] As the decade of the 1990s began, however, New York's economy had weakened again. The precipitous fall of the stock market in October 1987 signaled the end of a boom in the financial services sector that had brought the state several years of unprecedented growth in personal incomes. The consequences for New York of the stock market crash, "a loss in consumer confidence due to a decelerating national economy, and a sluggish high-tech industry . . . [were] the slowest growth in sales tax collections in over a decade, a dramatic decline in real estate–related taxes and erratic swings in personal income tax collections [and a decline of] corporate tax collections . . . to the lowest level in six years."[44]

By 1994, Governor Mario M. Cuomo suggested that "the worst of this challenging economic period is behind us," but warned that "encouraging statistics offer little relief to the many New Yorkers buffeted by corporate restructuring, military downsizing and other economic forces beyond their control."[45] His successor, Governor George E. Pataki, assigned blame for New York's economic problems not to external but to internal factors. The "entrepreneurial spirit," he asserted, "has been crushed by New York State regulation and taxation."[46] In his 1995 *Message to the Legislature*, Pataki, New York's first elected Republican governor since Nelson A. Rockefeller, called for "smaller, more effective, more efficient government."[47]

Collective Benevolence

New York's enthusiasm for individual competition, or capitalistic entrepreneurialism—"making money fast," in Talleyrand's words—is one of two dominant strands of the state's political culture. The other is collective benevolence, that is, compassion, toward those who are not able to compete— the "tired, poor, huddled masses yearning to breathe free," in the words of

Emma Lazarus. Long manifest in New York history, compassionate public policies can be explained by a combination of factors: liberal, moralistic elite values; pressure "from below," that is, from poor, immigrant groups; and political machine efforts to satisfy their constituents.

New York's reputation for collective benevolence dates to the late eighteenth century. New York was the first state to establish a public school system. "In 1782 Governor George Clinton urged the state legislature to establish schools and seminaries and two years later the lawmakers paid sufficient heed to his request to create the University of the State of New York, an organization supervised by a Board of Regents and authorized to establish secondary schools and colleges. . . . A permanent system of common schools, with school districts for each township, was set up by the legislature in 1812."[48]

More than a century after Clinton called for state schools, the state legislature, responding to the growing strength of the labor movement in the 1880s and the disastrous Triangle Shirt Waist Factory fire in 1910, regulated the hours and working conditions of women and children and adopted compulsory accident and unemployment insurance laws.[49]

New York's collective benevolence also extended early to mental and public health. "The care of the mentally disturbed became a special concern of the state because local communities had neither the funds nor the skilled staff to treat difficult cases. The first state mental hospital opened in Utica in 1843, accepting acute cases of insanity from county poorhouses." The state "began a public health program in 1850 by requiring each city and incorporated village to appoint a board of health and a health officer. The Health Department, which began in 1909, set up a sanitary code which it established as a minimum standard for localities to enforce."[50]

New York's compassion is reified in article 17 of the state constitution. Adopted by the Constitutional Convention of 1938 in the aftermath of the Great Depression, article 17 states: "The aid, care and support of the needy are public concerns and shall be provided by the state and by such of its subdivisions, and in such manner and by such means, as the legislature may from time to time determine." Although the Court of Appeals, New York's highest court, has issued both broad and more narrow interpretations of article 17, it has consistently asserted an affirmative duty for the state government to aid the needy.[51]

Spending for the needy has been particularly generous in New York since the administration of Governor Nelson A. Rockefeller (1959–73). Redistributional equity is demonstrated in efforts to target state aid to individuals or areas in the greatest need. New York, for example, which bases state aid largely on the ability of individual school districts to support education, is an exception to the general practice of American states to link education aid to pupil enrollment.[52] State laws that mandate special education services, preventive mental health services to families in crisis, and protective and health-care services for children and the elderly are, in many cases, more comprehensive than their federal counterparts.

New York's interventions into the economic and social affairs of its citizens translated in the 1950s and 1960s into public sector expenditures and taxes per capita that were among the highest in the nation. The fiscal crisis of 1975, which began in New York City and soon cast doubt on the state's financial solvency, was a rude awakening for New Yorkers. Governor Hugh L. Carey's initiatives (described in chapter 7) to strengthen and stabilize New York's private sector signaled a shift in the state government's agenda, a shift toward holding the line on taxes and spending while at the same time meeting the needs of citizens as generously as possible.

New York's responses to the budget cuts and decentralizing policies initiated by President Ronald Reagan in 1981 were consistent with the goal of balancing competition and compassion. New York did not replace all of the lost federal dollars; it did, however, substitute state funds for many programs targeted to poor New Yorkers—among them, social services, welfare, and compensatory education. In so doing, New York reinforced "characteristics of big state government and liberalism . . . that had long existed in the state."[53]

COMPETITION AND COMPASSION: THE VALUES JOINED

American political culture, according to Daniel J. Elazar, is rooted in two contrasting conceptions of the American political order—a marketplace and a commonwealth. In the marketplace, "the primary public relationships are products of bargaining among individuals and groups acting out of self-interest." In the commonwealth, "citizens cooperate in an effort to erect and maintain the best government in order to implement certain shared moral principles."[54]

Elazar asserts that three primary types of political subcultures flow from these contrasting conceptions—moralistic, individualistic, and traditionalistic. The moralistic political culture first developed in Puritan New England; the individualistic, in the Middle States; and the traditionalistic, in the South. The first two subcultures are applicable to the political culture of

New York. The moralistic political culture emphasizes the commonwealth concept. "Politics is considered one of the great human activities: the search for a good society. . . . Government is considered a positive instrument with a responsibility to promote the general welfare."[55]

The individualistic political culture, reflecting "commitment to commercialism and acceptance of ethnic, social, and religious pluralism," emphasizes the marketplace concept of the American political order. "Government is instituted for strictly utilitarian reasons, to handle those functions demanded by the people it serves. [It] places a premium on limiting community intervention into private activities, to the minimum degree necessary to keep the marketplace in proper working order."[56]

New York's enthusiasm for competition, grounded in the marketplace, and for compassion, grounded in the commonwealth, led Elazar to characterize New York's political culture as a combination of individualistic and moralist elements. The result of this odd mix of values is a distinctive orientation toward political action that combines the centrality of private concerns that would limit government intervention into private activities with a commitment to active government intervention in the economic and social life of the community.

Is contemporary New York both competitive and compassionate? The answer is yes, but it is also clear that the pursuit of both values has placed the state government in a "highly vulnerable financial position."[57] The pursuit, however, is not likely to be abandoned; New York's future is inextricably linked, as was its past, with the well-being and educational advancement of its diverse communities. At the same time, the tensions between the divergent roles implicit in New York's paradoxical political culture pose difficult choices for New Yorkers and their public officials. At the end of the twentieth century, the tensions between these choices are strong and are overtly played out within the labyrinth of politics that has long been characteristic of the Empire State.

CHAPTER TWO

Political Pluralism:
The Past in the Present

Sarah F. Liebschutz

New York's political system has long encompassed and reflected a wide variety of claims. Regional, economic, and ethnic interests, complicated by personality and ideology, have dotted the political landscape since the state's early history. Evidences of "tribalism," that often-volatile mixture of "land, blood and religion," abound throughout New York's history.[1]

"The mystery of colonial New York," Milton Klein observed, is "why its heterogeneous society did not come apart at the seams." New Yorkers, Klein contends, did not have the "sense of special mission of the New Englander nor the common racism of the Virginian to knit them together."[2] However, they did have "a bond of unity, perhaps only dimly perceived and certainly rarely articulated. *It was their common interest in making money and a set of political values which caused them to immerse their energies and diffuse their hostilities in politics.*"[3]

An early example of New York's political system in formation involved the clash of economic and security interests between upstate farmers and downstate merchants, Dutch settlers and upper-class Englishmen. In 1679, the British-appointed governor of New York granted millers in New York City exclusive right to mill and pack flour and biscuits for export and stipulated that all trade must funnel through the New York port. The monopoly was intended "to establish higher standards for New York flour and thereby increase the demand in the West Indies."[4] Upstate millers and Long Island shipowners were outraged.

Ten years later, New York City residents, the majority of them Dutch settlers, expressed their own grievances. Not only were they disaffected by the "hard times, monopolies, high taxes, and ineffective government" that emanated from Albany, but they were also fearful of the "hated Yankees" of

New England. After learning that the New York governor had been jailed by a revolutionary committee in Boston and hearing rumors that "a thousand French soldiers and Indian warriors were marching on Albany . . . [they] lit bonfires and paraded in the streets of New York City. Incensed by these demonstrations, [the] Lieutenant Governor threatened to burn New York City. The threat led the mob to storm the fort of New York, and power passed into the hands of the militia captains." Jacob Leisler, "one of their members . . . who stood for freedom, Protestantism, and the Dutch element," led the rebellion to "protect the upper Hudson from French attack."[5] When Leisler refused to surrender the fort's keys to the reasserted English royal authority, he was found guilty of treason and put to death. Additionally, the monopoly to the New York City millers was repealed. The governor subsequently regranted it, but in 1695 upstate representatives to the colonial legislature succeeded in reversing that action.

David Ellis contends that these "stirring events of the [late seventeenth century] gave New Yorkers many lessons in politics. They debated the merits of representative government, the dangers of mob rule, and the evils of entrenched privilege."[6]

From those early days to the present, New Yorkers have pressed their political claims by one or more of the following routes:

- Creating political parties with broad but distinct ideologies in affiliation with or in addition to the national Democratic and Republican parties
- Nurturing reform movements to educate the public and the government on particular issues
- Lobbying government officials directly to advance interests of specific populations within the state

EARLY POLITICAL PARTIES

Landowners and merchants who identified themselves with the Federalist and Antifederalist causes early on made their demands known. Thereafter, in 1800, during the election campaigns of Thomas Jefferson for president and John Jay for governor, the national Antifederalist party members began to call themselves the Democratic-Republicans (later, the Democrats). The state party followed suit. By 1814, the state Federalist party itself had split into two factions; the smaller faction joined the Democrats in supporting De Witt Clinton's two successful bids for the governorship. Clinton used his popularity to push through authorization and funding for the Erie Canal; after two terms, however, he was generally regarded as arrogant and offensive and was not encouraged to seek a third term in 1822.

During Clinton's second term, a constitutional convention was held to discuss the revision of the state constitution. Both parties—Democrat and Federalist—grappled with the issue of universal adult male suffrage. Martin Van Buren of the Democrats was in favor, but the Federalists offered strong opposition to expanding voting rights. Through adoption of a middle-ground strategy, Van Buren was able to reach an accord, and in 1821, 84 percent of adult white males in the state, nearly double the previous number, were allowed to vote for governor. Suffrage for black adult males was also granted, but with higher property qualifications.[7]

Van Buren flexed his political muscle in other areas and successfully ousted De Witt Clinton from his seat on the Canal Board of Directors. Public outcry against Van Buren's arrogance was so strong, however, that Clinton was able to take advantage of his newfound sympathy and run successfully for a third term as governor in 1824. Van Buren regained popularity by 1828, when he was elected governor; in 1836, Van Buren became the first of four New York governors to become president of the United States.

The Clinton–Van Buren story is typical of New York State politics in its joining of economic issues (the canal), political issues (suffrage), social issues (black men's voting rights), and simple personal popularity. As New Yorkers became more sophisticated in politics, their responses generated more sophisticated political solutions.

The state's first third party, the Anti-Mason party, was formed in 1826. Generated in the aftermath of the murder of William Morgan, a printer who had published an exposé on the Masons fraternal order, the party was an organizational outlet for strong Anti-Masonic feeling in western New York State. The new party won several assembly seats and by 1827 was attacking Governor Van Buren. Thurlow Weed, a publisher from Rochester, made an unsuccessful attempt to defeat Van Buren in 1828 through coordinating the efforts of the Anti-Mason and Federalist parties. In 1834, Weed organized the Whig party, which eventually became the present-day Republican party.

After 1830, the increasing diversity of the state's population forced a rethinking of the role of government. Before this time, government had generally been viewed in the context of the individualistic political culture—as a facilitator of commerce and general economic development. The singularity of that political culture was challenged from 1830 through the Civil War (1861–65), when New York's great influx of immigrants led to a doubling of its population. The newcomers expressed political ideas that frequently clashed with those of more established New Yorkers. Ellis provides a description of the period: "The Catholic majority in many cities . . . displayed class consciousness, organized unions, and demanded the 10-hour [work] day, all anathema to entrepreneurs. When old Knickerbocker [Protestant] families were not making snide comments about the 'nouveau riche,' they expressed shock at the uncouth behavior of Irish mobs brawling in the streets."[8]

The challenges to the prevailing order by the newcomers extended beyond the airing of ideas. Groups that initially formed to minister to the social and economic needs of the immigrants were transformed into overtly political organizations. By far, the most durable of these was Tammany Hall.

Tammany Hall

The Sons of St. Tammany—intended as a national fraternal and humanitarian order of working men—was organized in 1789 by William Mooney, an immigrant Irish upholsterer. The Sons of St. Tammany ministered to the poor and disadvantaged Irish immigrants who were ignored by philanthropists and who lacked a voice in government. Tammany's early ideals of equality and nationalism, borrowed from the French Revolution, were closely identified with Thomas Jefferson and his Antifederalist followers, who "were instinctively sympathetic to France." In contrast, prominent Federalists, such as Alexander Hamilton and John Jay, "looked just as fervently to England." The support by Federalists of the federal Alien and Sedition Acts of 1798 ("designed in part to prevent the absorption of immigrants into the Jeffersonian party") and their opposition in 1812 to universal white suffrage ("certain that it would swell the immigrant Irish vote of New York City") further strengthened the attachment of Tammany Hall to the Antifederalist party, precursor to the Democratic party.[9]

By 1812, the Irish vote was a factor in any election from New York City to Albany to Washington DC. The hierarchical way in which Tammany was organized was critical to its electoral success. Glazer and Moynihan describe the parallels between the Irish village and Tammany: "The Irish village was a place of stable, predictable social relations in which almost everyone had a role to play, under the surveillance of a stern oligarchy of elders, and in which, on the whole, a . . . person's position was likely to improve with time. Working from the original ward committees, [Tammany] slowly established . . . a political bureaucracy in which the prerogatives of rank were carefully observed. The hierarchy had to be maintained. For the group as a whole this served to take the risks out of politics. Each would get his desserts—in time."[10]

The principle of "Boss rule" was not tyranny, but order. "When Lincoln Steffens asked [early Tammany boss Richard] Croker, 'Why must there be a boss, when we've got a mayor and—a council and—' 'That's why,' Croker responded. 'It's because there's a mayor and a council and judges—and a hundred other men to deal with.' "[11]

Tammany Hall's best known "boss" was William March Tweed, who began his political climb in the mid-1800s by organizing a volunteer fire brigade. By 1863, he was put in charge of maintaining streets for the entire city. He issued paving and repair contracts to friends and collected a percentage of each contract. In order to ensure their continued spoils, Tweed's protégés stuffed ballot boxes for compatriot candidates for city offices. As public outrage grew, Boss Tweed became belligerent, challenging newspapers and reformers to "do something about it." They did. Thomas Nast of *Harper's Weekly* drew cartoons, the *New York Times* ran stories proving the graft and corruption, and reformers spoke out at every opportunity. Then a group of leading citizens, among them lawyer Samuel J. Tilden, brought Tweed to trial. He was convicted of stealing $6 million and put in prison, where he eventually died. Tilden himself became governor in 1874, running as a reformer on the Democrat ticket.

As the Tammany saga unfolded in New York City, party organizations proliferated throughout the state. The statewide Democratic party split into two factions: the Barnburners, who opposed downstate control of the party, and the Hunkers, who sought to "hunker down" and negotiate with downstate power brokers. Abolitionists formed yet another offshoot of the Democratic party, the Liberty party, which called for an end to slavery. This party gained little support; in 1848 it was supplanted by a Republican faction called the Free Soil party, which advocated slavery only where it already existed and rejected its introduction in any new states. Support of free public education and the suspension of laws mandating jail terms for debtors was the platform of another short-lived party, the Workingman's party based in New York City. In 1850, the Silver-Grays (named for their leader, Gideon Granger, who had distinctive silver-gray hair) opposed the inclusion of a fugitive slave law in the congressional Compromise of 1850. By the late 1800s, the Progressive party gained strength through its demands for workers' compensation; health, accident, and unemployment insurance; pensions; an eight-hour work day; and child-labor laws. In 1902, William Randolph Hearst formed the Municipal Ownership League to oppose Tammany boss Charles Murphy.

The progression has continued. Today, the Democratic and Republican parties dominate. But as chapter 5 elaborates, third parties, among them the Right-to-Life, Liberal, and Conservative parties, appear regularly on ballots for statewide and local elections.

Altogether, from the nineteenth century through the twentieth, New York's party organizations have advanced claims for compassion and competition. At times, the objective was to advance individual competitiveness; at other times, moralistic compassion; and sometimes—as in the case of Tammany Hall—both. Regardless of aim, such groups have infused, and continue to infuse, energy into the politics of the Empire State.

REFORM MOVEMENTS

New Yorkers have a long history of nurturing reform movements to educate the public and influence state and national governments. Three major reform movements of the nineteenth century—abolition of slavery, temperance, and women's suffrage—were encouraged and given political voice in the state. All three movements were a response to the "unsettling effect of the enormous transformation that the United States experienced" in the nineteenth century. "Population growth, immigration, internal migration, urbanization, the market economy, growing inequality, loosening family and community ties, the advancing frontier, and territorial expansion all contributed."[12]

Religious revivalism in the 1840s, known as the "Second Great Awakening" to heed the call to Christianity, was another "prime motivating force" for reform. Wherever evangelical Protestants preached, "voluntary reform societies arose. Evangelists organized an association for each issue—temperance, education, Sabbath observance, antidueling, and later antislavery; collectively, these groups formed a national web of benevolence and moral reform societies."[13]

Western New York was the site of intensive evangelical activities, particularly the preaching of Charles G. Finney, known as the "father of modern revivalism." In fact, "western New York experienced such continuous and heated waves of revivalism that it became known as the 'burned-over' district."[14]

Western New York women were among the most enthusiastic converts to the causes of abolition and temperance. One widely accepted explanation for the activism of such women as Susan B. Anthony, Elizabeth Cady Stanton, Lucretia Mott, and Elizabeth Blackwell is that "women's path to public

prominence began at the hearth of the privatized family and the altar of religious revivalism. . . . The historical image thus emerges of a relatively homogeneous body of women—white, middle class, Yankee, urban, and
evangelical—who left their private havens to purify the world under the ban-
ner of revivalism; they followed a lengthy, sometimes circuitous, but essentially singular path from benevolent associations through moral reform cru-
sades to women's rights campaigns."[15]

This "singular path" description of nineteenth-century activist women,
however, is misleading. Nancy Hewitt, in a case study of activist women in
Rochester, New York, from 1830 to 1870, depicts not one prototypical
woman but three self-consciously competing female networks. Although all
three networks drew from the "bourgeois," white middle class, they differed in their missions and styles of activism. Benevolent women, founders
of the "Female Charitable Society to aid the sick poor, [saw themselves] as
community caretakers and sources of social stability"; they sought continuity, not social change, through amelioration of existing social ills. Perfectionist women, who campaigned for "moral and social perfection—seeking
to rid the world of vice, intemperance, and slavery—" sought to eradicate
rather than ameliorate social problems. They did not seek to fundamentally
"alter basic institutions, but rather to institutionalize certain rights and privi-
leges supposed guaranteed by evangelical and constitutional doctrines." Finally, members of the third network rejected both continuity and reform
within the system. "Radical, or in nineteenth century terms, ultraist, women
. . . were far less committed to Constitutional traditions, horrified by 'what
laws our Fathers and brothers have enacted for mothers and sisters and wives
to [wear] as galling chains.' "[16] Ultraists challenged the system itself, demanding and agitating for sexual, religious, racial, and political equality.

Although the interests of benevolent, perfectionist, and ultraist women
converged from time to time—notably over the abolition of slavery—intemperance was the only "social problem that garnered significant attention
over a long period of time in all three networks. . . . Benevolent women
aided its victims, perfectionists first sought its eradication and later the salvation of its potential prey, and ultraists urged that it be accepted as grounds
for divorce."[17] The New York State Temperance Society, founded in 1829,
claimed over one hundred thousand members by 1850; while unsuccessful in
obtaining total statewide prohibition, the society did play a major role in
state regulation of the sale of alcohol.[18]

The most famous of the reform movements centered in New York State,
and one of the few to earn the wrath of religious reformers, was the feminist

movement. The movement's ultraist leaders, Susan B. Anthony and Elizabeth Cady Stanton, argued for the vote for women as well as for women's rights to higher education, legal control of their property and their children, and professional employment in the "Declaration of Independence for Women's Equality," the focus of the historic Woman's Rights Convention held in Seneca Falls in 1848. Although the movement had little tangible success in the nineteenth century, due mostly to the hostility from both religious leaders and the majority of women across the state, the state legislature did pass an "Earnings Bill" in 1860. This law guaranteed wives a life estate in one-third of real estate owned by a husband who died intestate, legal status as joint guardians with husbands, and the right to own and dispose of property acquired by inheritance or earnings.[19]

In addition to abolition of slavery, prohibition of alcohol, and women's suffrage, reformers in New York—men and women alike—focused on the abominable living conditions of the poor, the mentally ill, and criminals. Institutions established to house the latter two groups were often managed by political appointees with little training or sympathy for their charges. Liberal publishers in New York City, notably John Peter Zenger, William Cullen Bryant, Horace Greeley, Henry Raymond, Joseph Pulitzer, and William Randolph Hearst, exposed the scandals; reformers like Dorothea Dix, whose report of 1844 detailed and documented for the first time many of the atrocities, set about changing the conditions.

The reformers encountered much opposition. Nearly a century after the founding of the New York State Temperance Society, James J. "Jimmy" Walker, New York City's mayor from 1926 to 1932, defined a reformer as "a guy who rides through a sewer in a glass-bottomed boat."[20] His disparaging attitude toward the "do-gooders" was shared by many politicians. Thus, the successes of the reformers, in view of their limited numbers and the apathy or antagonism with which their zeal was met by the majority of New Yorkers, were all the more remarkable.

LOBBYING

The reform movements of the nineteenth century were themselves consistent with the state's moralistic political culture. Today, they have been superseded by numerous interest groups seeking to influence New York's public policy directions. Large and small industries, banks, public and private sector employees, insurance companies, veterans, religious charities, local governments, public utilities, senior citizens, hospitals, sportsmen, and lawyers are some of the organized interests regularly lobbying members of the legislature and the executive branch in Albany.

Interest groups have long been an accepted fact of New York's political life. Their visibility, diversity, numbers, and aggressive advocacy in Albany for a wide range of interests stem naturally from New York's rich cultural diversity and "the rough-and-tumble heritage of Tammany Hall."[21] Paul Smith describes the context for interest groups in New York: "The personal characteristics of assertiveness, knowledgeability, and so forth, when coupled with the intense competition among interests in the state, yield a political process marked by continual maneuverings, energetic discussions, and general activity. . . . The result is a good deal of vigorous debate, often punctuated by charge and counter-charge, that tends toward a process that is more open than closed, despite some incentives to the contrary."[22]

Warren Moscow, a newspaper reporter who covered New York State politics during the 1930s and 1940s, described the unusual access of one lobby, the New York State Federation of Labor: "Each day the members of the Legislature are furnished by their clerks with calendars of the day's bills. The labor group saw to it that the members received calendars on which the federation's stand was stamped in green ink alongside each measure. The notation read: 'approved by the State Federation of Labor' or 'opposed by the State Federation of Labor.' Members who knew nothing about some of the bills allowed themselves to be guided by the stamp, without asking questions. No other lobby ever obtained the privilege of so marking the calendars."[23]

Although no interest group, including the Federation of Labor, has had that sort of direct access and influence in many years, "interest groups are an accepted, welcomed [and growing] part of the state's political life."[24] In 1977, the legislature created the Temporary State Commission on Regulation of Lobbying and required lobbyists to disclose their activities and expenditures. In 1978, 941 lobbyists registered with the commission; by 1993, the number had doubled to 1,832. Lobbying expenses during the same time period increased by more than 550 percent, to $38 million.[25]

Groups most affected by the state budget consistently lead the way in lobbying expenditures. For example, "Philip Morris, fighting off a number of stringent anti-smoking measures, was the biggest spender" in 1993 on efforts to lobby members of the New York legislature.[26] In 1994, "amid concerns over budget cuts and health care overhaul, . . . health care providers, teachers and state workers" led the list of lobbyists.[27] A year later, hospitals, nursing homes, health-care providers, state employee organizations, and private employer groups lobbied the legislature on Medicaid reform (see chapter 12). Altogether, interest groups spent a record $47 million in 1995, with much of it focused on Governor Pataki's Medicaid reform proposals.[28]

In addition to direct lobbying to influence state legislators and agency officials, who "promulgate hundreds of rules, regulations, rates, and rate changes each year," interest groups "can also demonstrate the active commitment of the membership to the leadership's agenda through campaign contributions." Just under four hundred political action committees (PACs) in 1986 contributed millions of dollars—mainly to "majority-party incumbents who occupy safe seats or to campaign committees run by the Republican and Democrat leaders of the Senate and Assembly."[29] Such contributions enhance interest group influence and reinforce the strong leadership system of the New York State Legislature elaborated in chapter 6.

Within New York, a state of powerful interest groups and parties, two lobbies are commonly cited as the strongest: the business and public employee lobbies.[30] As David Cingranelli notes, the bases for their effectiveness differ: "Legislators thought unions were the most effective interest groups as elections approached, while business groups, such as the Business Council and banking and insurance associations, were often listed among the five most effective groups during more routine legislative sessions. This may indicate that at election time candidates may value campaign workers and votes (which unions may be able to supply) even more than PAC contributions."[31]

In summary, New York's reputation for convoluted and confusing political activity is well deserved. A complex mix of active New Yorkers reflecting the state's ethnic, regional, political, and cultural diversity has historically prevented assumption of complete control by any one group for any extended length of time. Yet two strong themes emerge as dominant across time: the entrepreneurial spirit of the capitalistic business community, arguing for the rugged individualist's right to succeed or fail by his or her own efforts, and the compassionate spirit of those concerned with the welfare of the group as a whole, whether persons unable to compete or persons whose well-being depends on state largesse. In the final analysis, the difference between the two positions is not whether those "unable to compete" should be helped at all; the difference, instead, revolves around who is deserving, and how and by whom he, she, or they should be advantaged in the New York political system.

CHAPTER THREE

Providing the Framework:
Constitution-Making

Joseph F. Zimmerman

The New York Constitution is the highest law of the state, the fundamental doctrine that sets "the ground rules for how public business is conducted and public policy is made."[1] Consistent with the constitutions of other states, the New York document is subordinate only to the guarantees of rights in the United States Constitution and the powers delegated to the Congress and backed by the "supremacy of the laws" clause in article 6. In brief, the New York Constitution establishes the government and determines the powers (reserved to the states by the tenth amendment to the U.S. Constitution) that may be exercised by the state and the forms of their exercise.

"Four factors in colonial New York," according to Peter Galie, "played a decisive role in shaping the first constitution of New York State in particular and the constitutional tradition in New York in general." Galie named as factors "the existence of a prominent and political active elite, many of whom were provincial gentry whose economic base consisted of large estates; the early development of a heterogeneous society with accompanying factional politics; the existence of a tradition of charters functioning as instruments of government; and a strong commitment to liberty protected by and rooted in the common law, Magna Carta, and various acts of parliament."[2]

Through the years, these factors have been transmuted into several key themes that characterize the current New York Constitution: compassion, competition, tension between centralization versus decentralization, and diversity.

The New York Constitution is replete with compassionate references. The most notable of its many enumerated social rights is found in article 17, section 1, which directs the state and its political subdivisions to care for the needy (see chapter 1 for elaboration). Article 11, section 1, requires the state legislature to provide for "a system of free common schools," the first such system in the United States. Other constitutional provisions protect rights of citizens not protected by the U.S. Constitution, including protection against discrimination by private individuals and corporations (article 1, section 11) and the right of employees to organize unions and to bargain collectively (article 1, section 17). Even where rights are not expressly guaranteed, the Court of Appeals has interpreted the constitution as guaranteeing them, as in the matter of adoption of children by a homosexual couple.

Competition for advantage is reflected in many provisions of the state constitution, from "a reapportionment policy [advocated by rural interests] . . . which made it virtually impossible for New York City to receive an appointment in the legislature commensurate to its population [to] a Labor Bill of Rights."[3]

Tensions between centralization and decentralization are reflected in the relative prerogatives vested in the governor and in the legislature within the state constitution, as well as those delegated to local governments and retained by the state legislature.

Finally, the constitution reflects New York's governmental and regional diversity. "Laws relating to the property affairs or government of cities" were divided into general and special city laws at the constitutional convention of 1894.[4] The state constitution contains numerous provisions specific to New York City, including local finance powers and a court structure that are distinct from those of other cities in the state.[5]

GENERAL PROVISIONS

The New York Constitution is organized in a manner similar to other state constitutions: a preamble followed by the bill of rights, the body, amendment articles, and schedule for implementation. The body is the heart of the constitution and provides for separation of powers between the state legislature, the governor, and the judiciary; a civil service system; debt and tax limits; functional responsibilities; and distribution of powers between the state and its political subdivisions.

New York's first state constitution was drafted and proclaimed to be in effect by a constitutional convention in 1777. Succeeding constitutions, drafted by popularly elected conventions, were approved by the voters in 1821, 1846, and 1894. The latter, currently in effect, has been enlarged considerably and complicated by subsequent amendments.

Constitution-making in New York can occur in two basic ways. One involves convening a constitutional convention and securing approval by the voters of a proposed new document or amendments issued by that convention. Every twenty years in the years ending in seven (e.g., 1957, 1977, 1997), the state's voters are asked whether they desire to call a constitutional convention. Their response usually is based on issues given wide publicity at the time. For example, voters rejected calling a convention in 1957, although

> Democratic Governor W. Averell Harriman supported the call for a convention. Furthermore he called for the adoption of a new procedure in changing the constitution, a constitutional initiative, whereby voters could initiate amendments to the constitution, thereby eliminating dependence on the legislature or a constitutional convention.
>
> [In contrast,] Republicans strongly opposed calling a convention, ostensibly on financial grounds, but more likely because a convention might redress the inequality in legislative reapportionment favoring upstate Republican areas. Republican leaders did not oppose revision altogether; they simply asserted that the legislative course was the better avenue for accomplishing needed revision.[6]

The state legislature is free to call a convention at any time subject to voter approval; in 1966, with voter approval, it called a convention to meet in 1967.

A convention, which bears a superficial resemblance to the state legislature, can submit its proposed constitution to the electorate as a series of questions or as a single question. Voters were asked in 1938 to approve nine heavily amended sections of the constitution; six were approved. In contrast, the convention of 1967 produced a constitution that voters were asked to approve or reject. Faced with this all-or-nothing choice, they rejected the document.

The state constitution can also be amended without calling a constitutional convention by majority vote of two separately elected legislatures approving an identical proposed amendment and its subsequent approval by the voters. The current (1894) constitution is a long (approximately 80,000 words), highly detailed document that has been amended more than two hundred times. The complex judiciary article, for example, contains approximately 15,800 words and is nearly two and one-half times the length of the entire Vermont constitution. New York's longstanding concerns for social welfare, education, conservation, and housing have all been incorporated in the constitution through the amendment process.

Thus, the New York Constitution is an evolving document embodying amendments, judicial interpretations, executive and legislative elaborations, and customs and traditions. In fact, judicial interpretations play a major role in New York because of the very complexity of the constitution.

CONSTITUTIONAL DEVELOPMENT

New York's first state constitution was written in 1776 by a 106-member "Convention of the Representatives of the State of New York," which promulgated the document in 1777 without a voter referendum. The 6,600-word document included the Declaration of Independence and established a strong bicameral legislature as the dominant branch. The power of appointment and the power to veto were confided in the Council of Appointment and the Council of Revision, respectively, thereby ensuring the governor would be a relatively weak officer.[7] Although the constitution contained no provision for amendment, the 1801 state legislature authorized the election of delegates to a convention that adopted five amendments without a referendum, including one increasing the number of members of the New York Assembly from 100 to 150.

The first constitution to be ratified by the voters (1822) was the product of the convention of 1821, which proposed abolishing the two councils and assigning their powers to the governor. The amendments were ratified by the voters, as were amendments reducing the governor's term of office from three years to two years and providing for the popular election of the attorney general, state comptroller, and secretary of state.

Commencing in 1790, the state legislature had made grants to private corporations undertaking public works that could not obtain adequate private financing. In addition, grants and loans of credit enabled firms to construct canals, highways, and railroads, and grants were made to help finance banks. The Panic of 1836–37 resulted in railroad companies defaulting on most of their state-supported bonds; the state legislature was forced to levy a special tax to obtain funds to meet the state obligations to bondholders.

A combination of factors—the state's fiscal problems, public displeasure with grants of funds and extension of state credit to private firms, and Jacksonian Democracy—induced the state legislature to call a convention that drafted a new document ratified by the voters in 1846. This constitution placed detailed restrictions on the state legislature relative to state finance, private corporations, and other matters. The 1846 constitution also provided for the popular election of several state officers—attorney general, state comptroller, secretary of state, judges, and others—and directed that the question of calling a convention be placed on the referendum ballot every twenty years.

The only voter-called convention in the nineteenth century met in 1867–68 and drafted a new constitution that was submitted as two questions to the voters. Only the judicial article was approved. However, Governor John T. Hoffman, with senate approval, appointed a constitutional commission in 1872 that recommended that the state legislature place on the referendum ballot many of the articles contained in the rejected part of the proposed constitution. Eleven amendments—among them an extension of the governor's term of office from two to three years—were placed on the ballot and ratified by the voters.

An additional six amendments restricting the powers of the state legislature were ratified by the voters in 1874. One granted the governor the item-veto power relative to appropriation bills, and one prohibited the auditing of private claims against the state. The latter amendment prompted the creation of the Board of Claims, which is now the Court of Claims. Another amendment prohibits the enactment of a bill by reference; that is, simply by referring to another law or section. This requirement necessitates that each bill include all provisions.

THE CURRENT CONSTITUTION

New York's current constitution is more than one hundred years old. When drafted by a convention and ratified by voters in 1894, it contained more than 20,000 words.[8] The new constitution (1) increased the size of the assembly from 128 to its current 150 members and the size of the senate from 32 to 50 members (currently 61); (2) reduced the term of the governor and lieutenant governor from three to two years (currently four years); (3) provided for state elections in even-numbered years and local government elections in odd-numbered years in an attempt to separate state issues from local issues; (4) stipulated that "no two counties . . . , which are separated only by public waters, shall have more than one-half of all the senators"; (5) required that all bills must be printed in their final forms and on members' desks three calendar days before being voted upon unless the governor issues a message of necessity waiving the requirement; (6) prohibited riders on appropriations bills; (7) made special laws affecting a single city subject to approval by the concerned city; and (8) incorporated the "Blaine amendment" forbidding the state to assist denominational institutions.

The Republican-controlled convention was allied with municipal reformers who desired to eliminate bosses, clean up corruption in large cities,
and protect cities against "ripper" laws (legislative interference). The convention also adopted a senate apportionment provision designed to ensure
Republican control in perpetuity.

Inclusion of numerous detailed provisions in the constitution facilitates
filing of lawsuits and ensures that provisions become archaic with the passage of time. One reason for the increasing length of the constitution is the
requirement for voter approval for the issuance of "full faith and credit"
bonds.[9] Examples include amendments authorizing "full faith and credit"
debt without voter approval for elimination of railroad grade crossings, bo-
nuses for certain World War I veterans, and expansion of the state university
system.[10] The only constitutional fiscal amendment that clearly belongs in
the fundamental document is the one establishing the executive budget system.[11]

Formation of the Progressive party by Theodore Roosevelt in 1912 split
the Republican party and led to Democratic party control of the governorship
and state legislature. Desiring to repeal the Republican-inserted apportionment provisions in the constitution, the state legislature placed on the 7 April
1914 ballot the question of calling a convention. The proposal was approved,
and the convention met in 1915. Republicans, benefitting from adverse public reaction to the impeachment of Democratic governor William J. Sulzer
and his removal from office, gained control of the 1915 convention, which
was dominated by supporters of state government administrative reorganization and municipal reformers. Voters, however, in 1915 rejected a proposed
new constitution that would have reorganized executive branch agencies,
authorized the executive budget system and issuance of serial bonds, incorporated a short ballot, and made changes in the judiciary. The 1921 state legislature called a convention that was limited to consideration of the judiciary
article and was not authorized to place proposed amendments on the referendum ballot. Several of the 1915 convention's recommendations, including
reorganization of the executive branch, were placed on the ballot by the legislature and ratified by the voters in 1925. In that same year, voters also approved an amendment limiting the number of civil departments to nineteen
(now twenty).

More significant was the 1927 ratification of a constitutional amendment,
proposed by the legislature, authorizing the executive budget system as a re-
placement for the legislative budget system. In 1936, voters approved an
amendment extending the term of office to four years for the governor, lieutenant governor, attorney general, and state comptroller.

A voter-called convention in 1937 submitted proposed amendments as a series of questions. The electorate ratified amendments relating to low-rent housing, railroad grade crossing elimination, social welfare, New York City debt limit, and hours, rights, and wages of public works employees.

Continuing unhappiness with the constitution, including the need for frequent amendment, and with the "one-person, one-vote" dictum of the U.S. Supreme Court induced the state legislature to place the question of calling a convention on the ballot in 1965.[12] Voters approved the calling of a convention and elected 186 delegates in 1966. The new constitution—a shorter, yet still detailed, document drafted by the convention—was submitted as one proposal and rejected by voters in 1967.

In the twenty-five years following the 1967 convention, sixty-five amendments were passed by the legislature, forty-three of which were approved by voters. "Over half (24) derived from four articles: VI (judiciary), VII (state finance), VIII (local finance), and XIX (conservation)."[13] The most significant changes pertained to the judicial article; they are elaborated in chapter 9.

THE NEED FOR REFORM

The critical need for constitutional revision in New York is highlighted by the constitution's many unintelligible provisions, as is illustrated by this example of convoluted language:

> Except for indebtedness contracted in anticipation of the collection of taxes actually levied and uncollected or to be levied for the year when such indebtedness is contracted and indebtedness contracted to be paid in one of the two fiscal years immediately succeeding the fiscal year in which such indebtedness was contracted, all such indebtedness and each portion thereof from time to time contracted, including any refunding thereof, shall be paid in annual installments, the first of which, except in the case of refunding of indebtedness heretofore contracted, shall be paid not more than two years after such indebtedness or portion thereof shall have been contracted, and no installment, except in the case of refunding of indebtedness heretofore contracted, shall be more than fifty per centum in excess of the smallest prior installment.[14]

Another problem is that the constitution's detailed, yet ephemeral, and statutory-type provisions necessitate the placement of proposed amendments on the ballot at every election dealing with relatively minor matters. Voters often do not understand the issues and frequently decline to vote on the questions.

Voters on 5 November 1974, for example, were faced with sixteen proposed constitutional amendments whose wording occupied nearly two full pages of fine print in the legal advertisement section of newspapers. Proposed amendment 4 provided:

> (b) whenever any county, city, other than the City of New York, village, or school district which is coterminous with, or partly within, or wholly within a city having less than one hundred twenty-five thousand inhabitants according to the latest federal census provides by direct budgetary appropriation for any fiscal year for the payment in such fiscal year or in any future fiscal year or years of all or any part of the cost of employer's contribution for pension, retirement, and social security liabilities, or an object or purpose for which a period of probable usefulness has been determined by law, the taxes required for such appropriation shall be excluded from the tax limitation prescribed by section ten of this article unless the Legislature otherwise provides.

Similarly, a current provision stipulates that corporations may not be formed by special act except "in cases where, in the judgment of the Legislature, the objects of the corporation cannot be attained under general laws."[15] In other words, the legislature can use its own judgment to determine whether a corporation is to be created by a general or a special law.

Additionally, the New York Constitution contains more prohibitions and restrictions than any other state constitution and reflects distrust of government and public officers. There are valid historical reasons for the encumbrances. When they were adopted, no other devices existed to prevent legislative abuses. Today, the direct accountability of public officers to the electorate can be achieved through the protest referendum, initiative, and recall—all explained in a subsequent section.

These prohibitions and restrictions, it can be argued, reduce the ability of the state legislature to respond to contemporary issues. In some cases, these encumbrances have been ineffective in achieving their goals because the legislature has found ways to circumvent them. For example, the requirement for voter approval for the issuance of "full faith and credit" bonds has been evaded by legislative creation of public authorities with the power to borrow funds backed by an indirect pledge of the state's credit. Such "moral obligation" bonds frequently pay a higher rate of interest than "full faith and credit" bonds and consequently are a more expensive method of financing public projects.

Constitutional provisions similarly hinder needed reorganization of the executive branch. There is no authorization for the governor to prepare executive branch reorganization plans that become effective after a specified number of days unless disallowed by the state legislature. The reality is that the legislature generally is not interested in the reorganization of the executive branch and does not initiate such reorganizations. As elaborated in chapter 8, the limit of twenty civil departments has been evaded by legislative creation of the executive department as a "holding company" for offices and divisions including ones that have larger appropriations and more personnel than the smallest department.

The massive judiciary article has been proposed for serious review and revision. Despite the constitutional stipulation that "there shall be a unified court system for the State," the judicial system is not fully unified. The widespread use of political party cross-endorsements of judicial candidates has made hollow the concept of elections. Finally, as judges cannot campaign on issues, the electorate is not able to evaluate judicial abilities and demeanor of candidates (see chapter 9 for elaboration of these points).

The simultaneous use of three methods—the *Ultra Vires* rule, *Imperium-in-Imperio*, and Devolution of powers—to allocate authority to municipal corporations produces confusion as to the extent of their discretionary authority, deters full use of such authority, and leads municipal attorneys to continually seek advisory opinions from the attorney general and the state comptroller (see chapter 10 for definitions and descriptions of these three methods).[16] In addition, restrictions upon the powers of these municipal governments prevent them from solving problems in the most economical and efficient manner. A related problem is the lack of constitutional protection for property taxpayers against expensive state mandates on local governments.

A CONSTITUTION FOR THE TWENTY-FIRST CENTURY

How can the Empire State achieve a constitution capable of responding effectively to the challenges of the twenty-first century? Many advocates for constitutional reform, among them former governor Mario M. Cuomo, argue that a convention is "the only way to overcome the legislative deadlock over issues such as state voter registration laws, campaign finance reform and the judicial selection process."[17] Cuomo, whose requests to the state legislature to call a convention were ignored, initiated action for constitutional reform in 1993 by executive order 172—four and one-half years in advance of the mandatory constitutional question. A Temporary Commission on Constitutional Revision, established pursuant to his order, was charged with "examining and evaluating the processes for convening, staffing, holding, and acting on the recommendations of a convention, and for developing a broad-based agenda of issues and concerns which might be considered by such a convention."

In 1995, the eighteen-member bipartisan commission issued an innovative report that diverged from the traditional section-by-section approach to constitutional reform. Instead, the commission, responding to public concerns about "deepening problems" and lack of confidence in current governmental institutions, proposed the appointment of four "Action Panels." These advisory groups to the governor and the legislature—modeled loosely on congressional commissions that have resolved such national issues as military base closing and Social Security reorganization—would propose fundamental restructuring of state fiscal practices, elementary and secondary education, the criminal justice system, and relations between the state and local governments.[18] Only if the state government failed to achieve "far-reaching reform" on these matters, the commission reported, would it favor convening a convention in 1999.[19] George E. Pataki, Cuomo's successor, stated when campaigning for governor in 1994 that he "did not have a problem with having a Constitutional Convention." He added that he would exclude "state legislators, lobbyists and commissioners as delegates . . . because the history has been that the Constitutional Convention is controlled by the same insiders who control the government anyway."[20] As governor, however, Pataki received the report of the Temporary Commission on Constitutional Revision without comment and maintained that silence through 1996. Nonetheless, whatever the outcome of the commission's work, the question of calling a convention will automatically appear on the ballot in 1997.

Despite agreement that reform of the New York Constitution is needed, there is no consensus "as to the direction of that reform and whether a convention is the best way to achieve it." Those who argue for a convention contend that "it would be able to clear the document of obsolete clauses, simplify its language, and, where applicable, align the document with the mandates of the Supreme Court. . . . It would provide the people the opportunity to decide the direction they wish to move concerning the major issues facing the state as it enters the new century. It would give citizens the opportunity to debate and decide issues such as reapportionment, campaign financing, and voter registration reform—issues the legislature has failed to address."[21]

Those who argue against a convention cite "the possibility of controversial and potentially dangerous proposals being placed before an electorate in the mood to entertain such measures." Abortion, rights of accused persons, recall, referendum, term limits, and spending and revenue caps are frequently mentioned among those controversial proposals. "With important and controversial issues to be decided, the convention could propose a constitution whose provisions address those issues, only to have the electorate reject its work, as it did in 1967."[22]

Unresolved issues about the convention process itself also complicate constitutional reform. "Should delegates be elected on a nonpartisan basis? Is the current selection method using senate districts as multi-member districts combined with at-large elections a violation of the [United States] Voting Rights act of 1965? Should there be limited or weighted voting to ensure the process results in a more diverse convention? Should public officials be barred from serving as delegates? Should amending the constitution by legislative initiative be simplified?"[23]

One suggested approach to avoid these obstacles to reform is to have a relatively brief document that guarantees civil liberties, establishes the framework of the state government, mandates civil service and executive budget systems, provides mechanisms that can be employed by voters to ensure continuing responsibility by government officers, devolves broad powers upon general purpose local governments subject to preemption by general law, prohibits enactment of special laws unless requested by the concerned local governments, requires state government reimbursement of specified types of new or enhanced state mandates, and contains general provisions facilitating flexible responses to rapidly changing conditions.

The Model State Constitution drafted by the National Municipal League, modified as needed as the constitutional convention in Alaska did, may be a reasonable guide for a New York constitution.[24] The Model State Constitution reflects the best judgments of leading state constitutional experts; it contains none of the prohibitions and restrictions that encumber New York state government.

Concern has been expressed that voters will not ratify a proposed constitution unless it contains many of the current prohibitions and restrictions. But voters may be persuaded to ratify a new document if it includes provisions enabling them to employ more effective devices for promoting citizen control of the government, such as the indirect initiative, protest referendum, and recall.[25]

The indirect initiative empowers voters to propose laws by petitions that must be considered by the state legislature. Its failure to enact the proposals into law within a specified number of days results in the proposals appearing on the referendum ballot. The protest referendum authorizes voters by petitions to delay the implementation of a new state law until a referendum is held to determine whether the law should be repealed. The recall allows the electorate by petitions to call a special election to determine whether an elected officer should be removed from office prior to the expiration of his or her term.

Reforming State Offices

A constitutional convention undoubtedly would propose a shorter document devoid of much of the detailed clutter and restrictions contained in the present document. A convention might also examine the provisions relating to the lieutenant governor, attorney general, and state comptroller.

The Model State Constitution does not provide for a lieutenant governor. Five states—Maine, New Hampshire, New Jersey, Tennessee, and West Virginia—experience no apparent difficulties in operating without this official. In Tennessee, the Speaker of the senate by statute has been assigned the additional title of lieutenant governor. Currently, the New York lieutenant governor has only one constitutionally assigned duty: presiding officer of the senate with a casting vote.[26] The constitution also assigns the lieutenant governor two "standby" duties. He or she automatically becomes governor if the elected governor dies; resigns; is impeached, convicted, and removed from office; is absent from the state; or is "unable to discharge the powers and duties of his office."[27] The second standby duty is service on the Court for the Trial of Impeachment except in a trial of an impeachment of the governor or the lieutenant governor.[28]

A strong case can be made for amending the constitution to remove the provision for the lieutenant governor to automatically become acting governor during the temporary absence of the governor from the state. Poor communications existing at the time the current provision was adopted explain the original rationale for the provision. With modern telecommunications permitting the governor to remain in contact with state officials while out-of-state, there appears to be no need for mandating that the lieutenant governor automatically become acting governor upon the governor's departure from the state. In practice, governors often fail to notify the lieutenant governor of out-of-state travel plans.

If the office of lieutenant governor is continued, it may be advisable to amend the constitution to mandate the joint nomination of the candidates for governor and lieutenant governor in the primary election. Currently, each voter casts one ballot in the general election to ensure that the candidates elected governor and lieutenant governor are members of the same political party. There is no joint nomination requirement for primary elections, and there have been instances where the winning candidates were members of competing slates who did not establish close relations.

In contrast to the office of lieutenant governor, the separately elected attorney general and state comptroller would seem to be important offices to retain. The federal model provides for the president to appoint the attorney general, subject to Senate confirmation, who serves as the president's chief legal adviser. The current independence of the New York attorney general has led each governor to appoint a counsel to the governor. At times, the attorney general may in fact serve as a counterweight to the governor. In 1984, for example, Attorney General Robert Abrams deflated Governor Mario M. Cuomo's proposal for a sports lottery to raise funds to support education by declaring the proposal violated the constitutional ban on gambling.[29]

The state comptroller achieved constitutional status in 1821 and became an elective officer in 1846. The comptroller's constitutional authority is limited to current or pre-auditing, post-auditing, and prescribing accounting methods.[30] Administrative experts recommend that current auditing be performed by a controller appointed by the governor and post-auditing by a state auditor elected by the state legislature and subject to its direction.

The current constitution, which blankly asserts "the executive power shall be vested in the Governor," suggests that the state has a single chief executive.[31] In fact, however—the constitution notwithstanding—the state has a plural executive, with executive functions assigned to the attorney general, state comptroller, and Board of Regents. A strong case can be made for centralizing all executive authority in the governor. If the state comptroller is divested of executive powers and confined to post-auditing, the office should be renamed state auditor and the state legislature should select the auditor.

The constitution creates a Board of Regents with at least nine members appointed by the legislature and authorizes the board to appoint the commissioner of education, but it delegates no other authority to the board.[32] The board and the Department of Education establish standards for and supervise all private and public education from kindergarten through postdoctoral programs.

Several governors have complained publicly about their lack of direct authority over the department that oversees educational spending, the function with the largest annual budget appropriation. In 1973, Governor Nelson A. Rockefeller created by executive order an Office of Education Performance

Review; it issued nine reports prior to its abolishment by Governor Hugh L. Carey in 1975.[33] Governor Mario M. Cuomo commented that education is "handled by people who are virtually unknown to the public at large and accountable to no one."[34] Governor George E. Pataki proposed abolishing the Board of Regents and replacing it with a commissioner responsible to the governor and the legislature. The board, he said, "can impose costs, they can impose programs, but they can't provide one nickel of aid."[35] A constitutional amendment would be required to remove the board's power to appoint the commissioner of education and transfer the power to the governor. The legislature by statute, however, could divest the board of its control of elementary and secondary education and other duties.

It is highly probable that if a group of constitutional law experts were asked to review the constitution of New York, they would rate its quality between a 1 and 2 on a scale of 1 (poor) to 10 (excellent). The experts would probably rate highly only the Bill of Rights and the executive budget provisions.

What is the best route for achieving basic constitutional reform in New York? The constitution recognizes the possible need for a major revision by directing that the question of calling a convention be placed on the referendum ballot every twenty years in the years ending in seven and by authorizing the state legislature at any time to place the question on the ballot.

The constitution, however, is the product of the interactions of political interest groups over the decades; a proposal for a constitutional convention to consider drafting a new document automatically results in opposition by interest groups seeking to protect provisions benefiting them. Citing the millions of dollars spent by the 1967 convention, which proposed a new document that was rejected by the voters, they argue that a convention is an extravagant method of proposing amendments. They also contend that needed amendments can be proposed by the state legislature.

However, reliance upon the legislature for basic constitutional reform has yielded only piecemeal and minor changes when fundamental changes are called for. Experience with the constitutions drafted by conventions in 1915 and 1967 indicates that the potential for voter approval is enhanced when a new fundamental document is presented to the voters as a series of separate questions. Ratification of even some of the proposed articles would improve the constitution. In addition, rejected proposals may serve as the basis for revised constitutional amendments that the legislature may propose in the future. Many provisions contained in the voter-rejected 1915 constitution, for example, were proposed as single amendments by the state legislature in the 1920s and subsequently were ratified by the voters.

A short constitution confined to fundamentals would facilitate citizen understanding of the state governance system and, of necessity, grant broad discretionary powers to the state legislature to enact statutes that would respond to the diverse problems in the Empire State. Potential abuses of legislative powers could be neutralized by inclusion of provisions authorizing the protest referendum, the initiative, and the recall.

No one, in sum, can deny either the need for constitutional change in New York or the fact that it is exceedingly difficult to accomplish.

CHAPTER FOUR

The State in the Federal System

Sarah F. Liebschutz

New York's place in the American federal system has been distinctive from the very beginning. New York City served as the nation's capital from 1785 until 1790, an honor marked by New Yorkers with a "concentration of energy, money, public spirit, and civic pride."[1] Yet New York was a "reluctant pillar" of the new federal union; it was the eleventh state to ratify the constitution, where nine states constituted the minimum necessary number. New York's ratification of the federal Constitution in 1788 came after careful assessment by delegates to the state's ratifying convention (a solid majority of whom were Antifederalists) of both the substance and the timing of ratification. The final pragmatic action was best captured in the words of Zephaniah Platt, an Antifederalist delegate who voted for unconditional ratification, he said, "not from a conviction that the Constitution was a good one or that the Liberties of men were secured. No—I voted for it as a Choice of evils in our own present Situation."[2]

The perspective of the federal government toward New York is equally intriguing. Some twenty years ago, it was most popularly captured in the 1975 *Daily News* headline, "Ford to City: Drop Dead," when federal assistance was sought to prevent the insolvency of New York City. Although the quote was incorrectly attributed to President Gerald R. Ford, Washington's disdain reflected the alienation of many Americans from the fast-talking, fast-thinking, fast-spending New Yorkers whose city and state, in the public mind, were undifferentiated.

Both characterizations, of New York's ambivalence and Washington's indifference, are overdrawn. New Yorkers have long played prominent roles in the political leadership of the nation, and New York has been a party in highly visible U.S. Supreme Court decisions. At the same time, New York and New Yorkers depend in significant ways on federal policies and programs. That dependence makes New York a competitor with other states and, at times, a challenger of presidents whose policies are perceived to threaten the state and its residents.

NEW YORK GOVERNORS AND THE PRESIDENCY

"After a narrow victory in his first race for the state's highest office during the height of the Republican ascendancy in Washington, New York's Democratic governor won an overwhelming reelection victory. The next day the state Democratic party chairman said he did not see how the governor could 'escape becoming the next presidential nominee of his party, even if no one should lift a finger to bring it about.' "[3]

That year was 1930; the governor was Franklin D. Roosevelt. But the assumption that New York's governorship is a springboard to the presidency has had much wider application. From Martin Van Buren, elected president of the United States in 1836, to Mario Cuomo, New York's governors have been identified as potential presidential candidates. Governors Van Buren, Grover Cleveland, Theodore Roosevelt, and Franklin D. Roosevelt actually served as president; Governors Horatio Seymour, Samuel J. Tilden, Alfred E. (Al) Smith, and Thomas E. Dewey were candidates for president. Republican Governor Nelson A. Rockefeller pursued the nomination of his party for almost all his fourteen years (1959–73) in office. And Governor Mario M. Cuomo was mentioned, virtually from his first election as governor in 1982, as a Democratic presidential candidate.

Even when not candidates, New York's governors have played major roles in their party's presidential candidate selection process. Their visibility is enhanced by their leadership of their state political party. At national nominating conventions, they command attention by controlling a significant bloc of delegates, a control that can leverage concessions from presidential hopefuls if the governor chooses to run on the first ballot as a "favorite son."

The high visibility of New York governors is grounded in an obvious fact: New York is a large and important state. Until the 1970s, when "the colossus of the Northeast [showed] unmistakable signs of decay,"[4] New York was the leader among the states in population and economic output. In the 1990s, with a population of nearly 18 million, still massive financial, agricultural, and manufacturing activity, and a congressional delegation of thirty-one members (second only to California), it is still formidable.

The visibility of the state and its governors is magnified because New

York City, the state's—and the nation's—largest city, is the communications and media capital of the United States. New York governors are thus more likely than other governors to command media attention. Coverage of their activities by the *New York Times*, the "hometown paper of record," and the national news networks based in New York City generate attention that extends far beyond the state's borders. When governors are adept at utilizing the media for their own purposes, the effect is magnified. Governor Cuomo's "skills at manipulating the media, assisted by a staff of 'spin doctors,' [were characterized as] superb."[5] His description of the "Decade of the Child" in his 1988 *State of the State Message*, for example, drew the nation's attention to his education, health, housing, and family proposals. His public opposition to President Ronald Reagan's 1985 tax reform proposal (elaborated later in this chapter), although viewed as a risky strategy for Cuomo's national political aspirations, heightened interest in the issue.

UNITED STATES SUPREME COURT DECISIONS

The national spotlight also derives from New York's association with seminal United States Supreme Court decisions. In four of the most famous such cases—*Gibbons* v. *Ogden*, *Lochner* v. *New York*, *New York Times Co.* v. *United States*, and *New York* v. *United States*—the court promulgated fundamental constitutional principles.

In 1824, the U.S. Supreme Court, in *Gibbons* v. *Ogden*, "determine[d] how far the local pride and self-interest of individual States would be permitted to hamper the development of one continentwide, free-trade market on which to build a unified Nation."[6] The case involved a monopoly of the right to operate steamboats on the waters of New York granted by the state legislature to Robert Livingston, the chief financier of steamboat inventor Robert Fulton. Livingston subsequently assigned a portion of his monopoly to Aaron Ogden. Ogden's monopoly was challenged by Thomas Gibbons, who sought to operate two ferries across the New York harbor. The basic constitutional question was whether "the grant to Congress of power to regulate interstate commerce means that only Congress can regulate . . . or [whether] the States are free to tax and regulate interstate commerce unless and until Congress ousts State law, thus retaining 'concurrent jurisdiction.' "[7]

The Supreme Court held that a prior act of Congress granting licenses to enrolled American vessels to enter the coastal trade conferred a federal right that, under the supremacy clause, prevailed over state law. Thus *Gibbons* v. *Ogden* swept away the steamboat monopolies and established an important constitutional principle.

Eighty-one years after *Gibbons*, the Supreme Court, in *Lochner* v. *New York* (1905), considered whether New York had legitimately exercised its police power to protect the safety, health, and morals of the public.[8] Joseph Lochner, the operator of a small bakery in Utica, challenged a New York law that limited a bakery worker's hours to sixty per week. The Court found that the law was "meddlesome," constituting "an illegal interference with the rights of individuals, both employers and employees, to make contracts regarding labor upon such terms as they may think best."[9] " 'Lochnerism' and 'Lochnerian' [came] to symbolize an era of conservative judicial intervention under the Due Process Clause, [which sought] to stem the flow of social and economic reform."[10]

Freedom of the press and national security were the core issues in *New York Times Co.* v. *United States*, decided by the Supreme Court in 1971.[11] This was the well-known case of the Pentagon Papers, an eighteen-volume "study, conducted by the Department of Defense, of the formulation and conduct of U.S. policy and military and diplomatic operations in Southeast Asia before and during the war in Vietnam."[12] President Richard M. Nixon sought to enjoin publication of the papers, contending that national security interests were at risk.[13] The Supreme Court ruled, 6–3, that these claims did not support an injunction against publication. Justices Hugo Black and William O. Douglas, in fact, declared that any prior restraint on the publication of any news "would make a shambles of the First Amendment."[14] Thus, this highly publicized case, which involved New York's most prominent newspaper, determined that "claims of the national interest in the preservation of secrecy [were inferior to] the values of publishing information about the conduct and plans of government in a democratic society."[15]

The constitutionality of federal legislation imposing a deadline for states to provide disposal sites for low-level radioactive waste generated within their borders was at issue in *New York* v. *United States* (1992). New York challenged the 1985 Low-Level Radioactive Waste Policy Amendments, contending that they violated its powers under the Tenth Amendment.[16] The Court, in an opinion written by Justice Sandra D. O'Connor, reaffirmed the authority of Congress "to preempt state laws and to render funding contingent on state compliance with congressional mandates" on the disposal of low-level radioactive waste.[17] At the same time, the Court struck down the provision that states failing to provide disposal sites by 1996 must take title of and assume liability for all undisposed waste. "The Constitution," O'Connor wrote, "has never been understood to confer upon Congress the ability to require the States to govern according to Congress' instructions."[18]

New York v. *United States*, with its twin rationales, thus may have signaled an important shift "in theoretical ground for the Court's defense of states' sovereignty."[19]

New York's presence in the Congress has always been substantial, with two senators and, until 1973, the largest delegation in the House of Representatives. But the state's size advantage has not been consistently translated into influence in either the Senate or the House.

United States Senators from New York

Seniority is crucial for assignment to influential committees and leadership positions. Turnover among members of the New York delegation historically has been high; hence, the number of New Yorkers holding leadership positions has been low. For example, only three New Yorkers, Robert F. Wagner (1927–49), Jacob K. Javits (1957–81), and Daniel Patrick Moynihan (1977–), made the list of 109 senators who, between 1789 and 1997, had served twenty or more years. When Senator Moynihan became chair of the Environment and Public Works Committee in 1991, he was the first New Yorker in forty-seven years to chair a Senate standing committee. Two years later, Moynihan became chair of the important Finance Committee. In 1995, with a Republican Senate majority, Senator Alfonse M. D'Amato became chair of the Banking, Housing and Urban Affairs Committee (and Moynihan reverted to ranking member of the Finance Committee). Prior to Moynihan's election as committee chair, the last New York senator to hold such a position had been Wagner, who chaired the Committee on Banking and Currency from 1937 to 1946. The last New Yorker to chair the Senate Finance Committee had been Daniel S. Dickinson in 1849.

Among New York's senators, Robert F. Wagner is most frequently acclaimed; Senator Robert C. Byrd, former majority leader of the U.S. Senate, characterized Wagner as one of the most "influential senators in the twentieth century."[20]

Born in Germany, Wagner immigrated to the United States at the age of nine with his family. Humble beginnings did not deter him from academic accomplishments (City College of New York and New York Law School) and political success. A Tammany Hall Democrat, Wagner was elected to the New York Assembly in 1904, where he chaired a special investigating commission to inquire into factory safety after the infamous Triangle Shirtwaist

Company fire, which killed 146 women workers. Subsequently, he and the commission's cochair, Alfred (Al) E. Smith, cosponsored some sixty bills "for more humane working conditions."[21] Wagner was elected to the U.S. Senate in 1926, where he "was speedily accepted into the Senate's inner club. . . . In 1935, Senator Wagner shepherded through Congress two of the most important bills ever passed during the New Deal—the Social Security Act and the National Labor Relations Act, better known as the Wagner Act. . . . The Wagner Act, as its author himself proclaimed, aimed to protect workers 'caught in the labyrinth of modern industrialism and dwarfed by the size of corporate enterprise,' to keep them from becoming the mere 'playthings of fate.' "[22]

Another New York senator was a potent force earlier in the twentieth century: Chauncey M. DePew. A two-term Republican senator, DePew effectively thwarted the will of the Senate majority from 1902 to 1912. Before his appointment by the New York legislature to the Senate in 1888, DePew had been a lobbyist and lawyer for the Vanderbilts and president of the New York Central Railroad; he was a defender of trust building "in an era of trust-busting."[23] DePew "prized [his] political freedom . . . and was not eager to subject [himself] to the discomforts of a public campaign, certainly not in response to jealous and malicious resolutions from the House."[24] He introduced an amendment in 1902 to a Senate bill to amend the U.S. Constitution to provide for the direct election of senators. His amendment, for the federal government "to enforce and to provide for . . . the conduct of elections," was viewed as friendly to black voters in the South (thus supported by Republicans), but as sanctioning the reimposition of Reconstruction on the South (thus ardently opposed by southern Democrats). DePew's parliamentary maneuvers were not overcome until ten years later, when the Senate finally secured the necessary two-thirds majority to pass the amendment for direct election of senators.

Since the late 1950s, New York has had one "national" senator (whose interests and perspective extend principally beyond New York) and one "local" senator (whose focus is mainly on the state) serving together. Jacob K. Javits, for example, a "national" senator,[25] represented New York in the Senate for twenty-three years, together with a succession of more "local" senators: Kenneth B. Keating (1959–65), Robert F. Kennedy (1965–68), Charles E. Goodell (1968–71), and James L. Buckley (1971–77). The term of a second "national" senator, Daniel P. Moynihan, overlapped for four years (1977–81) with that of Javits. Thereafter, Alfonse M. (Al) D'Amato, Javits's successor, assumed the "local" senator role.

Moynihan and D'Amato have been called an odd couple "with practically nothing in common."[26] Moynihan is a former Harvard professor and former ambassador to India and the United Nations, with service in the Kennedy, Johnson, Nixon, and Ford administrations. "A liberal but often unconventional Democrat," he has been the Senate's "resident intellectual, gadfly, and prophet" since his election in 1976.[27]

Moynihan is an effective advocate for New York. He was instrumental in retaining state and local tax deductibility from federal income taxes in 1986 and in securing $5 billion from the Federal Highway Trust Fund to repay New York for the Thruway in 1991.[28] But he is as well, or better, known as a statesman and intellectual whose writings, interests, and influence on the Environment and Public Works and the Finance Committees range widely across both domestic and foreign policy.

Senator D'Amato is also an effective advocate for New York. A conservative Republican with prior suburban, Long Island, local government experience, he is more "local" in outlook. Labeled "Senator Pothole" by the press, "an operator rather than a great legislator," and a "pitbull" by former New York City Mayor Edward I. Koch, D'Amato has long viewed constituent service, including the garnering of "pork" (federal funds for New York), as a high priority.[29] "If you put the pie out," D'Amato has said, "don't blame me for wanting a slice . . . for my people—who've got to eat also. . . . I may vote against the program, but if [it] gets passed, I'm going to fight for my fair share."[30] D'Amato's national profile was considerably heightened in 1995, when he assumed chairmanship of not only the Banking, Housing, and Urban Affairs Committee but also the Senate Whitewater and the National Republican Senatorial Committees. These positions, together with his close alliance with Governor George E. Pataki, made him, the *New York Times* asserted, "the most powerful politician in New York and the most important New Yorker in Washington."[31]

For all their differences in style, interests, and orientation, Moynihan and D'Amato work well together. For example, they collaborated on retention of deductibility of state and local taxes from federal taxation in the mid-1980s, a matter of very high priority for New York and New Yorkers, and they have amicably divided the nomination of judges to federal courts in New York by a formal quota.[32]

The House Delegation

New York's delegation to the U.S. House of Representatives, the largest until 1973 and second to California since then, has been less effective than its senators in promoting New York interests. The delegation was characterized in 1975 as a "helpless giant, scary to other members because of its size and roar, but basically ineffectual in passing legislation needed by the state."[33] Following the censuses of 1970, 1980, and 1990, the giant decreased from 41 to 34 to 31 members. Its roar was further diminished by the retirements in 1992 of twelve incumbents who represented 214 years of House seniority. New York's seniority disadvantage in the 103rd Congress that took office in 1993 was obvious: no New York representative chaired a major committee, and New York held fewer subcommittee chairmanships than did California or Texas.[34]

Two years later, however, after House control shifted to Republicans, New York's potential for influence increased considerably. Two New Yorkers were elected to chair standing committees: Gerald B. H. Solomon, House Rules, a committee central in setting the ground rules for floor consideration of legislation, and Benjamin A. Gilman, International Relations. Six Republican House members from New York were elected to chair subcommittees. Although the New York delegation continued to be dominated by Democrats (seventeen Democrats to fourteen Republicans), New Yorkers were better positioned in the Republican-controlled 104th Congress to advocate for the state.

Delegation cohesion is a key factor in delegation influence. The New York delegation has typically been schizophrenic. Upstate-downstate, Democratic-Republican, and liberal-conservative schisms have done little to promote civility or cohesion. Until the late 1970s, meetings of the whole delegation were rare and, when they did occur, were strident and boisterous. "To achieve some modicum of quiet, James Delaney, Brooklyn Democrat and longtime delegation dean, would call out 'One fool at a time!' "[35] The New York City fiscal crisis of 1975, which revealed the vulnerabilities of both New Yorks—city and state—was a "wake-up call" to the delegation to pull together on state and city priorities. In that crisis and the fight a decade later to retain state and local tax deductibility, the delegation was cohesive in advancing New York's interests. Such issues of high priority to the state, however, come along rarely.

In the 1990s, the delegation's level of internal civility is much higher than during the days of Representative Delaney; members, however, still divide along lines of ideology and partisanship on policy matters.[36] The delegation's vote on the Unfunded Mandates Reform Act of 1995, legislation that created "new procedures in the Congress to restrict the enactment of future unfunded mandates," is illustrative.[37] This legislation, part of the Republican majority's "Contract with America," was supported by state and local government officials, eager to reduce costs associated with federal regulations, and by President William J. Clinton.[38] The Unfunded Mandates Act passed the House by a wide margin—360 to 74. Yet the New York delegation was split largely along partisan lines: all 14 Republican members supported the act; a majority of Democrats (11–6) opposed it.[39]

New York City and the state are institutionally well poised to bargain in Washington. In addition to its large congressional delegation, New York's most important institutional representatives are the State Office of Federal Affairs (the governor's lobby) and the New York City Washington Office (the mayor's lobby).

The State Office of Federal Affairs—technically part of the "Second Floor" of the state capitol, but located in the Hall of States in the nation's capital—was established by Governor Nelson Rockefeller in 1971. His purpose was to enhance the state's competitive bargaining position vis-à-vis the Congress and administrative agencies. The governor's action reflected his disappointment with the inability of the National Governors Conference to surmount partisanship, his desire to "press for enactment of a federal revenue sharing program . . . [and his belief that] the state's large, but uncohesive, congressional delegation had the potential to influence a favorable outcome for such legislation."[40]

From 1971 to the present, the state office has monitored a wide range of issues that affect New York and New Yorkers, including cyclical (e.g., budget and tax policy), recurrent (e.g., immigration policy), and crisis (e.g., the New York City fiscal crisis) issues as they unfold in the legislative and regulatory processes. The state office plays multiple roles for the governor: collecting information, consulting with members of the New York congressional delegation, and developing strategy for the state to press its case in the appropriate arena.

The two cases that follow illustrate how Governors Hugh L. Carey and Mario M. Cuomo, working closely with the New York congressional delegation and the state office, advanced New York's interests in the federal system.

The New York City Fiscal Crisis of 1975

In the spring of 1975, New York City faced a fiscal crisis; put simply, the city was unable to borrow the cash it needed to pay current expenses and municipal debts falling due.[41] At the same time, the city's dire situation posed one of the most serious policy challenges to any New York governor in the twentieth century. The fate of the state and that of the city, both in desperate shape, "were inextricably intertwined."[42] Governor Carey played the central role in surmounting the city's fiscal crisis and, at the same time, preserving the fiscal integrity of the state. He personally engaged in intensive bargaining with city and union officials, state legislative leaders, the Ford administration, and members of the Congress. The New York Seasonal Financing Loan Act, signed by President Ford in December 1975, which provided for loans of $2.3 billion a year for three years to New York City, was one of Carey's greatest achievements as governor.

The New York City fiscal crisis of 1975 was a sobering experience for the city, the state, their representatives in the Congress, and the governor. First, it was patently clear that the fate of the state and that of its largest city were—and continue to be—inextricably intertwined. Second, it was obvious that New York, represented in the Congress by a delegation of strident, personally aloof, arrogant, and, above all, "different" members, was not beloved. "Fast-talking, fast-thinking, fast-spending New York [was] looked on as a foreign country."[43]

The strategic lessons learned from the fiscal crisis—to "tone down" behavior and to form coalitions within and outside the Congress in ways that "de-emphasize New York leadership and New York interests"[44]—were applied a decade later when Governor Cuomo played a highly visible role to retain deductibility of state and local taxes in federal tax reform.

State and Local Deductibility

Just as Governor Carey's role was essential in the resolution of the 1975 New York City fiscal crisis, so was that of Governor Cuomo in opposing the Reagan administration's tax-reform proposals of 1985 and 1986.[45] The elimination of deductibility of state and local taxes from federal income taxation was advocated by President Reagan on philosophical and pragmatic grounds. Governor Cuomo and other top state officials, Senators Moynihan and D'Amato, and nearly all the members of the New York congressional delegation viewed the elimination of deductibility as a direct threat to New York's taxpayers, public services, and competitive posture vis-à-vis other states. Cuomo's opposition to the popular president's proposal, although viewed as a risky strategy for his own national political aspirations, effectively drew national attention to the issues. The governor's public assertiveness and eloquence, as well as his role in developing the state's multilevel strategy that stressed internal delegation cohesiveness and downplayed deductibility as a New York issue so as to gain allies from other states, were pivotal for the retention of deductibility of state and local property and income taxes in the Tax Reform Act of 1986.[46]

INTERGOVERNMENTAL STAKES

The work of all New York's representatives in Washington—members of the Senate and the House of Representatives and staff of the "governor's lobby"—is important because the financial and regulatory stakes for New York in the federal system are very high.

Federal Regulations

No issue, on the whole, generates more intergovernmental conflict and competition than federal regulation. Since the 1960s, regulatory federalism has grown dramatically, and its nature has changed. Federal policies have been increasingly reoriented from places to persons, John Kincaid argues, and a historic shift from "cooperative" to "coercive" federalism has resulted.[47] The "shift and shaft" nature of mandates compels "state and local officials to raise taxes or cut other services in order to comply with [them] while the federal government declines to raise taxes or cut other programs to pay for its policy preferences."[48]

The U.S. Advisory Commission on Intergovernmental Relations (ACIR) identified thirty-six federal mandates affecting state and local governments as of 1980; a decade later, ACIR counted an additional twenty-seven, not including "a number of costly conditions that were added to existing grant-in-aid programs."[49] These mandates include requirements that cut across all federal grants ("crosscutting requirements"); grant conditions that impose fiscal sanctions in one program area for failure to comply with federal requirements under another separately authorized program ("crossover sanctions"); minimum national standards for certain programs, where administration and enforcement responsibilities may be delegated to states or localities ("partial preemptions"); and legal stipulations that are enforced by civil or criminal penalties ("direct orders").[50] During the 1980s, the increased use of crosscutting requirements, crossover sanctions, and partial preemptions was notable.

Federal mandates and grant-in-aid conditions affect the lives and fortunes of New Yorkers in many ways. From direct orders regulating disposal of New York City's sewage sludge to crossover sanctions affecting the designation of federal interstate highways within New York for use by tandem trucks, the costs of compliance—or noncompliance—are steep.[51] The following case examines intergovernmental relations in response to the 1986 federal Safe Drinking Water amendments.

New York City's Drinking Water Supply

New York City's water supply comes from a system of reservoirs, lakes, and tanks that store water drained from a 2000-square-mile watershed spread over three geographical areas in numerous towns and villages within eight upstate counties. The Croton watershed southeast of the Hudson, which supplies about 10 percent of the city's water, was completed in 1905; the Catskill watershed northwest of the Hudson, which supplies about 40 percent of the city's water, was completed in 1927; and the Delaware watershed, which supplies 50 percent of the city's water, was completed in 1964. Construction of all three watersheds had been specifically authorized by the state legislature.

The future of New York City's drinking water supply was challenged by the 1986 amendments to the federal Safe Drinking Water Act, amendments classified as both a direct order and a partial preemption. In 1989, the Environmental Protection Agency (EPA) issued its surface water treatment rule. The regulations stipulated that "surface water systems—like New York City's—must either filter or demonstrate that there hasn't been an outbreak of waterborne disease; that the water meets certain standards for bacteria levels; and that a program is in place to protect the watershed."[52] Because of deteriorated conditions in the small Croton watershed, a filtration plant costing about $600 million was already scheduled to be built. Cost projections for a massive filtration plant for the water from the Catskill and Delaware watersheds ranged from $4.5 billion to over $8 billion.

The 1989 EPA rule pitted New York City against local, state, and federal governments. The city sought, through acquiring thousands of acres in the Catskill and Delaware watersheds as a buffer against development, to avoid the costs of building and operating a massive filtration plant. Towns and villages in the watershed areas—many with inadequate sewage treatment systems—were concerned not only about adequate compensation for the land but also about constraints on their future economic development.

Between 1989 to 1993, officials from New York City, the state, watershed towns, and the EPA tried to work out their differences. Intergovernmental discussions among the EPA, the state, and city led to two formal EPA rulings in 1993: primary responsibility (primacy) for implementation of the 1989 drinking water regulations was delegated to the state Department of Health (DOH); and filtration avoidance status, pending compliance within eighteen months with sixty-six specific conditions, was granted for the Catskill and Delaware systems. Hostile negotiations between officials from New York City's Department of Environmental Protection (DEP) and a coalition of thirty-five Catskill watershed towns ensued; watershed representatives "recounted old war stories of land theft on the city's part [and by city officials], flagrant violations of water-protection rules upstate."[53] State government officials in the Cuomo administration "watched from the sidelines . . . [in these initial rounds as they] tried to work out their differences."[54] George E. Pataki, the new governor, took direct action. He secured a 180-day extension of the mid-April 1995 compliance deadline from the EPA. Then, after more than two hundred meetings, "many of them bitter and unproductive, [among] all the interested players," he succeeded in brokering an arrangement under which the city agreed to "spend more than $1.2 billion to acquire more than 100,000 acres of land from willing sellers, to upgrade 100 or so sewage treatment plants, to repair many of the region's 128,000 septic tanks and to underwrite a program to reduce runoff from farms. The project [would] be administered by a new Watershed Council made up of residents, city and EPA officials and environmentalists."[55] The estimated cost per New York City household of $7 per year was "a bargain in comparison with the cost of building and running a filtration plant that had threatened to triple water rates."[56] At the unveiling of the agreement in September 1996, the federal Environmental Protection Agency, representatives of the affected Catskills communities, and several environmental groups publicly endorsed the plan. One town supervisor "marveled at the breadth of support . . . [and said,] 'I remember when I said I wouldn't sit next to an environmentalist.' "[57]

Federal Spending in New York

Federal spending in all states goes to individuals for Social Security and Medicare benefits, to businesses for goods and services purchased by federal agencies, to military and civilian personnel for salaries and wages, and to state and local governments for grants-in-aid. Between 1981 and 1994, all such federal spending increased by 134 percent—from $562.2 billion to $1.3

Figure 1: Federal Government Expenditures in New York State, 1981–1994

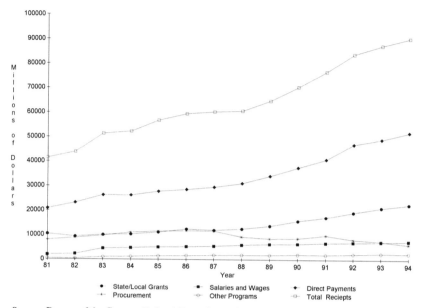

Source: Bureau of the Census, *Federal Expenditures by State* (various years).

trillion (in current dollars). During the same period, federal spending in New York grew by 118 percent. As shown in figure 1, however, spending trends differed by type of aid, increasing for direct payments to individuals (Medicare, Social Security) and grants to state and local governments, declining for procurements, and remaining flat for the other categories.

In 1994, the federal government spent $90.3 billion in New York, or 6.8 percent of its total expenditures in all fifty states. Given that 18.1 million New York residents accounted for 6.8 percent of the nation's total (estimated) population in 1994, New York State, on an overall basis, received a fair share of federal spending. In fact, from the mid-1970s to the present, per capita federal expenditures in New York have been very close to the national average.

However, the pattern of federal spending within New York is dramatically different from that of the nation as a whole. Direct federal spending in New York, for salaries and wages and for procurement and contract awards, is consistently lower than the national average, while indirect spending, through grants to state and local governments, is consistently higher. In 1994, for example, New York ranked third among the states in federal per

Table 3: Per Capita Federal Expenditures in New York, Federal Fiscal Year 1994

Expenditures	New York*	United States*	Rank for New York
Salaries and Wages	$ 408	$ 639	43
Procurement Contract Awards	338	749	35
Defense	196	476	
Direct Payments/Individuals	2,857	2,617	8
Food Stamps	107	86	
Medicare	887	688	
Social Security	1,186	1,289	
Grants to State and Local Governments	1,235	810	3
Medicaid	623	310	
AFDC	99	63	
Other	111	179	32
Total	4,972	4,996	22

Source: Bureau of the Census, Federal Expenditures by State for Fiscal Year 1994, April 1995.
*1994 U.S. population estimated at 18,169,000; 1994 New York State population estimated at 264,218,000 or 6.8% of total.

capita spending for grants to state and local governments; this ranking was largely driven by Medicaid spending. (New York's high Medicaid spending is explained in chapter 12.) At the same time, New York ranked forty-third in federal per capita spending for salaries and wages (see table 3).

The basic problem is that while New York receives its general share of federal social spending, it lags in areas perceived as more productive. As Senator Daniel Patrick Moynihan has put it, "Medicaid money . . . [is] really not the kind of money you want to get. . . . you want to get 18 percent of the procurement or federal employment, in terms of what helps your own economy."[58]

Since 1970, federal grants to the New York state government have fluctuated from 20 to 30 percent of state revenues. The state government received $21.4 billion in state fiscal year 1994–95, about 30 percent of total state revenues. The largest single sources of federal aid to New York are for three entitlement programs administered by all states—Medicaid, Food Stamps, and Aid for Families with Dependent Children, with Medicaid accounting for larger and larger shares. In 1981, federal Medicaid spending in New York was $2.6 billion, or 25 percent of all federal aid to the state government; by 1995, it had increased to $11.4 billion, or 58 percent of the total. New York's financial stakes in the federal system for the social welfare of its citizens, in sum, are enormous. The challenge for New York's representatives in Washington is to safeguard the state's share of social funding and, at the same time, secure a greater share of federal funds in more productive areas.

New York's place in the federal system, distinctive among the states at the beginning of the republic, remains distinctive more than two hundred years later. Springboard to the presidency for four New York governors and an aspiration for many more, New York has long played a prominent role in the formation of national policy by virtue of its large congressional delegation and involvement in Supreme Court cases with wide-reaching impacts. In the latter half of the twentieth century, New York's dependence on the national government has become more apparent; the state's effectiveness as national actor, however, has been hampered by a congressional delegation historically splintered by geography, ideology, and partisanship.

CHAPTER FIVE

Political Parties and Conflict

Jeffrey M. Stonecash

Political parties are central to New York politics. They draw their electoral bases from different constituencies and areas of the state. They "organize" political debates by taking differing positions on policies. Policy negotiations revolve around positions taken by the legislative parties. At the same time, however, parties are experiencing change. Public identification with parties has declined in recent decades, and split-ticket voting is on the rise. In many elections, independents are the pivotal group that candidates must win.

These two situations—the enduring dominance of parties while partisan attachments are declining—might be seen as contradictory. They are not, however. More voters are hesitant to identify with parties, but regional concentrations of partisan attachments persist. These regional divisions provide strong electoral bases for each party. There are areas where loyalties are divided, and these become political battlegrounds, but most areas have clear partisan inclinations. These differing electoral bases lead to parties taking differing policy positions and a continuing role for parties in the process.

This chapter reviews the electoral bases of the parties, the decline in attachment to the parties, and the response of party organizations to these changes over the years. The role of the parties in structuring the political debates within the state is then examined.

THIRD PARTIES

The focus in this chapter is on the two major parties. State law also allows for additional parties. Any party whose gubernatorial candidate receives at least 50,000 votes is certified as a legitimate party until the next election. In New

York, the current third parties are the Liberal, Conservative, and Right-to-Life parties. The Liberal party has been in existence for over fifty years. The Conservative party began in 1963 as a reaction to domination of the Republican party by the relatively liberal governor Nelson Rockefeller. The Right-to-Life party began in 1978 as an effort to make abortion issues an explicit part of campaigns. None of the third parties enrolls large numbers of individuals. As of 1995, the total number of party registrants was 8,856,289, with 4,091,740 enrolled as Democrats, 2,736,061 as Republicans, and 1,751,587 as Independents. The Conservative party had 142,548 enrollees, the Right-to-Life party, 37,548, the Independence party, 18,688, and the Freedom party, 2,006.

A candidate can be endorsed by more than one party, and candidates appear on the ballot on a separate line for each party line under which they are running. Voters can vote for a candidate under any line. Candidates seek to run on third-party lines because they believe it allows voters to register a more specific political message (for example, voting on the Conservative line) in addition to voting for a candidate. Candidates also do not want opponents to receive the endorsements.

Third parties have influence primarily through their strategies of endorsing major-party candidates. The Liberal party usually endorses Democrats, while the Conservative and Right-to-Life parties endorse Republicans.[1] The power to endorse is of some consequence because candidates believe an endorsement and the additional line on the ballot can provide more votes. While some candidates worry about endorsements a great deal, evidence from the last forty years indicates that votes on third-party lines provide the margin of victory in only about 3 percent of legislative races.[2] In gubernatorial and mayoral races, there are occasions where votes on third-party lines play a role, however. In 1982, Mario Cuomo won the governor's race with the votes on the Liberal line. The Liberal party also played a major role in helping Republican Rudolph Giuliani defeat incumbent Democrat David Dinkins for mayor of New York City in 1993. Republican George Pataki's votes on the Conservative party line (328,605) provided his margin of victory to beat Mario Cuomo in 1994. Thus while third parties can play a pivotal role in some races, the major parties continue to dominate the state.

THE DECLINE OF REPUBLICAN ENROLLMENT

The relative enrollment in the two major parties has changed over time. Figure 2 indicates the major trends in party enrollment since 1920. Two signifi-

Figure 2: Party Enrollment Trends in New York, 1920–1995

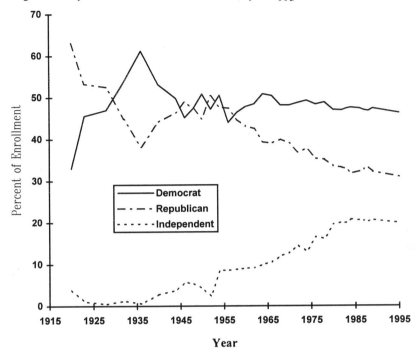

cant changes have occurred. First, Republicans once dominated the state, but their enrollment advantage has gradually declined since the late 1950s.[3] The impact of Watergate was devastating to the Republicans, and enormously helpful to Democrats, particularly in legislative elections. In 1974, Republicans controlled the legislature but lost control of the assembly when the nation voted against the Republican party because of the Watergate scandal.

The second significant change in party enrollment has been the increase in independents, or the proportion who choose not to enroll in any party. The decline in Republican enrollment did not produce a corresponding shift to the Democratic party. Instead, the movement has been into the Independent group, or those who decline to choose any party. By 1995, the percent in the Independent column had risen to 21.0 percent.

PARTY ELECTORAL BASES: REGIONALISM, CLASS, AND RACE

The important matter for politics is whether the parties represent different groups and serve as advocates of different policies. Political parties in New

Table 4: Bases of Partisan Identifications of New York Voters, 1980s

	Composition of Each Partisan Group (by percent)		
	Republican	Independent	Democrat
Political Persuasion			
Liberal	17.1	34.0	48.9
Moderate	29.0	32.9	38.1
Conservative	41.8	31.9	26.3
Income			
Low	30.5	26.8	42.7
Moderate	28.8	32.6	38.5
High	31.8	35.1	33.1

Sources: Gerald Wright, University of Indiana, and Robert Brown, University of Mississippi.

York draw upon very different constituencies. Table 4 indicates differences within the general public in identification with the two major parties by political persuasion and income. The results are from polls conducted by CBS and the *New York Times*.[4] Individuals were asked to define themselves as liberals, moderates, or conservatives and to indicate their income.[5] Liberals tend to identify with the Democratic party, while conservatives tend to identify with the Republican party. Differences by income are not as pronounced, but there are still differences. Low-income individuals are more likely to identify with the Democratic party.[6]

This aggregate portrait of party bases is helpful, but it is relevant primarily for statewide candidates. Legislative districts are more revealing of the regional, class, and race bases of the parties. Region has been significant for some time. Republicans do well upstate and in suburban areas around New York City. Democrats do well in New York City and a few upstate urban areas. There has been a longstanding division between upstate and downstate areas.

Much of this division has been driven by a sense among upstate residents that New York City is "different." The influx of immigrants, seen as "different," into the city in the late 1800s played a significant role in this. The Democratic Tammany machine built a strong base among immigrants, which further convinced Republicans upstate that New York City politicians and Democrats were not to be trusted.[7] This regional dominance was not complete, but it was sufficient for areas of the state to have clear political identities.[8] Republicans enjoyed an enormous edge in upstate areas in party enrollment and the ability to win legislative races. The regional dominance of the

Figure 3: Democratic Percentage of Assembly Seats by Area, 1990–1995

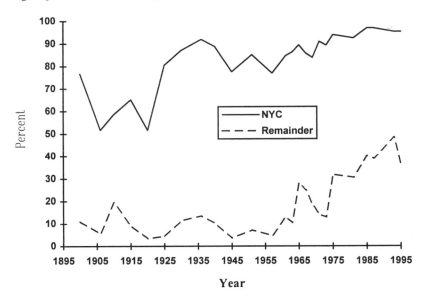

parties can be seen in the geographical bases of the legislative parties across time. Figure 3 presents the proportion of assembly seats held by Democrats representing New York City and the rest of the state since 1900. Democrats dominate New York City, whereas Republicans have dominated upstate. These regional differences in party support have also prevailed, with few exceptions, in gubernatorial elections.[9]

Because of these different party bases, many policy proposals were seen as benefiting either New York City or the rest of the state. Issue differences might have split along urban versus suburban-rural lines, with Buffalo and Rochester aligning with New York City, but, instead, the division between New York City and the remainder of the state dominated politics.

In turn, many people in each area who might normally have been in a different party stayed in the dominant party of their area because of hostility to the other area. Many blue-collar workers upstate, for example, might normally have been Democrats, but they were Republicans because their primary concern was opposition to New York City.[10] Many wealthy residents of New York City might have been Republicans, but they were Democrats because they felt that Republicans were unsympathetic to New York City needs.

As figure 3 indicates, the sharp division in support by area for the political

Table 5: Legislative Party Members by Area, 1994

Assembly

Area	Party		Democratic Percentage of Total Party Enrollment
	Republican	Democrat	
New York City	3 (4.9)	58 (91.1)	70.0
Remainder	53 (59.6)	36 (40.4)	
Long Island	15 (68.2)	7 (31.8)	28.1
Northern NYC			
Suburban	2 (25.0)	6 (75.0)	34.8
Upstate Urban	5 (23.8)	16 (76.2)	43.3
Upstate Rural	31 (81.6)	7 (18.4)	32.2

Income	Republican	Democrat
$0–31,99	8 (21.6)	29 (78.3)
$32,000–39,999	12 (31.6)	26 (68.4)
$40,000–54,999	19 (50.0)	19 (50.0)
$55,000+	17 (45.9)	20 (54.1)

Percentage of Minorities in District	Republican	Democrat
1–9	30 (75.0)	10 (25.0)
10–19	24 (63.2)	14 (36.8)
20–39	2 (5.6)	34 (94.4)
40+	0 (0)	36 (100.0)
Total	56 (37.3)	94 (62.7)

Senate

Area	Party		Democratic Percentage of Total Party Enrollment
	Republican	Democrat	
New York City	6 (24.0)	19 (76.0)	70.0
Remainder	29 (78.8)	7 (21.2)	
Long Island	9 (100.0)	0 (0)	27.9
Northern NYC			
Suburban	5 (83.3)	1 (16.7)	34.5
Upstate Urban	3 (40.0)	6 (60.0)	41.4
Upstate Rural	12 (100.0)	0 (0)	33.3

Income	Republican	Democrat
$0–31,99	4 (26.7)	11 (73.3)
$32,000–39,999	9 (56.3)	7 (43.8)
$40,000–54,999	10 (66.7)	5 (33.3)
$55,000+	12 (80.0)	3 (20.0)

Percentage of Minorities in District	Republican	Democrat
1–9	14 (93.3)	1 (6.8)
10–19	12 (75.0)	3 (25.0)
20–39	9 (60.0)	6 (40.0)
40+	0 (0)	15 (100.0)
Total	35 (57.4)	26 (42.6)

Sources: Reports prepared by the Reapportionment Task Force, 1992; official 1994 election results, New York State Board of Elections.

Notes: Figures are based on results of 1994 elections. For legislative seats, the first number for each area in columns one and two is the number of Republicans or Democrats from that area, followed by the percentage of legislators from that area who are Republicans or Democrats. The percentage of Democratic enrollment is presented in column three. Upstate Urban consists of Erie, Monroe, Niagara, Onondaga, Broome, and Albany Counties. Northern NYC Suburban includes Westchester, Orange, and Rockland Counties. Upstate Rural is composed of all other counties.

parties has declined in recent years. Democrats have been able to make some inroads into areas outside New York City. The 1974 election was particularly important for increasing Democratic success outside New York City. In 1975, the Democrats became the majority party in the assembly. Assembly Democrats took 21 seats that were held by Republicans and lost 2 to the Republicans for a net gain of 19. Most of these Democratic seat changes (14 of 21) were upstate. That election gave the party a significant base upstate. In 1974, Democrats held 10 of the 64 upstate seats (16 percent). After the 1974 elections, the Democrats held 24 of 64 seats (38 percent). In subsequent years the Democrats won even more seats upstate and expanded their legislative base. In 1982 and 1992, Democrats used their control over drawing district lines to create more districts favorable to Democrats, which increased the number of seats they held.[11] By 1995, they held 43 of 89 (52 percent) of the seats outside New York City. The assembly Democratic party is now more of an urban statewide party than a New York City party. Throughout these changes, the senate remained Republican and has been the enduring base for the party over time. Party success by area in the 1994 elections is shown in table 5.

The parties also differ in their class and racial bases. Table 5 presents party success by income level and percentage of minority residents within the district. Democrats in both houses do well in districts with lower incomes and with high percentages of minorities. Republicans in both houses do very well in more affluent, white districts.

PARTY BASES AND POSITION TAKING

Since 1974, the Democrats have had firm control of the assembly, while the Republicans held the senate. The parties, with differing electoral bases, have used their institutional bases to advocate different policy positions and negotiate legislation favorable to their constituencies.[12] Republicans have continually advocated policies that they believe will encourage more economic competition and new businesses within the state. They propose lower taxes because they argue that high taxes make it harder to retain business and professional workers.[13] They advocate fewer regulations on business and less government bureaucratic intervention into business practices. They advocate reductions in Medicaid and other social programs. Republicans consistently argue that too much is spent on welfare and Medicaid and that there should be limits on the benefits clients receive.

Democrats, on the other hand, have been much more likely to speak of compassion for the needs of workers and lower-class interests. They seek to restrain increases in tuition at the state universities. They consistently support social services and making the tax structure more progressive.[14] They seek to maintain welfare client benefits, while restraining the reimbursement paid to providers. They support building more public housing and preserving that public housing built in the past.

These party differences are reflected in the ratings that interest groups give the parties. Interest groups select bills important to their members and score legislators according to whether they vote "right." The higher the score, the more the legislator has voted in accordance with the interest group. Averages by party provide an indication of each party's compatibility with different interest group concerns.

The 1994 ratings indicate party differences. In the senate, Republicans averaged 57 for Conservative party ratings; Democrats averaged 22. For the Environmental Planning Lobby (EPL), Republicans averaged 58; Democrats averaged 78. In the assembly, Republicans averaged 74 for the Conservative party; Democrats averaged 10. For the EPL, Republicans averaged 72; Democrats averaged 88. Past ratings indicate the same differences between parties.[15] While some argue the parties do not differ,[16] interest group ratings indicate there are clear differences.

The parties in New York serve as vehicles for presenting different ideas about the role of government and its relationship to society. Republicans worry about the decline and stagnation of the state's economy; they think individualism and economic activity can be encouraged by cutting state programs and reducing tax and regulation burdens. Democrats argue for maintaining a greater state role to help people who are vulnerable and in need of assistance.

MODERATING PARTY DIFFERENCES

While New York's political parties are generally regarded as cohesive and different, there are tensions within each party that lead to some moderation of the general stances just described. Many assembly Democrats, particularly those from Queens and upstate, are moderate and conservative. This creates continual tensions within the party, which must be worked out in party conferences. Within the senate, upstate Republicans tend to be more conservative than those from the New York City metropolitan area. The nine Republicans on Long Island are continually seeking more school aid to hold down local property taxes. This requires maintaining state taxes to maintain revenue flows, which leads to a continuing tension within the party over whether to cut taxes or keep revenues at existing levels.

As table 5 indicates, each majority party does very well in its traditional areas, but to retain power, each party also needs seats in areas less receptive to its basic philosophy.[17] In the assembly, the Democrats hold almost all the seats in New York City. The key to their majority in the assembly, however, lies in the forty-three Democratic seats held outside New York City. These areas outside New York City are often not as liberal as the areas within the city. In the senate, the areas of Republican dominance are the upstate rural areas and Long Island, where they hold twenty-one out of twenty-one seats. But Republicans could not control the senate without the six seats they hold in New York City and their three seats in upstate urban areas. As with the Democrats, the Republicans control their house by being able to win seats in areas that are not inclined to elect Republicans. For both parties, some moderation of policy stances is forced on the "center" of the party because of the need to attract and accommodate party members from areas outside the party's strength.

There have also been tensions between the legislative and gubernatorial

Table 6: Gubernatorial Electoral Bases, 1990–1994

| | 1990 | | 1994 | | | |
| | Democratic Percentage of Vote | | Democratic Percentage of Vote | | Republican Percentage of Vote | |
Area	Within	From	Within	From	Within	From
New York City	73	35	70	45	28	17
NYC Suburban	50	25	41	25	55	31
Upstate Urban	48	20	38	17	51	21
Upstate Rural	43	21	27	14	65	32

Sources: Manual for the Use of the Legislature of the State of New York, various years; official 1994 election results, New York State Board of Elections.

Notes: The first column for each year indicates the percentage of the vote that each party won within each area. The second column for each year indicates the percentage of the party's entire vote that came from that area. (Separate figures are not given for the Republican party in 1990.) NYC Suburban includes Dutchess, Nassau, Orange, Rockland, Suffolk, and Westchester Counties. Upstate Urban consists of Albany, Broome, Erie, Monroe, and Onondaga Counties. Upstate Rural is composed of all other counties.

wings of each party. The Republican party's primary base of support is outside New York City, but for the last fifty years, Republican gubernatorial candidates have needed to win substantial votes in liberal New York City because the city constitutes 40 percent of the electorate. Governors such as Thomas E. Dewey and Nelson A. Rockefeller were able to get elected and reelected only by adopting relatively liberal Republican stances, which created clashes with their more conservative legislative party.[18] The Republican party was sometimes less conservative than it might have wanted to be because of the moderate to liberal leanings of the governor.

Democratic gubernatorial candidates also have tensions with wings of their party. The Democratic party's strongest base of support is in New York City, but Democratic candidates have usually had to be sensitive to the need to gather votes outside New York City. As New York City has declined in population, Democratic candidates have become even more concerned about winning votes outside the city. Lee Miringoff and Barbara Varvalho argued that the clue to Mario Cuomo's election success during the 1980s was his popularity in the suburbs around New York City.[19] Table 6 indicates how Cuomo depended on areas outside New York City in the 1990 election. The table presents the percentage of the vote that Cuomo received within each area and the percentage of his total vote that came from each area. Thus the first column indicates his popularity within an area, and the second indicates how much he relied on votes from each area. In 1990, Cuomo, facing Republican and Conservative party candidates, won with 53 percent of the vote. He received 50 percent of the vote in the New York City suburbs and upstate urban counties and derived about two-thirds of his total vote from areas outside New York City. In 1994, his support in the New York City suburbs and upstate urban areas declined, and his reliance on New York City increased. His inability to do well outside New York City led to his loss.

The 1994 election results suggest this tension to do well in areas outside the primary base of support *may* be declining in importance for Republicans. New York City was over 50 percent of the state population for many years, but that percentage has now declined to just over 40. The lower turnout in 1994 by New York City voters (just under 50 percent) compared to upstate voters (about 70 percent) reduced the importance of New York City and made it possible for Republican George Pataki to win the election while winning only 28 percent of the vote in New York City (see table 6). This was the lowest percentage won in New York City by a winning Republican candidate in over sixty years and suggested that the governor would not have to cater to New York City in the budget process.[20] This possibility of Republican political estrangement from New York City existed despite the presence of Rudolph Giuliani, the Republican mayor of New York City, elected in 1993. In the 1994 election, Giuliani endorsed Cuomo, further separating Pataki from New York City and leaving Pataki in a situation where he was not indebted to Giuliani. Pataki won the election although he received only 17 percent of his vote from the city.

The difficulty, however, with assuming that the 1994 election indicates a changed relationship to New York City for Republican governors is that the 1994 Democratic candidate, Mario Cuomo, had very high negative ratings by 1994, and much of the vote was interpreted as ABC ("anything but Cuomo"). Pataki may have won largely because of the hostility to Cuomo, who will not be present in 1998. Thus, New York City may once again be crucial for Republicans in 1998.

The minority parties in each house also have internal conflicts, but those conflicts are less significant because the minority party does not control policy decisions, so party members have more freedom to vote as they wish. There is less pressure to reconcile the conflicts within these party conferences.

Table 7: Age and Party Enrollment in Onondaga and Madison Counties, 1986

Age Group	Party Enrollment			Birth date
	Democrat	Republican	Independent	
18–24	32.6	27.9	32.6	1962–68
25–29	33.8	33.8	29.6	1957–61
30–39	29.6	36.0	29.1	1947–56
40–49	30.0	40.6	24.1	1937–46
50–59	28.6	52.2	13.0	1927–36
60–69	26.9	62.9	10.3	1917–26
70+	21.3	68.0	9.8	Prior to 1917

Source: Syracuse *Herald Journal–Herald American* telephone election poll of 900 registered voters, 8 October 1986.

POLITICAL CHANGE: PARTY VOTING AND ELECTORAL COMPETITION

The situations of New York political parties are in some ways very stable. The bases of the parties are relatively clear and stable, and divided control of the legislature has persisted for some time. But amid this continuity, considerable change is occurring. The attachment of the electorate to parties is declining, and the organizations through which parties work are changing. Three related changes in electoral behavior have emerged in recent decades. The proportion of independents has increased, split-ticket voting has increased, and party competition in legislative elections has declined in recent years.

The Rise of Independents

As noted earlier, the proportion of independent voters has increased. Voters without party attachments create problems for parties and their candidates because they are more variable than partisans in their vote choices. They rely on other criteria such as familiarity with the candidate, personalities, reactions to current events, along with positions on specific issues, rather than some enduring partisan attachment. The reliance on factors other than partisanship may make voting patterns more volatile from election to election and result in voters "splitting" their vote among candidates from different parties.

The impact of these independents in New York politics will also grow in the future. Enrollment in parties is strongly associated with age. Older individuals are more likely to be enrolled in a party, whereas younger individuals are much more likely to choose the independent category. An example of this decline in partisan enrollment is presented in table 7. The data are lim-

Figure 4: Split-Ticket Voting in New York Legislative Elections, 1910–1988

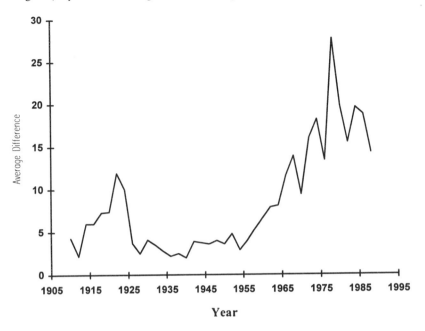

ited, but important. The results, from a survey conducted in the upstate counties of Madison and Onondaga during the 1986 election, present partisan attachment by age or year of birth. Registering as an independent is much higher among younger individuals.[21] If these younger voters maintain their independence as they get older, those without partisan attachments may constitute a larger part of the electorate. Unless something happens in future years to forge strong attachments to the parties, candidates will face an electorate less and less likely to vote regularly for one party.

The Rise of Split-Ticket Voting

Another change in state legislative elections has been a rise in split-ticket voting, defined here as the difference in the vote for assembly Democratic candidates and senate Democratic candidates within the same county.[22] Figure 4 presents the average difference between percentages for candidates in assembly and senate elections, collected by county for the years 1910–88. The trend is clearly toward more ticket splitting, as the party vote for an assembly candidate within a county often diverges considerably from the senate vote. If straight party voting is declining, then candidates can focus more on creating personal images. It may also lead legislators to have less inclination to work with and be associated with the party. If the electorate is not engaging in as much party voting, it may be politically expedient for legislators to be cautious about their association with the party and its image. This behavior makes it more difficult to create cohesive party positions within the legislature.

The Decline of Electoral Competition

One other change has affected the role of parties as organizers of issues in state politics. Many observers of politics argue that it is crucial to have competition between political parties within legislative districts so voters have a real choice. Electoral competition has changed dramatically in New York. Since 1900 the average margin of victory (percentage points by which the winner leads the loser) in legislative elections has steadily increased from a little over 20 to the current level of over 50 percentage points.[23] Few districts have close elections. As the proportion of independents has risen, and as split-ticket voting has increased, incumbents have been able to win with larger and larger margins. This decline in party competition within districts has occurred at the same time that the parties have continued to differ in the legislature. This seeming contradiction is discussed in a later section.

POLITICAL CHANGE: PARTY ORGANIZATIONS

The organizations that parties use to pursue their goals have also changed. Local county organizations have declined as the primary party organizations used by state politicians. The legislative parties have created legislative campaign committees, and legislative candidates now have their own campaign organizations. Governors have also created their own organizations to pursue political goals.

These changes have emerged gradually. At one time, most political party activity was organized by county organizations. We have no detailed studies of how significant their roles were, but numerous accounts of the county party organizations indicate they had a significant role in shaping nominations, mobilizing volunteers, and raising money for candidates from the local area.[24] Governors could negotiate state legislative agreement with county leaders and could count on the votes of that county's delegation.[25] That role has declined. County organizations have fewer patronage positions to distribute and have more difficulty attracting volunteers.[26] With the rise of independents, candidates now create organizations separate from county party organizations so they can make unique and personal presentations to the electorate. With the rise of television and direct mail campaigns, candidates raise their own funds and plan their own campaigns. All these changes have reduced the role of county organizations. They still play a role in interviewing candidates, gathering petition signatures, raising some funds, and performing various other activities, but candidates now can be, and generally must be, more independent and entrepreneurial in conducting their campaigns.

The legislative parties, responding to the decline of county organizations and desiring to affect the success of legislative candidates, formed legislative campaign committees. During the 1970s, the parties in the legislature became concerned about having the resources to conduct their own campaigns so they could preserve their incumbents and add new ones. These organizations have grown to considerable significance. Each party in each house has developed its own organization. The committees are directed by the leadership of each party in each house. They raise substantial funds within each election cycle (from $4 to $6 million for the majority party in each house in the late 1980s). They conduct their own polling, and they plan their own campaign strategies. Their primary focus is on marginal races, or races in which they face the greatest risk of losing a seat or have the greatest potential of gaining a seat.[27] The greatest resources go to the closest elections, and the organizations have sufficient discipline to deny resources to those who do not need them.[28]

These legislative campaign committees (LCCs) have become a significant part of the state party organization scheme. Legislative candidates receive virtually no funds from "state" committees and almost no direct financial support from gubernatorial candidates. LCCs have emerged to provide that assistance. The organizations raise their own funds, engage in recruiting candidates for office, and even help candidates who run for local offices. Although the point should not be stretched too far, the legislative campaign committees have become somewhat of the permanent party organization. They worry about recruiting candidates, raising funds, and maintaining the long-term position of the party.

These organizations have not completely replaced local organizations. Indeed, some research suggests that local organizations have revived somewhat from the decline that occurred during the 1960s and 1970s.[29] On many campaigns the local and state organizations work together. On other races and concerns there is some friction between the two.[30] While their status and significance is not entirely clear, it is clear that party organizations are changing in the state, and that healthy party organizations exist, but in more diverse forms.

The emergence of these organizations does not mean that legislators are less oriented to their constituents. Organizations in the capital may design strategy, write and print brochures, conduct polls, and mail literature, but all these activities are designed around the nature of the constituency in specific districts. Legislators receive assistance in passing legislation that is pertinent to their district. The focus continues to be on the local district, but the resources to respond to that constituency and to design a campaign for that constituency are more likely to come from Albany.

The effects of this transformation in party organizations are not entirely clear, but the transformation surely has contributed to maintaining party cohesion within each house of the legislature. The legislative parties have their own resources and organization. Legislators may have relied on these resources in the past or anticipate needing them in the future. Since this reliance is greatest among marginal legislators, it may create some loyalty among those most likely to otherwise be mavericks within the party. But this presumption of an impact on loyalty among these legislators must be tempered by a recognition that the party also is dependent on the survival of these marginal legislators and is more likely to understand that they need considerable autonomy from party discipline to survive.

These electoral trends and new party organizations have also increased the independence of the legislative parties from the governor. Legislators know their elections are not tied to gubernatorial results, and they have campaign resources independent of the governor.

Parties are significant in New York. They play a major role in organizing the electorate, but their political environment is changing. The electorate votes less on the basis of party. This discrepancy between partisan conflict in the legislature and the decline of party in the electorate may appear to be puzzling. If the electorate is less concerned with parties, then why does such strong party competition and conflict persist in the legislature? Why do legislators line up in opposition while the electorate is less concerned about such divisions?

The answer lies in the spatial clustering of the population. Areas of the state differ in their populations and dominant concerns. In turn, those areas elect legislators typical of the area. Rural areas tend to be Republican and relatively conservative; they invariably elect someone typical of their area, even if partisan competition within the area is low. Urban areas tend to be Democratic and relatively liberal; they also elect legislators typical of the area. Republicans tend to come from areas with more conservative attitudes on fiscal issues. Democrats tend to come from areas more liberal on fiscal issues.

When legislators assemble in Albany, members within each party find themselves in rough agreement with each other on many major issues, and they find themselves in opposition to legislators from other areas. Organized partisan competition persists in Albany even while partisan attachments are declining in the electorate.

CHAPTER SIX

The Rise of the Legislature

Jeffrey M. Stonecash

In the early 1950s when Thomas Dewey was governor, the legislative leaders were called to the governor's office after the budget was virtually settled. The leaders were told there was some discretionary money in the budget for small legislator projects. The leadership was expected to take the budget back to the members and pass it as it stood. They usually did so.[1]

In 1983 Mario Cuomo was the new governor. He presided over the passage of a budget negotiated among him, the Republican-held senate, and the Democratic-held assembly. Afterward he claimed considerable credit for the passage of the budget. The legislative leaders, angered by his claiming credit, negotiated the next budget between the two houses and then presented it to the governor with instructions to sign it.[2] The process had changed.

The New York legislature has emerged in recent decades as an equal partner with the governor in negotiations over state policy. Each house is dominated by parties that rely on strong leadership and that use their large staffs to develop policy proposals and to critique those presented by other political actors. The concern of this chapter is how the legislature has evolved from playing a marginal role in decision making to playing a central role, and why current practices of strong political leadership continue. The chapter first reviews the development of professional legislators—defined here as those who devote themselves full-time to the position and tend to stay in the legislature for numerous terms—and the growth of a large legislative staff capable of doing research to develop proposals and critiques and to review the actions of other state institutions. It discusses the role of the strong leadership system in creating cohesion among legislators. How these conditions affect the impact of the legislature in the political process in New York is then examined.

Table 8: Professionalism in the New York Legislature by Decade

	Percentage of Legislators:				Averages:	
	Seeking Reelection	Winning Reelection	In First Term	Listing Occupation as Legislator	Years Served	Age When First Elected
Assembly						
1870s	40.6	76.8	–	0	–	–
1880s	48.9	78.2	–	0	–	–
1890s	49.0	89.3	55.8	0	2.3	41.2
1900s	65.4	91.9	42.3	0	2.4	40.3
1910s	68.0	75.7	42.3	0	2.5	–
1920s	78.4	91.4	26.4	0	4.4	–
1930s	85.4	95.5	21.0	0	5.8	–
1940s	80.9	93.8	23.2	0	8.5	–
1950s	85.5	96.4	16.9	0	8.1	44.6
1960s	82.0	95.5	23.4	1.2	6.5	43.7
1970s	82.1	93.6	22.3	27.3	8.9	–
1980s	89.7	97.5	13.2	63.9	4.9	–
Senate						
1870s	43.1	68.6	67.3	0	2.9	–
1880s	42.5	78.1	67.7	0	3.1	–
1890s	51.2	79.3	58.5	0	4.6	43.7
1900s	61.0	90.1	44.8	0	3.9	43.7
1910s	62.0	82.8	45.9	0	4.7	44.6
1920s	76.1	85.9	30.7	0	6.0	42.9
1930s	82.4	92.4	24.9	0	6.4	44.1
1940s	84.1	90.7	24.9	0	7.4	44.7
1950s	87.4	91.5	18.9	0	8.3	45.0
1960s	81.6	93.6	22.0	0.4	8.3	43.6
1970s	81.9	93.4	16.6	27.6	9.6	38.7
1980s	92.6	98.2	10.2	44.5	4.4	48.4

Source: Data taken from *New York Red Book*, various years.
– not available

THE EMERGENCE OF PROFESSIONAL LEGISLATORS

Like most state legislatures, the New York legislature has changed over time. The legislature was once badly malapportioned, but court decisions in the 1960s resulted in apportionment plans that increased urban representation in the legislature.[3] There have also been some changes in size. The number of senate seats has increased from 32 in 1896 to 61 presently, while the assembly has been at 150 for a century.

Perhaps the most important change, however, has been the rise of legislators who seek to be reelected, who stay in office for numerous terms, and who devote themselves full-time to the position. Across the country there has been a gradual increase in the desire of legislators to remain in their legislatures.[4] New York has been no different. Several major changes have occurred in legislative careers in New York.[5] Table 8 presents these trends in a profile of professionalism in the legislature. First, in the latter 1800s and the early 1900s, there was a gradual and steady increase in the percentage of legislators seeking reelection—rising from about 40 percent to nearly 90 percent during that period. It has stayed at around that level since then. For reasons not entirely clear, the legislature became a very attractive place to remain, even though the real value of legislative salaries was gradually eroding due to inflation.[6]

Surprisingly, there has been little change since 1900 in the success of incumbents at getting reelected. The percentage of incumbents (among those seeking reelection) winning reelection has remained in the 80 to 90 percent range since about 1900. The major change has been in the interest in returning to the legislature. As this interest has increased, the percentage of new legislators has declined steadily. Table 8 shows the decline by decade in the percentage of all legislators at the beginning of legislative sessions who had no prior service in the legislature.[7]

The consequence of increased pursuit of office and a steady rate of success in retaining office has been a steady rise in the average number of years legislators remain in the legislature.[8] The fifth column in table 8 shows the average number of years served. Those coming to office have also gotten *relatively* younger. The last column shows the average age of legislators when they were first elected to the legislature.[9] Whereas the population has gotten older over the last century, legislators have remained at about the same age. Those individuals are also staying longer in the legislature, and many are making a career of the position. An indicator of this is the percentage of legislators listing their occupation as "legislator" in the *Manual for the Use of the Legislature of the State of New York*. This percentage has increased dramatically in the last two decades.[10] Informal discussions with legislators also suggest that relatively few of them have full-time occupations outside the legislature. In fact, many are dependent on the position for their living and have had little experience in the private sector. An analysis of the backgrounds of legislators in the 1890s and the 1980s indicates the changes that have occurred.[11] Figure 5 presents trends in the prior private and public sector experience of state senators over the last one hundred years.

Figure 5: Prior Work Experience of New York Senators, 1890–1990

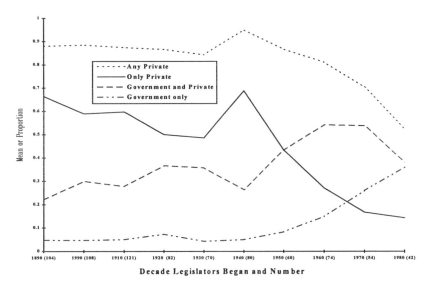

In the 1890s, almost all senators had private sector job experience, and two-thirds had only private sector experience. By the 1980s, only one-half had some private sector experience, and only 14 percent had exclusively private sector experience. While this private sector experience has declined, public sector experience has increased. The average number of public sector jobs has increased, as has the proportion of legislators with only public sector experience. Thus, more legislators are coming to office with extensive public sector experience, and fewer are coming directly from the business world.

The emergence of professional legislators has had two significant consequences for the legislature. The legislature is now composed of politicians who are very concerned about having an impact and who have a long-run focus on trying to affect policies. When legislators served for one or two terms and considered the job as part-time, this focus on having an impact was surely less. The first significant effect of increasing professionalization is that there is a greater collective desire to have the legislature play an equal role with the governor in making decisions.

On the other hand, it is probably more difficult to get these new legislators to form a policy consensus.[12] Almost all of them want to be reelected; they are more concerned with what is good for their districts and less concerned with just agreeing to keep the decision-making process moving along. They are seeking to have an impact, but reaching agreement about how to have an impact is not easy.

The desire to have an impact has led to a significant increase in the capacity of the legislature to play a role in policy debates. There has been a tremendous increase in legislative staff during the last several decades.[13] During the Rockefeller era the legislature was widely perceived as subordinate to the governor and as incapable of making policy initiatives in most areas. It was generally in a position of responding to gubernatorial initiatives.[14] This dependence was recognized by both legislative parties, and both parties have responded by supporting a significant increase in legislative resources.[15] Support for these changes also came from various groups outside the legislature, such as the New York Bar Association and academics.[16]

To increase the capability of the legislature, there has been a significant increase in the number of staff, in the amount of office space, and in the use of computers to handle information. These changes were intended to give the legislature the ability to conduct its own analyses and formulate its own policy positions. During the early 1970s, the legislature also created district offices so legislators could independently receive and respond to constituent concerns.

The legislature now also meets for a longer time each year. During the 1950s, it met for approximately one hundred days a year. Sessions usually ended sometime in March or April. During the 1960s, the number of session days began to increase, and by the end of the 1970s, the legislature was regularly in session until the beginning of July. Eventually the legislature decided not to adjourn at all so it could reconvene at its own discretion. Otherwise the legislators could meet only when the governor called them into session. This lack of adjournment reduces the ability of the governor to act without the involvement of the legislature.

To do all these things, the legislature has allocated itself more money. The salaries of legislators have increased, as have total expenditures by the legislature. Figure 6 presents the total legislative budget over time. The budget is divided into the amount devoted to legislator salaries and the amount devoted to staff purposes. The figures have been adjusted for inflation to provide an indication of the real resource increase over time.[17] There has been a remarkable increase in the staff budget from 1900 to 1996, with the most significant increases occurring during the last several decades. The increase has

Figure 6: Growth of New York Legislative Budget in Real Dollars, 1900–1996

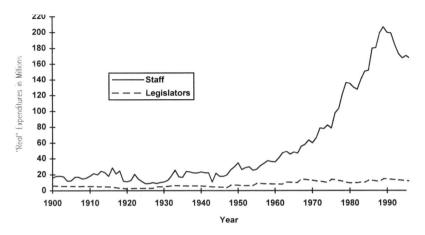

gone almost entirely into general legislative resources—staff, equipment, telephones, supplies. Even though legislators' salaries have increased over the years, they have consumed a smaller and smaller proportion of the total legislative budget.[18]

The legislature now has the staff to conduct its own analyses and to form its own proposals.[19] There are now staff members who have been through numerous budget negotiations and who are quickly able to determine the governor's position. They have "institutional memory" and are not ignorant of past debates and decisions. There are staff who conduct long-range studies on policy development and oversight. Staff of the Assembly Ways and Means Committee and the Senate Finance Committee either conduct or contract for economic forecasts for the state to help guide them in preparing analyses of anticipated revenues. Legislative staff members still rely on executive branch agencies for information, but the era when the legislature had to rely on executive branch personnel for interpreting that information is over.

All these changes have made the New York legislature a more active participant in the decision process.[20] The legislature is less passive and reactive than twenty years ago.

THE TRADITION OF STRONG LEADERSHIP IN THE LEGISLATURE

Bringing independent legislators together to make the legislature effective is not an easy task. The New York legislature has resolved this problem for some time by relying on strong leadership.[21] The leadership of each house allocates resources among members, presides over the party conferences, plays a major if not dominant role in setting party strategy, and represents the party in most policy negotiations. Although the leadership has considerable power, it does not "control" members. It is granted this power because the members generally support a significant leadership role in shaping behavior within the legislature.

One reason that the practice of granting the leadership such authority persists is that the formal rules of both houses grant the leadership considerable discretion in allocating resources and positions. No rules mandate relying on seniority for allocating influential positions within the legislature. Each member is guaranteed a minimal staff budget of around $40,000, but much larger staff budgets are awarded at the discretion of the leadership.

The more fundamental question is why do these rules exist and why do they persist? The practice of granting the leadership strong powers persists for one general reason: the majority of the members still find it suits their needs. As long as the leadership is responsive to member needs, the members are likely to continue to support a strong leadership system. There are several ways in which the leadership responds to the needs of the members.

First, leaders explicitly derive their ongoing policy positions from the members by consistently relying on party conferences to hear what the members are willing to accept as policy positions. Party conferences are closed-door sessions held off the floor on a regular basis for legislators only. In those sessions, members are free to make arguments about policy directions, and the limits of what the members can accept are determined. The leadership is then generally free within those limits to negotiate with the other house and the governor over policy. This reliance on member opinions is crucial for leadership legitimacy. Although the media tend to underplay the interaction between members and the leadership, it is essential to maintaining the system.

This practice of granting the leadership strong authority focuses the negotiating process and serves a purpose for the members. Legislators want some impact on policy and want to get reelected. Conference and informal discussions with the leadership give them opportunities to influence policy, yet turning over negotiations about specifics to the leadership gives the members more time to focus on and deal with district concerns, thus enhancing their reelection chances. With this arrangement, legislators do not need to be in the state capitol on a full-time basis because the leadership assumes responsibility for negotiations and the management of day-to-day legislative business.

Members also find the strong leadership system valuable because it "organizes" their concerns and constrains them from becoming fragmented as each seeks to pursue individual concerns. As Jim Tallon, the former majority leader of the assembly, put it, the party recognizes it must ultimately govern and make decisions. A strong leadership system allows members to speak, but it imposes the discipline needed for decision making. Many members look with dismay upon practices in Congress, where decision making is decentralized and members must spend all their time in Washington negotiating fine points of the law.[22] This is not to argue that all members of the New York legislature are equally happy with strong leadership, but enough are satisfied to continue the practice.

The strong leadership also uses its power to distribute resources to each member "according to need." More senior members, who understand the legislative process better and who may want to play a greater role in shaping policy, are allocated more leadership and committee chair positions. They also pass more bills.[23] This allows senior members to have more influence on legislation and to build records of passing and claiming credit for legislation. Regardless of whether members wish to actually change social conditions or just to claim credit for legislation, this satisfies more senior members.

Newer members of the legislature often have other concerns. Those who wish to focus on establishing some record of legislative accomplishments receive help from the leadership in terms of staff assistance with bills.[24] Others are more concerned with their next election. They may have faced a close election in their initial run for office, or they may want to build up their name recognition in the district. Their concern is likely to focus on receiving assistance in campaigns and obtaining aid from the legislative party campaign committees.[25] To be able to allocate campaign resources to these new and "marginal" members, the party leadership has to have enough discipline to deny resources to members who do not face close races.[26]

The party leadership continually faces the task of responding to the varying needs of the members. It must convince younger members and members with small electoral margins that the party will respond to their needs and try to enhance their reelection chances. It must also convince newer members that their policy views will be heard and their concerns accommodated. At the same time, the leadership must satisfy more senior members who have "waited their turn" and now want to have an impact. Thus far, leaders appear to have done this well.

The inclination of members to grant power to the leadership is increased because of the importance of majority control. The majority party controls the bulk of legislative resources. It determines which bills pass, and it is able to raise more money than the minority in its house because of that power. Strong desires to remain in the majority make legislators more inclined to work together as a party. The leader becomes the individual responsible for marshaling and distributing party resources to keep the party in power and preserve control over legislative resources.

There are, however, also political signs that legislators should be wary of being too amenable to leadership influence. Ticket splitting in voting has increased, negative ads can have a quick and devastating effect, and legislators always want to stress their independence. They know that it is important to fight for the needs of their district when decisions are made. All this makes them less amenable to leadership domination.

To execute all these responsibilities, the leadership must act with some skill. Leaders must listen and respond while pushing for consensus and party cohesion. In recent decades, exerting influence over legislators has been harder to wield because of the independence of legislators. As recent leaders have commented, it is now necessary to work very hard to make sure district needs are accommodated while seeking to form a consensus.

The greater independence of legislators is particularly important when the majority parties seek to reconcile their policy differences. As noted in chapter 5, each party has its internal tensions. The senate Republicans have nine incumbents on Long Island who want more money for school aid in order to restrain increases in property taxes on Long Island. The upstate delegation is more conservative and wants to cut taxes. The president of the senate during the early 1990s, Ralph Marino, found it difficult to get the nine Republicans on Long Island to accept tax cuts if it would mean less school aid. The Long Island delegation wanted to stay in office and saw school aid as a policy concern to which they had to respond. This made the leadership job's difficult.

In the assembly, the majority party must contend with the conflict between the many liberals from New York City and the less liberal upstate delegation. The Speaker, Sheldon Silver, must try to accommodate this diversity while negotiating with a more conservative senate.

To the extent leaders can accommodate these diverse needs, they are granted authority by members. Not all members are equally happy with this arrangement, of course, but it appears that enough have been placated that the tradition of strong leadership has persisted for some time. It may also be helped along by the fact that most legislators in New York do not have close elections. In 1994, for example, the average margin of victory in the senate and assembly was over 50 percentage points. That gives legislators more room to grant discretion in policy negotiations. There are also a limited number of new legislators entering the system every two years, which may make it easier to socialize new members into accepting this practice.

Regardless, strong leadership persists. The durability of this approach is indicated by the abrupt but smooth leadership transition in the assembly in 1991 from Mel Miller to Saul Weprin, and from Weprin to Sheldon Silver in 1994, when Weprin became incapacitated by illness. The dominant question was who would become Speaker, not whether there would be some sort of change in the system. When Joseph Bruno replaced Ralph Marino as president of the senate in a leadership battle in 1995, the strong leadership pattern persisted.

THE LEGISLATURE IN THE DECISION PROCESS

During the last several decades, the decision-making process has changed in Albany. Changes in the budget process illustrate the rise of the legislature as an equal partner in the process. In the 1950s, Governor Thomas E. Dewey regularly submitted the budget to the legislature only several days before it was due. He was able to get quick passage of his budget with few changes.[27] That is no longer true. The combination of a more professional legislature and divided control of the legislature has reshaped the decision process. There are now ongoing institutional battles between the houses and between the legislature and the governor.[28] Each house of the legislature first establishes its own positions internally and then begins negotiations with the other house and the governor. There is less willingness to make quick accommodations.

The combination of political parties with clearly different constituencies and policy concerns, divided control of the legislature, professional legislators, and strong leadership makes decision processes more difficult and more lengthy. In recent years, most budgets have not passed by the 1 April deadline, and the last decade has seen some significant delays. While much has been made of these delays, they are really part of a long-term trend of longer decision processes in Albany. The delays reflect significant partisan and institutional battles. Figure 7 presents the extent to which budgets have been completed before or after the budget deadline since the 1 April date was adopted in 1944. Over time there has been a gradual drift to a much later

Figure 7: New York Budget Passage: Number of Days Budget Early or Late, 1944–1996

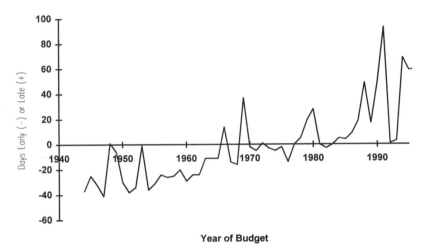

Year of Budget

date. The present divided control of the legislature has surely accentuated the problems of delay, but the primary change has been in the ability of the legislators to formulate their own proposals, pursue their objectives, and hold out until they get some of what they want.[29] Delays in the process are occurring, but they are a reflection of serious substantive disagreements that take time to resolve.

The 1986 tax reform in New York illustrates this. After the federal income tax laws were revised, the state needed to revise its tax laws to conform to federal laws because New York tax returns are based on federal returns. This change coincided with an ongoing debate among state officials about state tax levels. Republicans argued that taxes were too high and detrimental to the state. Democrats wanted to change the progressivity of the tax system by removing low-income individuals from the system.

Faced with the need to make some sort of change, the assembly leadership took the initiative to offer the senate Republicans lower tax rates and a simpler system with only two rates if lower-income individuals would be taxed at lower rates.[30] The result was an altered tax system in which each party got something it wanted. Overall tax levels were cut somewhat, which gave Republicans something. The progressivity of the tax system was preserved, which gave Democrats something. The significant aspect of this policy transition is that the initiative for the changes came from the legislature, and the subsequent negotiations were also handled by the legislature.[31]

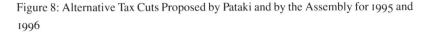

Figure 8: Alternative Tax Cuts Proposed by Pataki and by the Assembly for 1995 and 1996

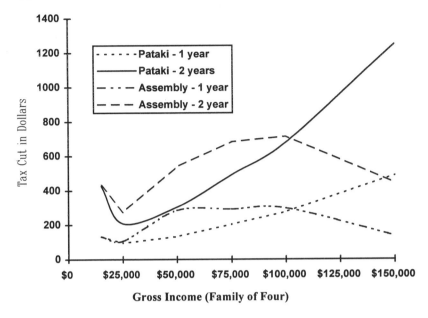

The independence of the legislature again became an issue in 1995, when George E. Pataki, the new Republican governor, proposed cuts in the state personal income tax. He had campaigned on a promise to improve the decision process in Albany and pass a budget on time, by 1 April. Democrats in the assembly recognized the widespread public support for reduced taxes but countered his proposal with proposed cuts that would give much less to those with higher incomes. Figure 8 indicates the alternative tax cuts by income levels proposed by Pataki and by the assembly. A lengthy battle ensued over these cuts, with the major disputes involving issues of tax progressivity and the desire of Democrats to indicate their institutional independence. A compromise was eventually arrived at in which the governor got a tax cut, but with reductions in the benefits to upper-income groups.

The legislature is now an equal partner with the governor in policy debates. The party conferences within the legislature serve as vehicles to form policy positions. The legislative staff generates information and studies to support party positions. At the same time, the legislators have sufficient staff to explore policy issues in new areas and to anticipate future situations. All this has allowed the legislative parties to participate in and structure policy debates within the state. There is now an ongoing dialogue between the houses and the political parties about what positions should be taken. The tradition of strong leadership allows legislators to create collective positions that allow a more focused debate.[32] The legislature has developed both as a professional political institution and as a body fully capable of playing a major role in affecting policy choices.

CHAPTER SEVEN

The New York Governorship

Sarah F. Liebschutz

Nelson A. Rockefeller, longest serving governor of New York, once observed that "great men are not drawn to small office."[1] The office of governor of the Empire State is surely not small. On the contrary, because of substantial grants of formal power in the state constitution, the historical exercise of such powers by formidable incumbents, and widespread expectations that the governor provide leadership, the New York governor is one of the strongest in the nation. At the same time, the potential for the New York governor to exercise this influence has become more constrained since Rockefeller took office in 1959. This is the result of the challenges from an increasingly assertive legislature, as discussed in chapter 6. It is also the result of heightened tension in the pursuit of competitive and compassionate policies.

THE GOVERNOR'S FORMAL POWERS

Formal grants of authority that make the position of New York governor one of the most powerful in the nation include four-year terms without limit on reelection, vast powers of appointment, broad budget and fiscal responsibilities, and a leading legislative role. The governor lacks only two formal powers that are held by some other governors: the ability to reduce items in appropriations bills and the option of returning bills to the legislature with suggested amendments as an alternative to vetoing them.[2]

Throughout its history, New York "has been less chary of a strong executive than most of its sister states. During the revolution, when the norm was a one-year gubernatorial term, limited succession, and legislative selection of the governor, the New York constitution, drafted later and in a more conservative political milieu than prevalent in the other original states, provided for a three-year term, unlimited succession, and popular election. At a time when the veto power was anathema, identified as it was with royal authority, New York nevertheless allowed its governor first to share such a negative with others on a Council of Revision and then, in 1821, made it his alone."[3]

Those powers were eroded in the mid-nineteenth century by the "tides of Jacksonian democracy that swept the rest of the nation. In 1821, the governor's term was shortened to two years and in 1846 the number of statewide elected officials was increased to thirteen, with a [devastating] impact on the power of the chief executive."[4]

The New York Constitutional Convention of 1915 was largely focused on strengthening the office of the governor. "At that convention, Elihu Root and others sought to re-empower the governorship by consolidating administrative agencies. . . , by adopting a 'short ballot' system to minimize the number of statewide elected officials, and by giving the executive budgeting authority. Ironically, the state constitution that emerged from this convention . . . failed of adoption."[5]

Later, Governor Alfred (Al) E. Smith (Democrat, 1919–20, 1923–29) successfully spearheaded separate adoption by voters of three constitutional amendments—the short ballot, government reorganization (both in 1925), and the executive budget (in 1927).[6]

Appointment Powers

The governor's appointment powers are considerable. Only two heads of executive agencies are directly elected by the people of New York: the attorney general (who heads the Department of Law) and the comptroller (who heads the Department of Audit and Control). In many states, the commissioner of agriculture, secretary of state, and commissioner (or supervisor) of education are also popularly elected; not so in New York. The New York commissioner of education is appointed by the state Department of Education's Board of Regents, themselves elected by the legislature. Heads of the remaining executive agencies, approximately sixty, are appointed directly by the governor. Most need senatorial confirmation, with its potential to set limits on the governor's authority.[7] However, the senate has "traditionally taken the view that a Governor is entitled to pick his own people as long as the nominees are neither dishonest nor incompetent,"[8] and has failed only in very rare instances to confirm a governor's appointee.[9]

Centrality in the Budgetary Process

The governor's preeminent role in budget making was set in 1927, with adoption by voters of the executive budget amendment to the state constitution. The amendment provided not only that the legislative budget would be replaced, but also that the executive budget had to be passed before other appropriations could be made.

The amendment, advocated by Governor Al Smith, was opposed by many legislators because of its challenge to the power of the legislature. The Republican party, which controlled both houses of the legislature, was split between progressives and conservatives; the conservatives were vehemently opposed. Theodore Roosevelt Jr., Governor Smith's Republican opponent in the 1924 election, campaigned against the budget amendment (although he promised to introduce a version of the federal budget system if elected).[10] Republican progressives, such as former governor Charles Evans Hughes and well-known New York City attorney Henry L. Stimson, favored it. Some Republicans in the legislature argued that a constitutional amendment was unnecessary; they said they would support a statute creating the executive budget.

Governor Smith's successful campaign for reelection in 1924 vindicated his call for a constitutional amendment to establish the executive budget. Working closely with Stimson and Hughes, Smith was able to persuade two successive sessions of the legislature and then the voters to approve the amendment.

Smith's immediate successors, Franklin D. Roosevelt (Democrat, 1929–32), Herbert H. Lehman (Democrat, 1933–42), and Thomas E. Dewey (Republican, 1943–54), all willingly exercised the prerogatives of the executive budget.[11] The Dewey administration, as discussed below, extended them.

Consolidation of State Government Departments

The executive budget amendment was closely linked to another of Governor Al Smith's important innovations in state government: the reorganization and consolidation of state government departments and the creation of an executive department headed by the governor. When first elected governor in 1918, Smith appointed a Reconstruction Commission to focus on post–World War I transition and government reorganization matters. He viewed as a matter of high priority the consolidation of more than one hundred agencies into a manageable number and their coordination through the executive office in order to reduce the size of government and to make it more efficient, economic, and accountable. The reorganization amendment, approved by voters in 1925, was, Smith said, "the most progressive step taken by the state in half a century."[12] After enactment of the state departments law by the legislature in 1926, Smith moved quickly to flesh out the concept of the executive department and to create a working cabinet of the most important agency heads.

The reorganization and the executive budget amendments strengthened the governor's position as chief executive of the state and laid the foundation for the modern governorship. Approval of four-year terms without limitation during Governor Lehman's tenure, with elections to be held in nonpresidential election years, further strengthened the governor's role. Since Lehman's time, most governors have served two or more terms. The only exceptions have been W. Averell Harriman (1955–58) and Malcolm Wilson (1973–74).

Legislative Powers

The governor plays a major role in the legislative process. "As a full-time state official, in contrast to the part-time legislature, it is not surprising that the governor has been labeled the [state's] chief legislator." The governor's perspective, deriving from a statewide constituency, tends to be broader than that of the legislature, and the governor "may call upon the entire state bureaucracy as well as special advisory commissions for assistance in preparing a legislative program." The governor is directed by the state constitution to present an annual state of the state message and state budget to the legislature. The state of the state message, compiled from proposals of executive agencies, provides a guide to issue areas the governor considers most important and to the legislation the executive office is likely to propose in the forthcoming legislative session. "Typically, the most important bills introduced in the legislature are sponsored by the governor, and his constitutional authority to prepare and execute the state budget allows him to play a preeminent role in policy-making."[13]

In addition to policy leadership, the governor's formal powers include the ability to call special sessions of the legislature, to bypass regular legislative procedure by declaring any bill to be a "message of necessity," which requires immediate action, and to veto bills in part or in whole.

The veto—over items in appropriations bills and over all other legislation in whole—is a particularly potent weapon. It can be exercised directly, with or without an explanatory memorandum, or indirectly, more than thirty days after the bill reaches the governor, by a "pocket veto." (The pocket veto has never been exercised.) Zimmerman and Prescott logged the number of the gubernatorial vetoes between 1875 and 1980 at nearly 25,000;[14] Zimmerman estimates that "in the typical year, the governor vetoes approximately one-fourth of the bills that reach his desk." In practice, he notes, "the governor's veto power has been nearly absolute, as evidenced by only sixteen . . . vetoes overridden by the legislature in the period 1823–72" and only a handful since then.[15]

In 1976, the legislature overrode Governor Hugh L. Carey's veto of a bill that required New York City "to appropriate a fixed proportion of its expense budget for education."[16] That override, the first such action by the New York legislature in 104 years, revealed both "an overwhelming hostility to Carey by members of his own party . . . and the realization that the veto would now be a somewhat less consequential gubernatorial power."[17] At the time, the *New York Times* characterized the veto override as a "farewell to ignominy," the start of a "legislative renaissance."[18] Subsequently, the legislature overrode several of Carey's vetoes of individual line items in the budget, but none of Governor Mario Cuomo's vetoes. In 1996, it overrode Governor George E. Pataki's veto of an entire bill—police arbitration legislation estimated to substantially increase New York City's public safety labor costs.[19] These veto overrides, although twenty years apart, had two key factors in common: each involved a New York City government under financial stress, and each occurred in an election year. Regardless of party, legislators were more concerned about reelection—and thus sympathetic to organized labor—than about the city's fiscal situation.

ENHANCING FORMAL POWERS

Within New York, the governor's formal powers are enhanced by both the breadth and the organization of the governor's office (i.e., the executive chamber or, more typically, "the Second Floor" of the state capitol) and the large number of agencies that report directly to the governor.[20] The scope and responsibility of these agencies—in particular, the central role of the Division of the Budget within the executive chamber and department and in the operations of all executive agencies—are examined in chapter 8.

Governor W. Averell Harriman (Democrat, 1955–58) first created a specialized staff within his office to serve as liaisons with the executive agencies. Governor Nelson Rockefeller (Republican, 1959–73) further expanded the office. He created a separate program office organized along functional lines; program staff not only developed legislative proposals, they also served as intermediaries between the governor, his top staff, and high-level agency officials.

The position of secretary to Governor Rockefeller, successively occupied by William Ronan, Alton Marshall, and T. Norman Hurd, was central, as the secretary had responsibilities for policy development, legislative communication, and overall coordination of the Second Floor activities. Robert Morgado, secretary during most of Governor Hugh Carey's two terms in office (1975–82), later reflected that his "greatest pleasure . . . was in melding the unique talents and perspectives of the permanent civil service and the policy apparatus."[21] Governor Mario M. Cuomo (Democrat, 1983–94) further refined the executive office. Today the Second Floor includes not only such offices as press, appointments, counsel, program, and the New York State office in Washington (see chapter 4) but also a system of subcabinets.[22]

While the governor does meet once or twice a year with the full cabinet, composed of more than sixty agency heads, these sessions are too large to be working meetings. Subcabinet meetings bring together heads of relevant agencies to work out important policy initiatives as well as to coordinate activities among the agencies. By coordinating the policy formulation and implementation of the agencies on the Second Floor, the governor is able to deal more effectively with the legislature and is more visible to the media and the public.

EXERCISING LEADERSHIP

New York's governors represent diversity in priorities and personal style. But they also represent an appreciation of the potential that the office of governor offers for action and a willingness to take action. Governor Thomas Dewey played an important role in consolidating the powers secured under the leadership of Governor Al Smith. Governors Rockefeller, Carey, and Cuomo yielded the tools of governing with vigor and enthusiasm and, in so doing, affected the policy balance between compassion and competition. The following sketches of four modern New York governors illustrate these points. The efforts of Governor George E. Pataki, elected in 1994, to redirect that balance are discussed in chapter 12.

Thomas E. Dewey (1943–1955)

Thomas Dewey, a Republican, brought to the governorship a reputation for personal integrity, administrative efficiency, and executive-style policy making. A passionate advocate of good management, he declared it "the single greatest need . . . in government."[23] With John E. Burton as director of the budget for most of the Dewey years, both the structure and process of executive budgeting were revolutionized. Burton's additions to the budget system included revenue estimating, expenditure-control systems, estab-

lishment of a detailed classification and salary plan for the state's civil service, and a reorientation of the state's local assistance activities. The results
were a strengthened executive branch vis-à-vis the legislature and bolstered
authority and prominence of the governor.

Dewey's style was "exhaustive preparation, attention to detail, and mas-
tery of the subject at hand."[24] In addition to a much-strengthened Division of
the Budget, Dewey's legacy from twelve years in office included the New
York State Thruway, new approaches to industrial-labor cooperation, and
legislation to prevent discrimination in employment.

Dewey, educated at the University of Michigan and Columbia Law
School, came to the New York governorship after extraordinary success as
special prosecutor in New York City. As such, Dewey was charged with
breaking up organized crime; he pursued this goal with relentless determina-
tion, gaining press attention and public recognition. Dewey's first elective
office was district attorney for New York City (1937–41). He ran unsuc-
cessfully for governor in 1938 against Governor Herbert Lehman, but succeeded in 1942, 1946, and 1950. While governor of New York, he was the
unsuccessful Republican nominee for president in 1944 and 1948.

Unlike Al Smith, who worked with a Republican-controlled assembly all
of his years as governor and a Republican senate for most of them, Dewey
was the undisputed leader of his party when he became governor, with control over both party and state patronage. In filling state positions, he report-
edly moved as carefully and methodically as when he had been special prosecutor and district attorney.

Dewey's collaborative relationship with the legislature was very different
from Smith's adversarial style. Dewey, with his top aides in attendance, held
weekly meetings at the executive mansion with the leaders of the Republican-controlled legislature. These sessions were patterned after parliamentary negotiations; executive and legislative leaders debated both short- and
long-term policies.[25] Dewey sought unanimity from legislative leaders on
policy matters, although this did not always translate into bills he was willing to sign into law.[26]

Nelson A. Rockefeller (1959–1973)

Nelson Rockefeller is often numbered "among America's greatest governors—
one who . . . built the 'most socially advanced state government in United
States history and changed the physical face of New York more than any Governor since DeWitt Clinton built the Erie Canal.'" A "pragmatic liberal," Rock-

efeller's "consuming concern was policy, problem solving and program-setting."[27] "His drive as an executive, his use of his position as the elected executive . . . resulted," a close associate remarked, "in one of the greatest assaults on the variety of diverse social programs that any state has undertaken."[28]

Born into a family of immense wealth in 1908, Rockefeller was educated at Dartmouth. After a stint with family businesses, he embarked on a career of public service, holding appointments as coordinator of inter-American affairs during much of World War II and undersecretary of Health, Education, and Welfare (HEW) for two years in the Eisenhower administration. Rockefeller's experiences in the latter position led to his pursuit of the governorship. According to Malcolm Wilson, who served as lieutenant governor during the entire Rockefeller governorship, Rockefeller "threw himself with great vigor into [his role as undersecretary] as he did with every undertaking. He proposed legislative approaches to the problems faced by [HEW]; he went to Capitol Hill and talked to congressmen and to chairmen of committees, and he testified before committees. He felt totally frustrated because, with few exceptions, his proposals met with something less than enthusiasm on Capitol Hill. And so he decided that the way to get things done was by the executive branch, and that's why he decided he would seek the governorship of New York."[29]

As governor, Rockefeller extended the state's role into new areas. His first campaign in 1958 offered the vision of a broad state agenda "geared toward growth and development" in education, transportation, labor, banking, health, and mental health.[30] That vision, translated into policies by task forces of persons inside and outside the state government, was implemented over the next fourteen years. Programs in all of these fields were begun or extended; mental health facilities, hospitals, nursing homes, daycare centers, senior citizen centers, and low-income housing units were built. The State University of New York (SUNY) was expanded from 38,000 students on twenty-eight campuses to 246,000 on sixty-four; the South Mall, a massive $1.5 billion state office building complex adjoining the historic capitol building—Rockefeller's single most visible construction project—was built.

Revenues to support these programs came from increased tax rates on personal and business income, new tax sources, and creative financing mechanisms. State agencies with independent authority to issue capital financing instruments were conceived; among them were the State University Construction Fund, the Housing Finance Agency, and the Urban Develop-

Figure 9: Ratio of State Government Tax Revenue to Per Capita Personal Income, 1960–1994

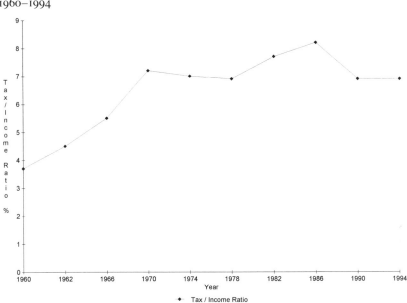

Source: State of New York, *Annual Reports of the Comptroller.*

ment Corporation (UDC). Bonds issued by these agencies did not require legislative or public approval. Many of their projects were financed with moral obligation bonds, a device that did not obligate the state government in the same way that general obligation bonds did.

Rockefeller courted the legislative leadership in the years when Republicans controlled both houses and when they did not. In the early years of his administration, Rockefeller was generally able to secure the agreement of Republican legislative leaders on bills important to him. Later, Rockefeller's deft personal skills—his ability to work with Democrats as well as Republicans, to circumvent leaders when necessary, and to always transmit excitement about his proposals—led Stanley Steingut, former Speaker of the assembly, to characterize the legislature, even when both houses had Democratic majorities, as "a Nelson Rockefeller legislature."[31]

The Rockefeller years were marked by growth of the state's population (from 16.6 million to 18.5 million) and personal income (from $41.8 billion to $97.7 billion). They were also marked by growth in taxes and debt. In

Figure 10: New York State Government Debt Per Capita, 1959–1973

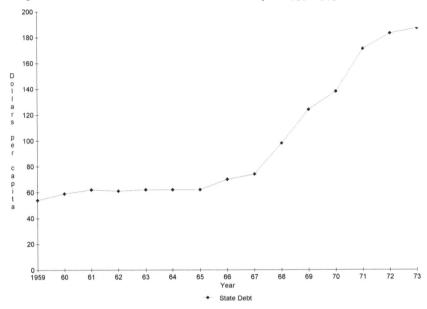

Source: State of New York, *Annual Reports of the Comptroller.*

fact, state tax revenues and state debt grew faster than population and income. On a per capita basis, personal income increased by 110 percent between 1959 and 1973, state tax collections by 350 percent, and state debt by 250 percent. The net result was a ratio of per capita state tax revenues to per capita personal income that almost doubled during the Rockefeller years (see figure 9) and a per capita debt burden that more than tripled (see figure 10).

Rockefeller himself acknowledged in his last state of the state message in 1973 that "the costs of social programs were exhausting our State and local tax revenue sources [and the] state tax structure was getting out of line with that of most other states."[32] Two years after Rockefeller left the governorship to assume the appointed position of vice-president of the United States, New York's state and local tax effort score of 160—compared to a national average of 100—far exceeded its tax capacity of 99.[33] For the average New Yorker, this high tax burden was Rockefeller's chief legacy, the legacy that contributed to the decline in New York's competitive economic position during two subsequent decades.

Hugh L. Carey (1975–1982)

"Not only was it a new feeling to sleep in the mansion," Hugh Carey reflected long after he had left the governorship, "I had a year-long insomnia because Robert, the House Manager, waited for a full year to tell me the bed I was using was a leftover hard mattress that a doctor had prescribed for Governor Rockefeller's chronic back problem. But I didn't run for Governor to seek a soft berth."[34]

Carey did not find a soft berth. Shortly after assuming office in 1975, he stated bluntly that strong action was necessary to avert a financial crisis caused by excessive government growth and inefficiencies and a stagnant private economy. For New York, he asserted, "the days of plenty, the days of wine and roses, are over."[35] Carey inherited "extraordinary and unprecedented burdens as governor . . . a real, but hidden budget gap, State agencies in trouble (i.e., UDC collapse), a flat economy, jobs and business leaving, New York City's near collapse and a state badly over-extended with costly borrowing."[36]

Carey, a law graduate of St. John's University and long active in Brooklyn Democratic politics, served seven terms in the U.S. House of Representatives before winning the Democratic primary nomination and subsequent election as governor. His record in the House was "that of a mainstream liberal Democrat, with special interests in education, health, and mental health." However, his record also reflected the interests of his conservative, white, working-class Brooklyn district; "he opposed busing, supported parochial school aid, and spoke against a civil review board for the police in New York City."[37]

Just as Carey balanced liberal and conservative positions in the Congress, so did he pursue both compassionate and competitive policies as governor. "There is no contradiction," he commented at the outset of his first term, "between having a liberal philosophy and a concern and compassion for people and at the same time being realistic enough to know that you have to pay the bills or the people aren't going to get the programs."[38] On the compassion side, Carey initiated reforms in the state's mental health institutions and services, implemented the state's 1979 Child Welfare Reform Act, improved licensing and inspection procedures for nursing homes, and vetoed the death penalty passed each year by the legislature.[39] On the competition side, Carey's most acclaimed achievements were saving New York City from bankruptcy, UDC from failure, and the state from defaulting on its obligations. (See chapter 4 for a discussion of Carey's pivotal role in the resolution of New York City's fiscal crisis.) To strengthen New York's economy, Carey instituted, with the legislature's approval, a four-year personal and business tax-reduction program in 1977; two years later, he announced a multifaceted strategy to retain existing jobs and create new ones in the private sector.[40]

During his two terms as governor, Carey's style frequently overshadowed his accomplishments. "Self-consciously Irish . . . with the extremes of temperament so often identified with the Irish heritage," he was characterized as moody, remote, and arrogant in his relationships within the executive branch and with state legislators. Unlike Rockefeller, whose courting of the legislature was legendary, Carey's style was confrontational. "In fact, Carey prided himself as a 'no deals' governor, one who would not play the 'Albany game.' " Carey's twin goals of fiscal stability and tax cuts to restore the New York economy also contributed to the tensions. Left with "little money for the increased local assistance payments or enriched state programs for which legislators like to take credit in their districts when running for reelection," the legislature asserted its own institutional priorities.[41] It overrode five of Carey's vetoes and won the right to appropriate federal funds.[42] It did not accept the "institutionalization of taxing or spending limits through legislation or constitutional amendment" that the governor proposed.[43] The real expenditure reductions accomplished during the first Carey administration "turned out to be more of a minor blip than a major turnabout in fiscal philosophy."[44] As Benjamin points out, whereas past governors "proposed policy innovations and the legislature accepted them or cut, guarding the purse strings, [u]nder Carey, the governor imposed austerity, and the legislature became the restoring branch, adding money and programs to satisfy group and constituency pressures."[45] In this sense, Carey promoted programs to make New York competitive, and the legislature promoted programs to keep New York compassionate.

Mario M. Cuomo (1983–1994)

Mario M. Cuomo was once described as an "inspiring and exasperating leader."[46] In 1984, at the height of his popularity, his words were applauded by New Yorkers and Democrats across the nation. A decade later, when he sought a fourth term as governor, he was decisively rejected by voters and replaced by a relatively unknown Republican state senator, George E. Pataki, whose campaign theme, simply put, was "I'm not Cuomo."

Cuomo, the son of Italian immigrants, graduated with highest honors from St. John's University and its law school. He attracted the interest of the state Democratic party for his representation of citizen groups in court battles over public housing in Queens. Cuomo was defeated in his first two tries for public office—Democratic primaries in 1974 for the nomination as lieutenant governor and in 1977 for New York City mayor. Hugh Carey appointed Cuomo as secretary of state in 1975 and selected him as his running mate in 1978. Mario Cuomo assumed his first elected office as lieutenant governor in 1979.[47]

The 1982 gubernatorial election set the stage for Cuomo's emergence as a successful political leader. He secured the Democratic nomination for governor after a fiercely competitive primary campaign against New York City Mayor Ed Koch (who had bested him in the mayoral primary in 1977). He won the first of his three elections as governor of New York by defeating Republican Lewis Lehrman, a businessman making his first run for public office.[48]

In his first inaugural address, Cuomo articulated a "progressive pragmatic" philosophy of government that joined compassion and competition. The duty of government, like that of a family, he asserted, is to allow successful citizens to expand their horizons and at the same time provide assistance to those not able to succeed on their own.[49] Stressing social and fiscal responsibility and common sense in the formulation of spending proposals, Cuomo urged the cooperation of business interests, government, labor organizations, and the public. These themes of family, compassion, and cooperation were frequently articulated during his twelve years as governor.

Cuomo had some successes in his dealings with the state legislature. Social programs to deal with health-care problems, drug abuse, and poverty were expanded. To promote the climate for private investment in New York, Cuomo persuaded the legislature and then voters to approve transportation bond issues to repair New York's highways and bridges. The legislature also extended tax-rate reduction programs begun by Carey and approved new initiatives such as economic development zones. To Cuomo's dismay, but because "it had to be done," New York's prison system was also greatly expanded to meet increased demand.[50] Cuomo also led successful efforts to establish a mandatory seat belt law and to raise the legal drinking age from nineteen to twenty-one.[51]

His relationship with the legislature, which began amicably, deteriorated over the course of his tenure. Cuomo typically presented dozens of proposals in his annual state of the state address but failed to secure enactment of most of them. Unlike Nelson Rockefeller, whose personal contacts with legislators were well known, Cuomo tended to rely on a very small group of advisers. His social contact with state legislators or other government officials was minimal; he made little attempt to lobby for his proposals on a daily basis or to create coalitions of support for specific programs. Further, he often responded poorly to criticism from others by lashing out at the media or those voicing objections to his programs.[52]

The adoption of the annual budget became the battleground between the governor and legislature. Cuomo's early achievements in 1983 and 1984 of timely legislative budget adoption seemed to presage greater executive-legislative civility than his predecessor had experienced, perhaps even a reversal of the long-term late-budget trend described in chapter 6. Such optimism, however, was short-lived. After growing tensions, and later and later budgets, the battle was fully joined in January 1991 when Governor Cuomo, projecting a $6 billion expenditure/revenue gap, proposed a budget "recommending the deepest cuts for the Legislature's most cherished programs—school aid, local government assistance and Medicaid. Then, to preempt the most obvious solutions, he threatened to veto any rise in broad-based taxes, including the personal income tax." The ensuing budget talks resembled "the Iran-Iraq war in one of its stalemates. After about a month of fruitless negotiations, Mr. Cuomo absented himself. . . . Left to their own devices, the legislative leaders decided to slice state agencies, which are controlled by the governor, as a way to restore local programs that are so important to locally elected officials."[53]

When the budget finally reached his desk in June, Governor Cuomo vetoed all $937 million in additional spending items as a "response to a potent mixture of fiscal concerns, institutional interests, and sheer personal pique."[54] The legislature did not attempt to override any of the governor's item vetoes; instead, with the fiscal year already two months underway, the legislative leaders negotiated with the governor for some funding restorations.

Cuomo gained national prominence largely because of his oratorical skills. His keynote address at the 1984 Democratic National Convention was a stirring denunciation of the Reagan administration and a defense of liberal principles.[55] The governor's keynote speech did not affect the outcome of the 1984 presidential election—Ronald Reagan easily defeated Democratic challenger Walter Mondale to win a second term. It did, however, catapult Cuomo into the national spotlight and make him a potential presidential candidate. His articulation of federalism themes around the 1986 Tax Reform Act, discussed in chapter 4, helped maintain his visibility.

Cuomo's publicly expressed indecision about whether he would run for president earned him the epithet "Hamlet on the Hudson." When he declined to run in 1988 and 1992, many Americans, although baffled, continued to admire him. But the governor's national popularity did little to enhance his standing in New York. In fact, criticism of his leadership grew as the problems faced by the state seemed to explode.

Cuomo's speaking ability seemed to become a liability as his tenure in office progressed. Because his speeches created high expectations, disappointment in the state's deteriorating economic and social conditions was magnified.[56] The growing disillusionment was reflected in his reelection bids. In 1986, Cuomo was returned to office with 65 percent of votes cast—the largest margin of victory in New York state history. In 1990, he won with a reduced margin—53 percent of the vote. In 1994, he received only 45 percent of the vote and was defeated.[57]

Factors both internal and external to New York were at work during Cuomo's tenure. Decentralizing policies initiated by the Reagan administration, an increasingly assertive state legislature, and Governor Cuomo's personality all contributed to the inability of the state to solve many of its serious problems during his tenure.

During the Cuomo years, the ratio of state tax collections to personal income was decreased from its high in 1986 (see figure 9); in 1992, New York ranked twenty-second highest among the states, with a state tax burden of $74.21 per $1000 personal income—down from fifteenth a decade earlier.[58] However, with state and local taxes combined at 68 percent above the national average, New Yorkers still bore a heavy tax burden. Only Alaska, whose revenues come largely from levies on oil and gas companies, ranked higher.[59] Cuomo failed to convince New Yorkers that it was increased local taxes that drove up their tax burden and contributed to the state's economic woes.[60] George Pataki, running for governor in 1994 as "not Cuomo," successfully exploited those issues and, as discussed in chapter 12, laid the blame at Cuomo's feet.

The governorship of New York, newspaperman Warren Moscow asserted in 1948, "compared with the [physical strain of the] Presidency or the [New York City] mayoralty . . . is a soft snap."[61] In 1975, when newly inaugurated governor Carey bore the burden of ensuring the "integrity of both the City of New York budget and the New York State budget and the coordination of the New York City and state financial plans,"[62] Moscow's contention was arguable. Twenty years later, when George E. Pataki assumed office to face an assertive legislature and public demands to solve problems, continue and even expand services, and still hold the line on taxes, the position (although still less demanding relative to that of president or mayor of New York City) was clearly not a "soft snap." At the end of the twentieth century, the governor of New York faces greater challenges and has more difficulty in resolving them than did many of his counterparts in the years from the American Revolution to the mid-1950s.

Contemporary policy responsibilities on the nation's governors stem from the current stage of American federalism, where "the states are resurgent and Washington reluctant."[63] In the domains of welfare, the environment, public health, growth management, and job training, states are playing a more active role in policymaking, administration, and funding than they did some twenty years ago. In the public policy areas of education, criminal justice, and transportation, where the states have always played a dominant role, their responsibilities have been heightened. These challenges have all been compounded by serious revenue shortfalls.[64]

Nelson Rockefeller, Hugh Carey, and Mario Cuomo demonstrated strong executive leadership on policy matters of considerable importance to New York State. In the intergovernmental arena, their leadership, as in the 1975 New York City fiscal crisis and 1986 tax reform bargaining, was undisputed. Within the state policy arena, however, the upper hand exerted by New York's governors from Smith to Rockefeller has been challenged by a legislature with considerably enhanced institutional capacity.

At the end of the twentieth century, the governor of New York remains a powerful figure. Opportunities for leadership remain considerable. The paradox, however, is that such leadership has become "more difficult just as it has become more necessary."[65]

CHAPTER EIGHT

The Executive Branch

Jane Shapiro Zacek

"Energy in the executive is a leading character in the definition of good government."[1] So observed Alexander Hamilton, New York delegate to the U.S. Constitutional Convention of 1787. New York's twentieth-century governors, from Al Smith to George Pataki, have all approached with vigor the challenge of organizing and administering the executive branch. Their efforts have flowed naturally from the state's moralistic political culture, which supports government intervention to enhance the economic and social well-being of New Yorkers.

The Executive Department

The Executive Department was created during the governorship of Al Smith, subject to the constitutional limitation of no more than twenty departments. (The twentieth, the Department of Motor Vehicles, was created in 1959.) All except three departments—Law, Education, and Audit and Control—report directly to the governor. The state Department of Education, the administrative agency to the Board of Regents, who are elected by the legislature, is not directly responsible to the governor. The Law and the Audit and Control Departments are headed, respectively, by the independently elected attorney general and comptroller. All three departments, however, are subject to the same budget process as "regular" executive agencies.

New York's executive branch agencies range in purpose from tax collection and enforcement to provision of social services, from veterans' affairs to registration of motor vehicles and their drivers. Some agencies receive substantial funding from nonstate sources; others charge fees to offset the costs

Figure 11: Functional Distribution of State Executive Agencies

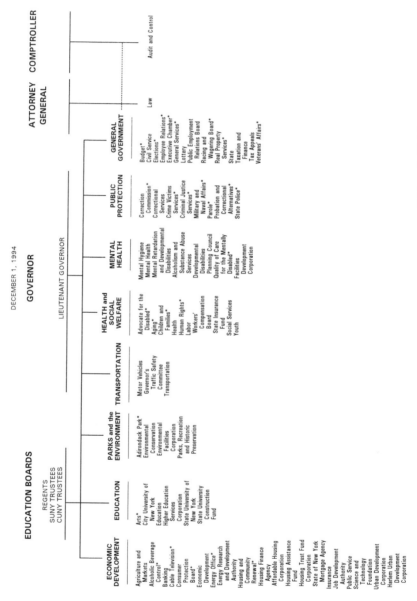

DECEMBER 1, 1994

GOVERNOR

ATTORNEY GENERAL

COMPTROLLER

LIEUTENANT GOVERNOR

EDUCATION BOARDS

REGENTS
SUNY TRUSTEES
CUNY TRUSTEES

Audit and Control

Law

ECONOMIC DEVELOPMENT

Agriculture and Markets
Alcoholic Beverage Control*
Banking
Cable Television*
Consumer Protection Board*
Economic Development
Energy Office*
Energy Research and Development Authority
Housing and Community Renewal*
Housing Finance Agency
Affordable Housing Corporation
Housing Assistance Fund
Housing Trust Fund Corporation
State of New York Mortgage Agency
Insurance
Job Development Authority
Public Service
Science and Technology Foundation
Urban Development Corporation
Harlem Urban Development Corporation

EDUCATION

Arts*
City University of New York
Education
Higher Education Services Corporation
State University of New York
State University Construction Fund

PARKS and the ENVIRONMENT

Adirondack Park*
Environmental Conservation
Environmental Facilities Corporation
Parks, Recreation and Historic Preservation

TRANSPORTATION

Motor Vehicles
Governor's Traffic Safety Committee
Transportation

HEALTH and SOCIAL WELFARE

Advocate for the Disabled*
Aging*
Children and Families*
Health
Human Rights*
Labor
Workers' Compensation Board
State Insurance Fund
Social Services
Youth

MENTAL HEALTH

Mental Hygiene
Mental Health
Mental Retardation and Developmental Disabilities
Alcoholism and Substance Abuse Services
Developmental Disabilities Planning Council
Quality of Care for the Mentally Disabled*
Facilities Development Corporation

PUBLIC PROTECTION

Correction Commission*
Correctional Services
Crime Victims Services*
Criminal Justice Services*
Military and Naval Affairs*
Parole*
Probation and Correctional Alternatives*
State Police*

GENERAL GOVERNMENT

Budget*
Civil Service
Elections*
Employee Relations*
Executive Chamber*
General Services*
Lottery
Public Employment Relations Board
Racing and Wagering Board*
Real Property Services*
State
Taxation and Finance
Tax Appeals
Veterans' Affairs*

*Indicates agencies within the Executive Department

of providing services. Irrespective of funding source, each agency is subject to the executive budget process, bound by the restrictions of civil service regulations, influenced by periodic public employee union negotiations with state management, and subject to audit processes from the state comptroller's Department of Audit and Control. (See figure II for a listing of state executive agencies.)

Although state agencies' major responsibilities are indicated by their titles, some departments have expanded, taken on, or been assigned additional duties and responsibilities. Others have shared duties with newly created agencies. The Department of Correctional Services illustrates the latter point.

Correctional Services

Only the Department of Correctional Services (DOCS) is a constitutionally established executive agency. However, increased pressures on the criminal justice system, together with shifts in philosophy toward persons convicted of wrongdoing, have resulted in a proliferation of agencies providing correctional services.

DOCS, for example, is responsible for the confinement of all convicted offenders. As elaborated in chapter 9, the number of such offenders has grown enormously since the 1970s. Because of shortages of prison space, despite additional building, expansion, and staffing of facilities, the department has been charged with developing and implementing programs to provide alternatives to incarceration when appropriate. The department makes recommendations about parole and probation but is responsible for neither of these areas.[2]

A separate Division of Parole assesses incarcerated offenders and determines when and under what conditions inmates may be released on parole. The division also decides when the terms of parole have been violated and the offender must return to prison. As part of its mission, the division works to counteract drug and alcohol abuse, which contribute substantially to parole violations.

Until 1992, a separate Division of Probation and Correctional Alternatives, working closely with local probation services, was responsible for assisting offenders not sentenced to incarceration. As this agency's functions and clientele did not differ greatly from that of the Division of Parole, the two agencies were merged with the expectation that additional services could be provided and, at the same time, that the combined agency would generate cost savings of more than $2 million annually.[3]

Finally, the Commission of Correction supervises the operations of state and local correctional facilities. It is responsible for recommending and overseeing implementation of improvements in correctional facilities' management and operations.

The development of this myriad of parole, probation, and correctional services agencies has been accompanied by a shift in emphasis away from nearly exclusively resorting to incarceration. The shift involves more effective supervision and rehabilitative services for nonviolent offenders, for whom supervised structured living within the community is better than prison.

Circumventing the Constitutional Limitation

During his long tenure as governor, Nelson Rockefeller reshaped and enlarged the executive branch of state government to implement new programs and to expand others. When he believed new agencies were needed to handle public programs, he created them. When new programs were developed, he enlarged existing agencies and opened new offices throughout the state. When traditional agencies were deemed inappropriate to handle new challenges, Rockefeller turned to the concept of public authorities. All of these actions added to the governor's authority and prestige within the governmental system. Rockefeller managed to stay within the constitutional limitations by creating offices, divisions, and boards to serve similar purposes as executive departments.

Public authorities also proliferated during the Rockefeller years, as the executive branch sought to use creative means (and often creative financing) to undertake urban renewal projects, build housing, establish transportation networks, and construct medical and other facilities. State public authorities are entities loosely grouped within the executive branch; they are responsible, not to the governor, but to their boards of directors.

William Ronan, secretary to Governor Rockefeller from 1959 to 1966, describes how Rockefeller outflanked the Public Service Commission, part of the Department of Public Service, to achieve his own policy goals:

> Coming into office with the avowed purposes of improving rail transportation and adding to the State's electric power resources, Rockefeller understood he could expect little positive action by the Public Service Commission. . . . So he looked elsewhere to encourage electric power development, as had Governor Dewey before him, to the State Power Authority, which was then completing its monumental hydro works at the Saint Lawrence and Niagara. He also sponsored the State Office for Atomic Development to pursue nuclear research and nuclear industry. . . . To improve transportation, he sponsored the legislation that created the Metropolitan Transportation Authority in New York and transportation authorities in the Niagara Frontier, the Rochester area, Syr-

acuse, and then Albany-Troy-Schenectady and other areas. All were exempted from Public Service Commission regulation.[4]

Governor Hugh Carey (1975–82) continued the practice of creating new
agencies to meet his programmatic goals. For example, in 1978, following a
highly publicized series of revelations about shocking conditions at Willowbrook, a major state facility serving the mentally retarded, Carey reorganized the administration of mental health. The Department of Mental Hygiene, which Carey characterized early in his administration as "in
disarray,"[5] was divided into an Office of Mental Health (with responsibility
for operating an increasing number of state psychiatric hospitals), an Office
of Mental Retardation and Developmental Disabilities (with responsibility
for operating a growing number of facilities for the mentally retarded), and
an Office of Alcoholism and Substance Abuse. The latter, in turn, was divided into separate alcoholism and substance abuse divisions. In 1991–92,
Carey's successor, Governor Mario Cuomo, reconsolidated these two divisions into a single office in response to pressures for budgetary savings.

In the late 1970s, the independence of several New York public authorities created during the Rockefeller years was curtailed. The impetus for creating supervisory control systems was the default, thirty days after Hugh
Carey became governor, of the Urban Development Corporation (UDC),
"the largest, most heavily financed development facility in the United
States." Because Carey "saw in this agency, if properly conducted, a great
potential for economic recovery and housing development," he and his key
advisers developed a "rescue plan [that involved] executive and budgetary
control and invited closer legislative oversight."[6] This approach to reining
in the UDC, detailed later in this chapter, was subsequently extended to some
other New York public authorities.

The Executive Budget Process

The Division of the Budget is at the very center of executive branch operations. Although senate confirmation is not needed, the director of the budget
is recognized as one of the most powerful and influential persons within the
executive branch. Created by constitutional amendment in 1927, the division was strengthened greatly during both the Dewey and Rockefeller administrations. Its role is central during times of increased government spending as well as in times of fiscal constraint.

New York's fiscal year begins on 1 April, and the state budget is normally
expected to be in place on that date. That expectation, however, has been

largely ignored by the legislature, with budget adoption occurring increasingly later since 1980 (see figure 7).

Most states have moved to a 1 July fiscal year, which reduces the need for spring borrowing for school districts and local governments. For New York, still reluctant to change its fiscal year, spring borrowing is now administered under the auspices of the 1990 Fiscal Reform Act, which created the Local Government Assistance Corporation, with authority to issue long-term bonds. This financing system was designed to be a less expensive and more stable method of providing funding for the school districts and the localities at the end of the state's fiscal year.[7]

The governor is mandated by the state constitution to submit the executive budget and the accompanying appropriation bills to the legislature on or before the second Tuesday following the first day of the newly convened legislative session (and somewhat later in years following gubernatorial elections). The constitution also requires a balanced budget. The legislature has from eight to ten weeks to examine the proposed budget as well as the accompanying bills. During the year, the fiscal committees of both the senate and the assembly conduct their own studies. Through informal meetings with executive chamber staff and in other informal settings, legislative staff develop a knowledge of the governor's priorities and how the legislature might appropriately respond.

The executive budget process extends year round, through execution of the existing budget and planning for the next one. Planning includes both expenditure calculations and revenue estimation—both part of the state's financial plan, which is updated on a quarterly basis.[8]

Executive agencies prepare their budget requests in late summer for submission to the Division of the Budget (DOB) by mid-September. The division is organized along functional lines, and agencies are assigned accordingly. Each agency is assigned a budget examiner with responsibility to review all agency requests, especially those for new programs. Budget examiners meet with agency officials to gather additional relevant information on which their recommendations to higher-level DOB officials will be based. Ultimately, the entire budget document is prepared in accordance with the governor's particular priorities for the next fiscal year.

In fact, agency fiscal officers are in continual contact with "their" budget examiner all year round. The more knowledgeable budget examiners are about existing and proposed programs, the more comfortable they are with supporting these programs within DOB. Ultimately, the governor and his or her top staff members (including the director of the budget) determine what will be included or excluded before the budget document is printed and submitted to the legislature.

DOB is responsible for ensuring that agencies spend monies allocated to them for the specified purposes. It also monitors revenue and expenditure estimates continually throughout the year. At any moment throughout a given fiscal year, the division is working on three budget cycles: the year just passed, the current year, and the following year. There is little question that the division plays the central role among executive agencies in executive branch operations.

Other Central Control Agencies

Three other control agencies are central in the operations of all executive agencies, including the Department of Civil Service, which is responsible for maintaining the merit system of personnel selection and promotion, and the Governor's Office of Employee Relations, which negotiates with the unions representing more than 90 percent of the state's approximately 185,000 employees.[9] Unionization began in 1967, after the passage of the Public Employees' Fair Employment Act (commonly known as the Taylor Law), which recognized the legality of public sector employee unions and, at the same time, prohibited strikes. This law replaced the 1947 Condon-Wadlin Act, which prohibited strikes but, in fact, did not prevent them. The governor appoints the heads of each of these agencies; Employee Relations is an agency within the executive department, whereas Civil Service is one of the enumerated twenty executive departments.

The third central control agency is the Department of Audit and Control, headed by the independently elected state comptroller. Audit and Control is responsible for both pre-audits (i.e., before authorizing disbursement of state funds) and post-audits within agencies. It also audits selected programs of various agencies. The department itself is audited by an external accounting firm every two years.[10]

Since the Rockefeller administration, New York voters have elected a fiscal watchdog from a party different from that of the governor. Arthur Levitt, state comptroller from 1955 to 1979, was routinely returned to office, the only Democrat to be reelected. During the Cuomo years, Levitt's successor, Republican Edward V. Regan (1979–93) was reelected repeatedly, right along with Democrats Cuomo and Attorney General Robert Abrams. H. Carl McCall, who was appointed comptroller by the legislature in 1993 when Regan resigned, was elected to a full term in 1994, the only Democrat to survive the statewide Republican sweep.

DELIVERY OF SERVICES AND ECONOMIC REGULATION

In the twentieth century, particularly since the 1930s, New York state government built an increasingly strong presence in providing services to its citizens and residents. From Franklin Roosevelt on, regardless of political party affiliation, New York's governors have believed in government's broad responsibilities toward the citizenry. Sometimes agencies' responsibilities were increased because the governors successfully sought legislation to expand their role in current or additional areas. At other times, the initiative to better serve citizens' needs came from the legislature. But the objective was the same.

Economic Development

One agency whose role and responsibilities have increased dramatically is the Empire State Development Department (ESD), the 1996 successor to the Department of Economic Development (and its predecessor, the Department of Commerce). ESD's ambitious mandate is to increase investment within the state from local, national, and international sources. During Governor Mario Cuomo's administration, that mandate was coupled with oversight of the state's economic development zones program, a program established in 1986 to stimulate investment and job creation in distressed areas through tax and financing incentives to the private sector. Cuomo reorganized all the state's major economic development agencies—the Department of Economic Development, the Office for Regulatory and Management Assistance, and the formerly autonomous Urban Development Corporation (UDC), Science and Technology Foundation, and Job Development Authority (JDA)—under the aegis of an office of economic development, with Vincent Tese as director. Governor George Pataki further reorganized the economic development function in 1995. This time, three separate agencies were created. The Empire State Department of Economic Development (encompassing the Department of Economic Development and the Science and Technology Foundation), and the Empire State Economic Development Corporation (encompassing UDC and JDA) were headed by the commissioner of economic development, Charles A. Gargano. The Office of Regulatory Reform, with considerably strengthened authority, was located in the governor's office and headed by Robert King. This restructuring was intended to advance Pataki's commitments to reduce administrative costs, provide easier access for businesses to economic development assistance, and "work with state agencies to eliminate regulations that unnecessarily add to the cost of doing business in New York."[11]

Mental Health

Since the 1970s, New York, as suggested in the earlier discussion of the Department of Mental Hygiene, has provided comprehensive services for the mentally ill, the developmentally disabled, alcoholics, and drug abusers. While the locus of services provided has shifted from institutional settings to community homes and individual family living, the number of people served has increased dramatically. According to the Office of Mental Retardation and Developmental Disabilities (OMRDD), approximately 29,000 people were assisted in 1982, and more than twice that number a decade later.[12] The downsizing or closing of OMRDD's developmental centers began in the 1960s following court orders that grew out of the scandalous conditions at Willowbrook Developmental Center on Staten Island. The availability of Medicaid reimbursement for people living in their own homes or in community residential placements administered by OMRDD also accelerated the process.

Much the same trend was in evidence for the mentally ill population in state facilities. Despite the move from institutionalization to community-based care, New York still spends more per capita on mental health than does any other state. Between 1987 and 1992, the inpatient population in state-funded mental health facilities declined by 7,700; such former patients are now treated through community-based care. Additional reductions to an adult inpatient population of 8,000 were anticipated, pending the availability of "adequate community services."[13] The costs of providing community-based support services are lower than those of institutionalization; simultaneous with deinstitutionalization, the Office of Mental Health expanded its operation of residential services. As with OMRDD, Medicaid reimbursements were expected to be extended to community- or individual-based mentally ill persons, with the latter in "assisted living" arrangements.

Nearly two million New York adult residents were estimated in 1992 to have serious alcohol problems. The Division of Alcoholism, now reconsolidated with the Division of Substance Abuse Services into the Office of Alcoholism and Substance Abuse Services (OASAS), operates residential alcohol treatment centers (handling 5,000 patients annually) as well as several research centers. Most of its activities are focused at the local level, with federal funds picking up almost 50 percent of the costs.

The Division of Substance Abuse Services provided support services for more than 50,000 clients in 1992 and expects, given continued societal needs, to expand its services. Half of the estimated 260,000 intravenous drug users in the state in 1992 are believed to be HIV positive, adding to the enormity of the problem.

Social Services

New York's largest single provider of services, historically, has been the Department of Social Services (DSS). This department, whose operating expenditures at more than $23 billion in 1995–96 represented nearly 40 percent of total state appropriations, was responsible for administering income transfer (Aid to Families with Dependent Children, Home Relief, and Supplemental Security Income), Medicaid, and other social services. The shift in 1996 of New York's very large Medicaid program from DSS to the Department of Health meant that DSS no longer had budgetary dominance.

Health

The Department of Health has historically had responsibility for the promotion and supervision of public health activities within New York. In that capacity, the department works to combat communicable diseases, administers the federally funded WIC (women, infants, and children) nutritional program, and is the major regulator of hospitals, public water systems, food service establishments, and children's camps. Through its community health programs, the department monitors nutritional programs for children, the frail elderly, and the homeless, also funded in part by federal grants. The AIDS Institute, created in 1983, focuses mainly on prevention and on providing services for HIV-infected people and their families through local organizations. The department runs a nationally prominent laboratory that conducts research on various diseases, offers HIV screening programs, and seeks to identify congenital disorders in newborns, among other items on its crowded agenda. The department also stipulates health-care standards, monitors the quality and availability of care within the state, and provides financing for nonprofit health-care facilities. With the assumption of responsibility for management of New York's large Medicaid program in 1996, the Department of Health's expenditures were projected to increase from $1.4 billion in 1995–96 to over $17 billion in 1996–97.

In summary, these and other executive branch agencies provide extensive services to the state's residents, much of it through local offices and facilities. Many state agencies have regional offices that provide linkages directly with local service providers. The reduction in size of institutionalized populations in facilities administered directly by the state in favor of community residential placement has resulted in more services being offered at the local level. At the same time that they deliver services, these agencies are also regulators: they establish procedures, inspect, license, and periodically review programs and personnel responsible for delivering services. The vast network of agencies' central and regional offices, facilities, and community-based operations ensures a substantial and continued presence of the executive branch throughout the state.

Public Authorities: The Fourth Branch of Government?

There are literally hundreds of public authorities in New York State. Many, such as municipal and industrial development authorities, are locally operated and generally are locally financed. Despite their disparate structures and purposes, authorities share two common characteristics: they are distinct and separate from general government, with the power to issue tax-exempt bonds to finance their activities and to set fees and charges for their services.[14] As of 1995, there were thirty-two major debt-issuing state public authorities.[15]

Public authorities are not new in New York. In 1921, the Port of New York Authority (its name later changed to the Port Authority of New York and New Jersey) was the first to be established. The Power Authority was created in 1931, and the State Bridge Authority in 1932. Other early authorities include the Dormitory Authority (1944), and the Thruway and New York City Transit Authorities (1950). While public authorities are included in the executive branch, for lack of another neatly defined "home," in fact, once they have been established, the governor has relatively little control over their activities and often has little input into their range of responsibilities.

Public authorities are created to circumvent procurement, personnel, and budgetary requirements that restrain state agencies. The justification for the autonomy of authorities is that they operate with greater efficiency and flexibility than government agencies. Public authorities typically are established to focus on single issues such as transportation and housing, although they may later expand their responsibilities. They generally recruit staff from the nongovernmental sector and are free of the restrictions of the civil service system. The creation of a public authority to develop and manage a regional or metropolitan activity, such as mass transit, that cuts across local governmental jurisdictional boundaries suggests that local government restructuring is overdue and that regional authorities are responding to a real need. When authorities are created to avoid constitutional, statutory, or budgetary restrictions, the rationale often is based on expedience and a drive to "get something done" that is difficult to achieve within the existing governmental structure.

After voters rejected "Rockefeller-initiated multimillion-dollar and multibillion-dollar bond issues for housing four times, for transportation two times, and for higher education four times, . . . the frustrated governor turned to John A. Mitchell, then an eminent Wall Street bond counsel"[16] (later, the discredited attorney general in the Nixon administration). Mitchell developed the concept of "moral obligation bonds," which required a public authority to maintain reserves to cover only one year's principal and interest on its debts. The governor could ask the legislature for additional funding if needed to cover unexpected debts. In fact, legislatures cannot compel future legislatures to appropriate funds for such purposes, so the bonds issued were not backed by anything except the issuing authority's ability to keep itself solvent. As such, the state was "morally" but not legally responsible for backing the bonds.

Governor Rockefeller well understood the utility of "moral obligation" bonds to "give the voters what they wanted but refused to pay for." As he testified to Congress during his vice-presidential hearings in 1974, "I was unable to obtain public approval of state bond issues. We therefore devised an innovative approach."[17]

Curbing State Authorities

The failure of the Urban Development Corporation in 1975 to redeem its bonds as well as its inability to meet debt service and operating expenses led to greater oversight of public authorities. The UDC default led Governor Hugh Carey to appoint a commission (under the state's Moreland Commission Act) in 1975 to investigate the operations of UDC and public authorities in the state in general. The commission concluded that there was "inadequate consideration, supervision, and control by the executive and legislative branches of government" over the activities of state public authorities.[18] It recommended a variety of controls on public authorities, including the creation of the Public Authorities Control Commission and an end to the use of moral obligation bonds.

The Public Authorities Control Board, created by the legislature in 1976, is charged with regulating the finances and development of ten major authorities. It reviews and must grant approval before any of the authorities it monitors "can require, finance, or construct any project."[19] Other "safeguards" that have been put in place include mandated annual external audit and budget reports, and authority for the state comptroller to examine accounts. The control board establishes debt ceilings for the authorities monitored but has no authority to review authorities' performance or the projects they undertake.[20] The Division of the Budget, with its oversight over budgets and capital plans of authorities, further limits their autonomy.

Despite the Moreland Commission's recommendations, moral obligation bonds continue to be used. The possibility of public authorities making bad investment decisions with dubious government securities firms also proceeds unchecked. In 1982, for example, the Dormitory Authority invested some of its cash on hand and ultimately lost $21 million; it could have lost more than double that amount when the securities firm with which it was doing business went bankrupt.[21] Despite investigations by the legislature and others, greater accountability has yet to be put into place.

Public authorities continue to assume functions of rejected bond issues. In the mid-1980s, for example, at Governor Cuomo's request, UDC was given additional authority to issue bonds to build correctional facilities. The Department of Correctional Services and the Office of General Services (responsible for all state-owned or leased space) leased the facilities; ultimately both the state and the public authority will own these new (and expanded) facilities.

UDC also purchased the Attica correctional facility by floating a $200 million bond issue. The state thus was able to reduce its deficit by this amount in the 1991 executive budget; it is estimated, however, that the sale will ultimately cost $290 million because of the lease-back arrangement.[22]

A Success Story: The Environmental Facilities Corporation

The New York State Environmental Facilities Corporation (EFC) is viewed by many as a public authorities' success story. Proposed by Governor Cuomo for elimination in 1988, the EFC got a new lease on life as a consequence of national environmental policy. In its early years, the EFC designed a few facilities and provided much technical advice to localities but did little else. In 1989, Congress created a state revolving-fund concept for the U.S. Environmental Protection Agency, designed to assist states in environmental improvement projects (water, sewage, and solid waste). That agency provides grants to the states, which states must match 20 percent. States can then provide loans to localities for the purposes of the fund as stated. Through wise investment strategies and issuance of bonds, EFC has increased the amount of financing it has available to loan. By keeping bad-risk localities out of the bond pool, EFC has been able to maintain an Aa bond rating. Loans are offered to localities at low interest rates. Because localities need to repay the loan in a timely manner, there is greater attention to completing the project for which they received the loan than if they had received a grant. EFC estimates that by 1999, it will have awarded up to $4 billion in loans. Part of EFC's current success is a consequence of an infusion of environmental, technical, and financial experts from the state's Department of Environmental Conservation, with which it works very closely.[23]

In summary, despite recently imposed controls and monitoring procedures, many New York public authorities have too much clout and too little accountability. Some have assumed responsibilities in areas in which they were not designed to operate. Others have usurped responsibilities from state agencies to which those responsibilities properly belong. To closely monitor the activities of a large number of public authorities and to hold them accountable, while still providing the flexibility that executive agencies do not have, is a continuing challenge for elected officials.

New York's executive branch exercises responsibilities and activities consistent with the state's twin policy goals of meeting social needs and fostering competition. Its more than sixty agencies employed a full-time equivalent workforce of 267,000 in 1992. The range of services extends from repairing roads to financing community residences for the developmentally disabled. In many sectors, New York has chosen to provide services that are not offered in most other states. It spends more per capita for mental health patients; it provides more extensive Medicaid services; it undertakes more research in such health-related areas as alcoholism and communicable diseases. The state's regulatory functions are also extensive and range from requiring a variety of permits to set up or expand a business to inspecting children's camps.

Over the years, a system of external controls has been developed and refined to regulate and supervise agency operations. Chief among these is the budgetary and program review responsibility that the Division of the Budget exercises over all state agencies as it reviews budgetary and spending requests. The Department of Audit and Control must authorize all payments for goods and services before the agreement to purchase is finalized as well as when the bills are to be paid. Both the civil service merit selection system and the public employee union/state agreements (usually three-year contracts) limit agencies' capabilities in personnel recruitment, selection, and retention.

For these reasons as well as other restrictions put upon the activities of executive agencies in carrying out their responsibilities, governors have sometimes chosen to recommend creation or expansion of a public authority to "get the job done." When funding is unavailable or the electorate fails to support a bond issue, a public authority can take on the task by issuing tax-exempt bonds of its own. Although public authorities are not directly responsible to the governor, both the credit and the blame for their activities and operations accrue to the chief executive.

CHAPTER NINE

The Challenges of Dispensing Justice

Sarah F. Liebschutz

They hauled in the guilt by the ton. . . . Forty-thousand people, forty-thousand incompetents, dimwits, alcoholics, psychopaths, knockabouts, good souls driven to some terminal anger, and people who could only be described as stone evil, were arrested. . . . Seven thousand of them were indicted and arraigned, and then they entered the maw of the justice system. . . . And to what end? The same stupid, dismal, pathetic, horrifying, crimes were committed day in and day out, all the same.—Tom Wolfe, The Bonfire of the Vanities

Tom Wolfe's description of New York City's legal system reflects literary license. At the same time, it captures many realities of dispensing justice in New York, including "the drug culture [that] produces violence at every level, from the kingpins to the dealers to the addicts, from gangland slayings to robbery to child abuse."[1] Such realities also include the homelessness that is associated with mental illness, alcoholism and drug dependency, and unemployment. For these and other realities, violent as well as victimless, New Yorkers seek justice from overworked judges and overcrowded prisons.

New York's judicial system reflects preferences for both competition and compassion. Competitive, partisan elections determine the selection of most of the state's judges. The high court's reputation is liberal, especially in protecting the rights of defendants. However, New York's harsh penalties for drug-related crimes that date from the 1960s, its adoption of the death penalty in 1995, and Governor George Pataki's 1996 proposals to close "criminal friendly loopholes" in state laws contrast with the high court's compassion.[2] Three factors complicate the dispensing of justice in New York: the

Table 9: Structure and Composition of New York Courts

Appeals Level

Name of Court:	**Court of Appeals**
Number of Judges:	7
Selection Method:	Appointment by governor with consent of senate
Term:	14 years
Jurisdiction:	State
Subject Matter:	Constitutional issues
Name of Court:	**Appellate Division of Supreme Court**
Number of Judges:	54
Selection Method:	Appointment by governor from Supreme Court justices
Term:	5 years
Jurisdiction:	Department (4 departments)
Subject Matter:	Appeals of judgments and orders from superior trial courts
Name of Court:	**Appellate Term of Supreme Court**
Number of Judges:	15
Selection Method:	Appointment by chief administrator from superior court judiciary
Term:	5 years
Jurisdiction:	Department (first and second departments only)
Subject Matter:	Appeals from judgments or orders from inferior trial courts

Trial Superior Level

Name of Court:	**Supreme Court**
Number of Judges:	325
Selection Method:	Partisan election*
Term:	14 years
Jurisdiction:	Judicial districts (12 districts)
Subject Matter:	Unlimited
Name of Court:	**County Court**
Number of Judges:	120
Selection Method:	Partisan election
Term:	10 years
Jurisdiction:	County (57 of 62 counties—all except New York City)
Subject Matter:	Felonies and civil action up to $25,000
Name of Court:	**Family Court**
Number of Judges:	123
Selection Method:	Partisan election outside New York City; appointed by New York City mayor
Term:	10 years
Jurisdiction:	County (57 counties) and New York City
Subject Matter:	Matters concerning families and children
Name of Court:	**Court of Claims**
Number of Judges:	54
Selection Method:	Appointed by governor
Term:	9 years
Jurisdiction:	State
Subject Matter:	Tort and contract claims against the state
Name of Court:	**Surrogate's Court**
Number of Judges:	74

Selection Method:	Partisan election
Term:	10 years, outside New York City; 14 years, New York City
Jurisdiction:	County (57 counties) and New York City
Subject Matter:	Affairs of decedents; including probate of wills, estate administration, and adoptions

Trial Inferior Level

Name of Court:	**New York City Civil Court**
Number of Judges:	120
Selection Method:	Partisan election
Term:	10 years
Jurisdiction:	New York City
Subject Matter:	Civil actions up to $25,000; small claims
Name of Court:	**New York City Criminal Court**
Number of Judges:	108
Selection Method:	Appointed by Mayor
Term:	10 years
Jurisdiction:	New York City
Subject Matter:	Misdemeanors, felony arraignments
Name of Court:	**District Court**
Number of Judges:	51
Selection Method:	Partisan election
Term:	6 years
Jurisdiction:	County (Nassau and Suffolk only)
Subject Matter:	Misdemeanors, felony arraignments
Name of Court:	**City Court**
Number of Judges:	155
Selection Method:	Varies by locality
Term:	Varies by locality
Jurisdiction:	City (outside New York City)
Subject Matter:	Misdemeanors, felony arraignments
Name of Court:	**Town Court**
Number of Judges:	2,327
Selection Method:	Partisan election
Term:	4 years
Jurisdiction:	Town (931 towns)
Subject Matter:	Misdemeanors, felony arraignments
Name of Court:	**Village Court**
Number of Judges:	750
Selection Method:	Partisan election
Term:	Varies by location
Jurisdiction:	Village (more than 500)
Subject Matter:	Misdemeanors, felony arraignments

Source: New York State, Office of Court Administration.

*Acting Supreme Court justices are appointed from the Court of Claims and New York City Civil Court to hold temporary appointments.

fact that New York has "arguably the most complex [court structure] in the United States";[3] the ongoing controversy over election or appointment of judges that was not settled by a 1977 amendment providing for appointment to the Court of Appeals, the state's highest court, by the governor; and the huge, expensive, and overcrowded prisons resulting from "unrelenting demand for prison capacity [growing out of] the continuing drug epidemic and the inflexibility of the State's sentencing laws."[4] These factors link past and present New York politics.

NEW YORK STATE COURTS: STRUCTURE, COMPOSITION, AND FUNCTION

The court system of New York, the origins of which date back to the state's revolutionary constitution of 1777, is today one of the largest and busiest in the nation. In 1995, more than 1,200 full-time and 2,500 part-time (town and village) judges, 13,000 nonjudicial employees, and 450,000 jurors, whose activities were funded by a budget of nearly $1 billion, handled 3.3 million cases.[5] The court system is also one of the most complex. In contrast with California, the nation's largest court system, which has "five identifiable courts from municipal court to the supreme court, New York has at least 13 different varieties of courts statewide, depending upon how one is counting."[6]

The New York State court system can be visualized as a hierarchical pyramid with three tiers. As detailed in table 9, the upper tier represents the appellate courts, the middle tier the trial courts of superior jurisdiction, and the bottom tier the trial courts of limited jurisdiction. The tiers are based upon geography and types of cases heard. Within tiers, the number of judges per court and method of selection, by appointment or election, vary widely.

Another important distinction is between the trial courts of New York City and those in the rest of the state. Felony cases, for example, are heard in New York City by criminal court judges appointed by the mayor; elsewhere such cases are tried before elected judges in county courts. Civil suits up to $25,000, on the other hand, are brought before elected judges in New York City's civil courts and in county courts in other areas of the state.

The Court of Appeals, the state's highest court, is at the apex of the system; the Chief Judge of the Court of Appeals is the chief judge of New York and its chief judicial officer. The chief administrator of the state's unified court system, appointed by the Chief Judge, exercises oversight, through the Office of Court Administration, of the entire judicial system.

The current New York state court system and its administrative structure are relatively recent, dating from 1977, when the state constitution was amended to provide for appointment of judges of the Court of Appeals by the governor and centralized administration of the state courts system. Before 1846, judges had been appointed by the senate and then by the governor. Then "in the midst of the era of Jacksonian Democracy when non-owners of land protested against judges whom they felt were too closely allied with the landed gentry, New York switched to an elective system."[7]

Prior to 1977, court administration was lodged in four offices, one in each of the appellate divisions of the Supreme Court. The Office of Court Administration created in 1977 was "a new figure in a tradition-bound setting in which the courts had been highly autonomous entities."[8]

New York's court system, with its many different trial courts, has been called "a classic instance of how not to construct a modern justice system." A 1993 Court Management Study Committee appointed by the Chief Judge cited "duplication of services and offices incumbent in the [present] structure [and] disruptive, expensive . . . time-consuming . . . inordinate and ongoing litigation over pay parity among courts and judges."[9] Governor Mario Cuomo long contended that New York's "inefficiently organized trial court system actually foments additional litigation, keeps citizens from obtaining complete relief in one court, creates confusion for litigants, and unnecessarily delays the delivery of justice."[10]

The New York State Bar Association, the Association of the Bar of the City of New York, the Committee for Modern Courts, the League of Women Voters, and other public interest organizations have long pressed for merger of all or some of the state's trial courts (County Court, Family Court, Surrogate's Court, Court of Claims, New York City Civil Court, New York City Criminal Court, and District Court) into a single-tier trial court.

Governor Cuomo in 1986 proposed a constitutional amendment to allow court merger. Both houses of the state legislature approved first passage of the merger amendment that year, but they failed in 1987 to support the second passage necessary to put the matter to voters. Cuomo subsequently broadened his strategy, calling for merger of the state's trial courts at a 1998 state constitutional convention. Court merger in New York has powerful opponents. Resistance comes from supporters of specialized jurisdiction, such as represented in Family Court, Surrogate's Court, and the Court of Claims; from the Civil Service Employees Union, whose employees staff the courts; and even from some Supreme Court justices who perceive that their elite status on the trial bench would be threatened. But the most intense opposition comes from local political parties. A single, unified trial court would not long tolerate the diverse judicial selection methods currently used; merit selection of judges, the method preferred by merger advocates, reduces the potential for partisan political influence. Thus the merger of New York's trial courts poses a direct challenge to the present system by which most New York trial court judges are selected. As discussed later in this chapter, the power of political leaders would be seriously eroded.

THE COURT OF APPEALS

Until 1977, when voters approved a state constitutional amendment that replaced partisan elections to the Court of Appeals with a modified Missouri Plan, the state's highest court had remained virtually unchanged in number of members and jurisdiction for more than a century.[11] For the first decades of New York's history as a state, justices of the Supreme (trial) Court, the chancellor (a judicial officer), and members of the state senate composed the membership of the state's highest court. The Court of Appeals, with eight elected judges, was itself established at the Constitutional Convention of 1846. At the Constitutional Convention of 1869, the present-day Court of Appeals was mandated with one Chief Judge and six associate judges.[12]

The 1977 amendment was not without controversy. Supporters—including Charles D. Breitel, Chief Judge of the Court of Appeals at the time, Governor Hugh Carey, most major bar associations, and public interest organizations—argued that "campaigns are demeaning and costly . . . [and] voters are unaware of the qualifications of judicial candidates and unable to evaluate judges' legal ability because the Code of Judicial Conduct bars candidates from taking stances on substantial issues [so that they do not appear to prejudge future cases]." Opponents, among them Charles Desmond, a former Chief Judge, "argued that none of the supporters of the amendment [had] demonstrated that it [would] improve the quality of the bench." Other opponents contended that judicial appointment would favor the "economic and social elite."[13]

The 1977 amendment, as approved by voters, established the new system of appointing judges of the Court of Appeals, including a twelve-member Commission on Judicial Nomination. Four commission members are appointed by the Court of Appeals Chief Judge, four by the governor, and one appointment each is reserved for the Speaker of the assembly, the minority leader of the assembly, the senate president, and the minority leader of the senate. Each commissioner serves a four-year term, at the end of which he or she may be re-appointed by one of the designated appointers.[14]

When a Court of Appeals vacancy occurs, the governor chooses a nominee from a list of seven names submitted to him by the Commission on Judicial Nomination. The state senate then confirms or rejects the governor's nominee. If confirmed, the judge is appointed for a fourteen-year term, with no limit on the number of terms that can be served. Since the inception of the new system, the senate has confirmed every nominee, after hearings that, on the whole, have reflected bipartisan support.[15]

The Commission on Judicial Nomination was designed to maximize citizen participation and minimize political influence.[16] No more than two of the four appointments made by the governor and Chief Judge can be lawyers, and no more than two can be of the same political party. Further, commissioners are ineligible for elective office while on the commission and for one year after their departure.

The 1977 constitutional amendment has not been completely successful in insulating either the commission or the process from politics. There are numerous points of entry where politics can be injected into the system, such as in the search for nominees by the commission and in the governor's selection. Shortly after the new system came into effect, a member of the state legislature complained, "I think we have brought more politics into the process than . . . we ever did when judges were elected."[17] Although the governor's four appointees assure him influence in the commission, this has not always resulted in nominees satisfactory to the governor. Early in his first term, Governor Cuomo expressed dissatisfaction with some of the lists of Court of Appeals nominees he received.[18]

These comments aside, the modified Missouri Plan for appointment of judges to the New York State Court of Appeals is generally praised as superior to the partisan election process that preceded it. The current Court of Appeals—eight appointed by Cuomo and one by Pataki since 1983—with two female judges, one of them Hispanic, and a male African-American judge, better reflects the state's ethnic diversity than the all-white, male Courts of Appeals that preceded the 1977 amendment. Chief Judge Judith S. Kaye, the first woman to serve on the Court of Appeals, appointed by Cuomo in 1983 as associate judge and in 1993 as Chief Judge, is unlikely to have attained either position under a partisan electoral system. At the time of her nomination for Chief Judge, the *New York Times* lauded her as "a conscientious judge with an active interest in court administration as well as wisdom in deciding cases. Her presence on the Court of Appeals has already vindicated the merit selection system."[19]

The Court of Appeals and Judicial Federalism

Under the U.S. Constitution, states cannot deny their citizens rights protected by the federal government. State courts, however, basing their judgments on "independent and adequate" state constitutional grounds, can set rights standards that are higher, but not lower, than those established under the U.S. Constitution. They can "choose to follow federal precedent or take a higher road and expand rights protections." The new judicial federalism "conforms to an old principle of American federalism: that states may act where the U.S. government has elected not to act, so long as state action does not violate the U.S. Constitution or federal law."[20]

The New York Court of Appeals, long in the forefront of the new judicial federalism, is generally viewed as liberal. Scholars of the court cite its "rich tradition of independent constitutional adjudication, of safeguarding individual liberties beyond federal requirements, and of exerting considerable influence on the other state courts and the United States Supreme Court as well. . . . When the Supreme Court became more conservative in the 1970s, the Court of Appeals simply proceeded apace in its own rights-protective direction. This was consistent with the court's practice, since early in its history, when it established a tradition of defining and extending rights as a matter of independent state fundamental law."[21] U.S. Supreme Court Justice William J. Brennan Jr. in 1986 characterized the New York Court of Appeals as the "acknowledged leader" in guarding civil rights and liberties through reliance on state constitutional law.[22]

The rights-protective tenor of the court was well articulated by Sol Wachtler, former Chief Judge of the Court of Appeals.[23] In *Arcara* v. *Cloud Books, Inc.*, the Court of Appeals held that closure of an adult bookstore where prostitution and other illicit sexual activities occurred was an unconstitutional restraint of the owners' rights to freedom of speech. Judge Wachtler wrote: "The Supreme Court's role in construing the federal bill of rights is to establish minimal standards for individual rights throughout the nation. The function of the comparable provisions of the state constitution, if they are not to be considered purely redundant, is to supplement those rights to meet the needs and expectations of the particular state."[24] The subsequent interpretation by the U.S. Supreme Court of the First Amendment to the Bill of Rights was narrower than that of the state's highest court. The six-member Supreme Court majority, reversing the Court of Appeals, asserted that "the closure sanction was directed at unlawful conduct having nothing to do with books or expressive activity."[25]

During the last years of Sol Wachtler's tenure as Chief Judge (1985–93), the Court of Appeals seemed to "reverse the course on which it had been proceeding for the previous quarter century" in safeguarding individual rights and liberties beyond federal requirements. Vincent Martin Bonventre, in an analysis of right to counsel, fair trial protection, and free expression decisions during 1990–91, concluded that "the court [was] simply more pro-government and less pro-individual across the board."[26]

The reversal of the high court's historic liberalism, however, was temporary. Under the leadership of Chief Judge Judith S. Kaye, who had "objected to the Court's 'about face' and 'break with its proud tradition' of ensuring protection of fundamental rights, the Court of Appeals . . . adjusted its course." Bonventre and John Powell, in an analysis of the court's rulings for the fifteen-month period after the resignation of former Chief Judge Wachtler, found a shift away from a "lopsided siding with the government or prosecution" and toward greater protection of individual rights and liberties."[27]

ELECTION OR APPOINTMENT OF JUDGES?

Political competitions determine how the vast majority of New York's judges come to the bench; they must secure political party nominations and win partisan elections. The exceptions are the 7 members of the Court of Appeals and 33 members of the Court of Claims, appointed by the governor, and 25 judges of the New York City Family Court and 107 judges of the New York City Criminal Court, appointed by the mayor. In addition, justices of the Appellate Division are appointed by the governor from among sitting (elected) Supreme Court justices.

New York is one of only thirteen states that use partisan elections for the regular selection of judges. The reason for the elections is that judgeships are the most attractive of the few sources of patronage that remain for parties to distribute; their "prestige and power . . . make them alluring prizes."[28] Where political parties are strong, as in New York, "political service and influence in the party organization are almost always prerequisites to receiving the organization's support." Even so, as Bruce Green's description of the judicial selection process in the New York City borough of Queens indicates, party loyalty is not enough to secure a judicial nomination, let alone superior qualifications: "First, past political service to a local club or the county organization is of paramount importance in the selection of judges; second, in the discussions leading to the selection of the party organization's candidates, political leaders often bargain over judgeships; and third, there is no assurance that the political leaders will select the most qualified judicial candidates."[29]

Three criticisms have been leveled at the current selection process for New York state judges. The first criticism is that it is undemocratic. The New York State Commission on Government Integrity concluded in a 1990 report, "Most judges in New York are chosen by elections that are almost totally dominated by political party leaders."[30]

The second criticism is that the current system produces judges of lower quality than those selected in a merit process. A 1992 study comparing the characteristics and behavior of elected and appointed judges in New York City concluded that merit selection produced a "younger, more representative, better educated, highly qualified and more politically diverse judiciary."[31] Further, the number of elected judges in New York City who were disciplined for misconduct violations was six times higher than that of merit-selected judges.

The third criticism of the partisan election process is that it excludes women and minorities. The New York City study found "that more minorities (African-American, Hispanics, Asian or Pacific Islanders, and Native Americans/Alaskans) came to the bench through an appointive system . . . than [from] any form of election."[32] For the state as a whole, the current judicial selection process has yielded a bench that in 1991 was 92 percent white, 6 percent African-American, 2 percent Hispanic, less than 1 percent Asian-American, and less than 15 percent women. Deviations from the general population were particularly striking in some judicial districts. For example, 85 percent of the Supreme Court justices in the Second State Judicial District (Staten Island and Brooklyn) were white, 13 percent were black, and 2 percent were Hispanic. This contrasts with the district's population—46 percent white, 31 percent black, and 18 percent Hispanic. Even more marked was the deviation in the Twelfth Judicial District, with 66 percent white justices and 77 percent nonwhite population.[33] The report of the Task Force on Judicial Diversity, appointed by Governor Cuomo, laid the blame at the feet of machine politics: "The perception that a political entree is required restricts the pool of talent across the board. But restricting the pool of minority and women lawyers is of particular concern to us because that pool of talent is already restricted by the deprivations of prejudice and social disadvantage. It is fundamentally unfair . . . to compound the problem by imposing on the strong talent pool that does exist the totally irrelevant requirements of having a political entree."[34]

The task force, in its February 1992 report, concluded that New York's system of electing judges "cannot pass muster" under the federal Voting Rights Act, interpreted just eight months earlier by the U.S. Supreme Court to apply to election of judges. Rather than recommend dismantling the election system, however, the task force proposed a constitutional amendment to increase minority voting strength by creating small, single-member judicial election districts.

Responses to the report of the Task Force on Judicial Diversity were swift. On 19 February 1992, one week after the report was issued, the Center for Constitutional Rights initiated a class-action suit in Federal District Court in Manhattan, "charging the way [state supreme court] justices are nominated and elected in New York City violates the Voting Rights Act." Acting on behalf of six black and Hispanic voters, the center alleged that racial minorities "are denied the right to elect justices of their choice because [they] are nominated by tightly controlled party organizations and then elected at large in mostly countywide judicial voting districts." The center supported the task force's recommendation for small, single-member judicial districts, agreeing they "would give black and Hispanic areas of the city a much stronger voice in the nomination and election of justices."[35]

While Governor Cuomo used the task force findings to buttress his advocacy of court reform, he did not support the recommendation for smaller judicial districts. Rather, he continued to press for merger of the trial courts and merit selection of judges by the legislature or a constitutional convention.

Does the merit system yield better judges and better judging? Opponents of the governor's "merger and merit" proposal in 1994 reiterated an argument they made in 1977: there is no conclusive evidence to support that contention. At the same time, they strongly emphasized that the conditions under which judges labor need immediate attention. As the head of the Association of Justices of the Supreme Court put it, "Do you know that many of us have seen our caseloads increase dramatically? That we still have rotary phone systems, word processors and computers so obsolete we have trouble getting them repaired; dirty, infested courthouses and a morale at its lowest due largely to no salary increase since 1987 while everyone else in the court system has received increases?"[36]

THE HARD-PRESSED CORRECTIONS SYSTEM

The administration of justice does not stop with the decisions of judges and juries; it shifts to implementation of those decisions by the New York Department of Correctional Services, with responsibility for "the secure confinement of offenders and the preparation of these individuals for successful reintegration into the community upon their release."[37]

New York State's prison population more than doubled between 1974 to 1984, from 12,000 prisoners to over 31,000, and then doubled again in the next decade, to nearly 65,000. Construction of new prisons kept pace with the increasing demand through the 1980s. After 1990, however, in the absence of continued prison expansion, the system was absorbing thousands of new inmates by housing them in temporary facilities or double-bunking them in medium security facilities.[38]

The unrelenting demand for prison capacity has been driven, not "by the need to remove violent offenders from the community, but rather by the spiraling number of drug-related, non-violent offenders serving mandatory prison sentences."[39] Harsh penalties were contained in legislation enacted in 1973 at the behest of Governor Nelson Rockefeller, who viewed them as the way to "defeat drug abuse before it destroys America."[40] The so-called Rockefeller drug laws increased the number of offenses requiring incarceration and mandated that any ex-convict convicted of a second felony within ten years automatically be sent to jail.[41] It is estimated that more than 50 percent of the New York state prison population was incarcerated in the 1990s because of crimes associated with substance abuse and punishable under laws enacted thirty years earlier, during the administration of Nelson Rockefeller.

The high recidivism rate among New York prisoners also contributes to prison overcrowding. Sixty percent of ex-convicts are re-arrested for felonies within five years of release, and 47 percent are convicted of new infractions. The more extensive a prisoner's prior arrest record, the higher the rate of recidivism. Recidivism is a function of prior socialization. New York's prison population consists largely of black and Hispanic young men "who have had unsuccessful experiences in their families, schools, military services, and the labor force. They suffer disproportionately from child abuse, alcohol and drug abuse, poor self-concept, and deficient social skills."[42]

Probation is the most traditional alternative to incarceration. "Originally intended to provide help and counseling, probation now concentrates on supervision. The system is so overloaded that serious felons, with criminal histories similar to the probationer who was recently arrested for killing a street vendor, now comprise 70 percent of the probationers in New York City.[43]

The trade-offs for New York's corrections policymakers are costly and difficult. More prison cells, which cost between "$80,000 to $100,000 to build and $26,000 a year to maintain," generate more prisoners with attendant recidivism.[44] At the same time, initiatives such as reforms in sentencing second-felony offenders, to shift "the emphasis in applying sanctions against low-level, non-violent offenders from the prison to the community,'' meet with resistance from a public fearful of crime.[45] Proposals, such as those Governor George Pataki advanced early in his administration, to permanently deny parole for criminals who commit one violent felony, to hold juvenile offenders to adult standards in certain cases, and to liberalize criminal evidence procedures—all of which have the potential to increase the demand for prison cells—resonate more positively with New Yorkers.

Dispensing justice in New York involves political control over the courts and public attitudes toward crimes and criminals. These are not new issues. On the contrary, as shown in this chapter, contemporary positions on court organization, judicial selection, and crimes and punishments are all influenced by past political preferences and choices. In consequence, New York attempts to mete out justice competitively and compassionately within a judicial system with such notable internal contradictions as a liberal high court, a judiciary chosen in partisan elections, and a huge corrections system reflective of longstanding and conservative attitudes toward offenders.

CHAPTER TEN

The Local Governance System

Joseph F. Zimmerman

General purpose local governments are the most important suppliers of services to the public and are the units with the greatest degree of citizen participation in policymaking and implementation. Diversity is a key descriptor of the local governance system in New York State, with its 932 towns, 556 villages, 62 cities, 57 counties, 712 school districts, and 998 other special districts.[1] Although each type of local government has a number of uniform characteristics, there are variations within cities operating with the mayor-council, or council-manager, or commission forms (for details on New York City, see chapter 11).

The state government plays a key role relative to the operation of the local governance system. As noted in chapter 3, the state constitution employs simultaneously three methods—*ultra vires* rule, *imperium in imperio*, and devolution of powers—for distributing political power between the state and its political subdivisions. Competition between supporters of centralization and decentralization of political power has been a common theme throughout the history of New York State. Furthermore, the development of suburban areas has led to competition between them and the large central cities for state financial assistance. The suburbs generally have been successful in their quest for additional state financial aid for public schools. Local governments also compete for industries and tourists.

New York is a highly partisan state, and most local government elections are partisan. In consequence, the nature of local government politics differs sharply from such politics in states where all or most general purpose local government officials are elected by nonpartisan ballots. Partisanship also explains in part why only a small number of local governments have professional managers as chief executive officers.

This chapter focuses upon the constitutional and statutory grants of political power to various types of local governments, state and federal mandates and restraints, structural variations among general purpose local governments, the future of small rural local governments, and the need for professional management in these units.

The state constitution, statutes, and administrative rules and regulations—as interpreted by the courts, attorney general, commissioner of education, and state comptroller—determine the amount of discretionary authority possessed by each type of local government with respect to structure of government, property, personnel, finance, and functions. As explained in a subsequent section, the powers of the four types of general purpose local governments are not identical, and specific exceptions are made for named units.

A study published in 1981 ranked New York thirty-fifth relative to the amount of discretionary authority granted to its general purpose political subdivisions.[2] These units have the least amount of discretionary authority in the areas of finance and personnel, and the broadest authority in the area of structure of government. Reviewing the development of constitutional provisions granting authority to general purpose local governments facilitates an understanding of their current powers.

CONSTITUTIONAL AUTHORITY

Cities during the colonial period possessed limited discretionary authority, and their mayors were appointed by the royal governor.[3] The constitution of 1777 continued this policy by vesting the appointment of mayors in the Council of Appointment, composed of the governor and four senators.[4] The system was changed by the constitution of 1822, which provided for the mayor to be appointed by the common council.[5] A constitutional amendment ratified in 1833 authorized voters to elect the mayor of New York City, and a second amendment, ratified in 1839, authorized the state legislature to provide for the election of the mayor in other cities by the voters.[6]

Historically, local governments were subject to the *ultra vires* rule (later known as Dillon's Rule), which held that they could only exercise delegated powers and that these powers were to be interpreted narrowly. The state legislature's power to control local governments, including chartering of cities and villages, first was restricted in 1874 when voters ratified a constitutional amendment forbidding the enactment of a special law affecting a named subdivision in seven areas, including roads and incorporations of villages.[7] A voter-ratified new constitution in 1894 contained a stipulation that all "special city" acts were subject to a suspensory veto by the concerned cities.[8] An enacted bill was sent to the governor only if the mayor or city council approved the bill. If the city rejected the bill within fifteen days, it could be approved a second time by the state legislature and sent to the governor.

A 1923 constitutional amendment established an *imperium in imperio* (an empire within an empire) or federal system for cities by stipulating that the state legislature could not enact a law concerning the "property, affairs, or government" of a city if the law was "special or local either in its terms or effects" unless the law was enacted by a two-thirds vote of the members of each house pursuant to an emergency message from the governor.[9] The amendment, implemented by the City Home Rule Law, authorized cities for the first time to draft, adopt, and amend charters.

Cities also were authorized to enact local laws in nine specified areas, provided the laws were not inconsistent with the constitution or general laws. A local law supersedes the corresponding state law relative to the city enacting the local law. The 1928 state legislature amended the City Home Rule Law and authorized cities to enact local laws relating to "property, affairs, or government," provided the local laws were consistent with general laws.[10]

The constitutional amendment, however, was emasculated by the Court of Appeals, which opined in 1929 that the words "property, affairs, or government" had been placed in the constitution "with a Court of Appeal's definition and not that of Webster's dictionary."[11] Writing for the court, Judge Benjamin N. Cardozo developed the "state concern" doctrine by holding that the state legislature may enact a law in a functional area, multiple-dwelling housing in this case, provided there is a substantial state concern even "though intermingled with it are concerns of the locality."[12]

A constitutional amendment ratified by the voters in 1935 extended the *imperium in imperio* system to counties.[13] Voter-ratified 1938 constitutional amendments forbade the state legislature to enact a special city law unless its enactment had been requested by the concerned city, and authorized a city, with specified exceptions, to enact local laws superseding special laws enacted by the state legislature following receipt of emergency messages issued by the governor in the period 1894 to 1938.[14] Another voter-ratified 1938 constitutional amendment extended the *imperium in imperio* system to villages with a population exceeding 5,000.[15] This amendment also directed the state legislature to confer, by general law, upon these villages the power to adopt and amend local laws relating to their "property, affairs, or government," provided the local laws did not conflict with the constitution or a general law.

A 1958 voter-ratified amendment authorized counties and villages to draft, adopt, and amend charters and forbade the state legislature to enact a special law relative to a county or a village unless the concerned governing bodies requested enactment of the law.[16]

The most recent constitutional amendment affecting the discretionary authority of general purpose local governments was ratified by the voters in 1963 and became effective on 1 January 1964. The amendment continues the *imperium in imperio* system and the prohibition of the enactment of a special law unless requested by the concerned local government; it also directs the state legislature to enact a "Statute of Local Governments" broadening the powers of general purpose political subdivisions (devolution of powers), authorizes local governments to act relative to ten specified matters beyond "property, affairs, or government," and stipulates that the grants of power are to be interpreted broadly.[17] Devolved powers can be preempted only by general law. In other words, the state legislature could not take a specific power away from a single city, but the legislature could remove the power from all cities.

This amendment is particularly significant for towns because it confers home rule powers upon them. Previously, a 1962 amendment had broadened appreciably the authority of suburban towns, which are defined as towns with a population of 25,000, or fast-growing towns with a population of 7,500 if located within fifteen miles of a city with a population of 100,000 or more.[18] A 1976 amendment to the Municipal Home Rule Law enhanced the power of nonsuburban towns by authorizing them to supersede provisions of the Town Law relating to "the property, affairs, or government of the town . . . unless the Legislature expressly" forbids the enactment of such local laws.[19]

A COMPLEX LEGAL SYSTEM

The state constitution currently distributes political powers between the state government and its general purpose local governments by the simultaneous employment of the *ultra vires* rule, *imperium in imperio*, and devolution of powers, which produces confusion as to the extent of the discretionary authority of the various types of general purpose local governments.

The inclusion of three methods of distributing powers between the state and its general purpose local governments is attributable to competition between the supporters of political centralization and supporters of two methods to achieve political decentralization, and the tendency to add provisions to the constitution without deleting existing provisions. The degree of discretionary authority varies by function, structure of government, property of government, and "local affairs."

The legal confusion, relative to the discretionary authority of general purpose local governments, is increased by the enactment of a number of general laws—Municipal Home Rule Law, General Municipal Law, First Class Cities Law, Second Class Cities Law, General City Law, County Law, Town Law, Village Law, Public Officers Law, and other laws—containing, in certain instances, conflicting provisions.

Municipal attorneys seek advisory opinions from the attorney general, state comptroller, and commissioner of education relative to complex legal issues. It was not uncommon for a municipal attorney to seek an opinion simultaneously from the attorney general and the state comptroller and occasionally also from the commissioner of education. The opinions rendered were not always uniform. If a mayor received two conflicting opinions and decided to initiate the action in question, the mayor could always point to the favorable opinion or provision of a state statute if questioned about the legality of the action.

Until 1979, these state officials generally had been conservative in interpreting the powers of local governments. The election victories of Robert Abrams as attorney general and Edward V. Regan as state comptroller in 1978 led to the appointment of a new assistant attorney general in charge of advisory opinions and a new counsel to the comptroller. The new appointees were committed to a broad interpretation of the powers of general purpose local governments and also agreed to coordinate their responses to requests for advisory opinions. In 1980, for example, Assistant Attorney General George D. Braden advised that "when the Legislature exercises state power over local governments in the area of 'property, affairs, or government,' article IX requires the Legislature to cover all cities, all towns, all villages, or all counties; and if the Legislature fails to cover them all, local governments have the power to enact local laws amending the state law."[20]

STATE MANDATES AND RESTRAINTS

Constitutional and statutory provisions broadened the discretionary authority of general purpose local governments in the twentieth century, yet the state legislature retains the power to enact general laws mandating that these governments initiate specified actions or restraining their freedom to initiate action.

The term *state mandate* commonly is employed loosely by many local government officials when they refer to costs that must be financed by their governments. We define a state mandate as a legal order—constitutional provision, statutory provision, or administrative regulation—requiring a local government to undertake a specified activity or to provide a service meeting minimum state standards. In contrast, a state restraint prevents or restricts the ability of a local government to initiate or continue an action. Although tax limits are state restraints, they often are described by local government officials as state mandates.

A state mandate also must be distinguished from a condition-of-aid. A mandate cannot be avoided, but a local government can refuse to apply for a grant-in-aid and hence avoid the conditions attached to the grant.

The first and only national study of state mandates on local government revealed that New York State had mandates in more functional areas—sixty of seventy-six surveyed—than any other state.[21] Mandates are the products of interest group activities (see chapter 2). An interest group unsuccessful in persuading local government bodies to provide a service or a benefit often will attempt to persuade the state legislature to mandate that local governments provide a specified service or benefit. Police and firefighter unions, for example, persuaded the state legislature to enact a law mandating the use of compulsory binding arbitration to settle collective bargaining impasses between municipal employers and their police and firefighter unions.[22]

Associations of local governments lobby the state legislature for the repeal of certain mandates and restraints. Local governments generally have been ineffective in securing relief because they do not speak with a single voice. There are three associations representing general purpose local governments—the Association of Counties, Association of Towns, and Conference of Mayors and Other Municipal Officials (cities and villages). In 1991, however, the state legislature enacted a law requiring all state agencies to identify clearly all state mandates contained in proposed rules and regulations and a second law containing several mandate relief provisions developed by associations of local governments in conjunction with the governor.[23]

Local government associations have been seeking partial or total state reimbursement of state-mandated costs. Their pleas have fallen upon deaf ears in the state legislature in part because New York is experiencing fiscal problems. Furthermore, state officials stress that the state is generous in sharing its revenues with local governments, as explained in chapter 15.

A number of restraints were added to the state constitution in response to corruption or financial irregularities in the nineteenth century. Constitutional tax limits, defined in terms of percentages of average full valuation of taxable real estate and excluding taxes levied to raise funds for debt service, apply to all local governments except towns and noncity school districts. The limit is 2.5 percent for New York City, 2.0 percent for other cities and villages, 1.5–2.0 percent for upstate counties, and 1.25–2.0 percent for school districts in cities with a population under 125,000.[24] Debt limits are established by the state constitution for all local governments except noncity school districts.[25] The budgets of these school districts are subject to voter referenda. Debt limits range from 5 percent for school districts in cities to 10 percent for New York City and Nassau County.

The state constitution also contains restraints on the adoption of a county charter and transfer of functional responsibilities from cities, towns, and villages to a county. A proposed county charter or transfer of a city or town function to a county is subject to a concurrent majority in a referendum; that is, voters in cities, if any, in the county and in towns must give their separate consent before a proposal can be effectuated. If a proposed charter contains a provision for the transfer of a village function to a county, a triple concurrent majority is required—separate approvals by city, town, and village voters. The latter also vote as town voters since all villages are located within towns. The U.S. Supreme Court in 1977 upheld the constitutionality of the concurrent majority requirement by ruling it did not violate the Court's "one-person, one-vote" dictum.[26]

Other restraints include requirements for formal competitive bidding on local government contracts and dedication of revenue from a locally levied tax to certain functions. Illustrative of restraints impeding local government economy in providing a service is the lack of authority for a county sheriff to enter into a contract for police protection with a town or village desiring to abolish its police department. The Village Law, for example, authorizes a village to create or abolish a police force, but the state comptroller opined in 1962 that a "sheriff may not enter into a contract with a village or town in order to receive compensation for the added expense of furnishing additional police protection."[27]

The plethora of local governments affords ample opportunity for interested citizens to become involved personally in policymaking and politics. Local government elected positions often are characterized by low or no salaries, frequent public criticism, long hours, and the need to carry out responsibilities on a part-time, after-hours basis. Nevertheless, elected officeholders generally find rewards and stimulation as they deliberate on issues, such as environmental problems, that most directly affect the quality of life of their constituents. On occasion, a local government lacks a candidate for an important office. In 1993, for example, no citizen sought the nomination of the Democratic or the Republican party for the position of town supervisor in Berlin.[28]

All elections, including local government ones, are conducted by the state in accordance with the Election Law. School district, fire district, and village board elections are nonpartisan in contrast to most county, city, and town elections, which are partisan. Voter qualifications are common for all elections—national, state, and local.

County (with a few exceptions), town, and city elections are held on the first Tuesday after the first Monday in an odd-number year, whereas village elections are held on the third Tuesday in March or June unless a village selects a different date.[29] Holding local government elections in odd-numbered years results in a lower voter turnout compared to local elections held in conjunction with state and national elections and in a divorce between local issues and national and state issues.

Local governments possess relatively little power to initiate referenda. State law, however, requires a referendum before certain actions can be initiated. Adoption of a city or county charter or a noncity school district budget is subject to a mandatory referendum, as is the creation or abolition of an elective office. Certain actions by state law are subject to a permissive referendum; that is, either the governing body places a question on the referendum ballot or voters petition to place the question on the ballot. The initiative, which permits voters by petition to place a proposed law on the ballot, is not authorized except in Suffolk County, where the initiative can be employed to place proposed charter amendments on the ballot.

Candidates, political committees, and contributors are subject to the State Corrupt Practices Act, which regulates campaign contributions. The restrictions upon the amount of money a candidate or a political committee could spend in an election campaign have been repealed.

The Campaigns, Elections, and Procedures Law of 1974 for the first time allowed corporations to contribute funds—up to $5,000—to any election campaign.[30] Previously, corporate officials gave funds in their own names or in the names of family members. One result of the 1974 law is a masking of the names of individual contributors since donations are made in the names of companies. Adding confusion relative to contributors is a proliferation of fund-raising committees organized by a candidate; each committee files campaign receipts with the State Board of Elections.

TYPES OF LOCAL GOVERNMENTS

New York contains counties, cities, towns, villages, and special districts. The type of government does not necessarily indicate either population or services provided. Montague, the state's smallest town, has less than fifty residents; Hempstead, the largest town, has a population twice the population of Buffalo, the state's second largest city. Many New York counties, cities, towns, and villages provide public safety, transportation, and parks services; counties alone have responsibility for administration of income maintenance, Medicaid, and other social services. Public education is the responsibility of school districts except in Buffalo, New York City, Rochester, Syracuse, and Yonkers, whose school districts are fiscally dependent on the city government.

The organizational structure of general purpose local governments is reflective of the prevailing political culture and historical patterns. Counties historically lacked legislative powers; towns historically and today lack separation of executive and legislative powers. Traditional town government organization is decentralized, with several elected officers who would be appointed officers in a city.

The principal source of revenue for general purpose local governments is the real property tax. These units also receive state revenue-sharing funds and grants, and federal grants. If a county levies a sales tax, the proceeds are shared with the cities, towns, and villages within the county. Special districts rely upon the real property tax and fees for revenue.

Towns

Towns initially were quasi-municipal corporations possessing limited powers, but towns today are municipal corporations possessing constitutional home rule powers. The Town Law classifies towns as first or second class.[31] Towns with a population exceeding 10,000—with the exceptions of towns in Broome and Suffolk Counties and the towns of Potsdam and Ulster—are first-class towns, as are all towns in Westchester County, even if their respective populations are below the threshold. Towns with a population of 5,000 or more, assessed real property values exceeding ten million dollars, and adjoining a city with a population exceeding 300,000 may become a first-class town by a local law, subject to a permissive referendum. As noted, certain towns are classified as suburban towns.

Towns lack separation of powers, as the town board exercises legislative and executive powers. The typical board is composed of the town supervisor and four council members. The supervisor is chair of the board and is delegated several financial powers, including those of town treasurer, by the Town Law.[32] Although the supervisor is not the chief executive, he or she may be a de facto chief executive because of his or her position as head of the dominant political party. Furthermore, long service enables a number of supervisors to gain knowledge that increases their ability to influence the conduct of town affairs. The Suburban Town Law designates the supervisor as the ''chief executive officer'' but does not confer major executive powers upon the supervisor.[33]

By exercising its home rule powers, a town could establish by local law a separate executive branch headed by a town manager.[34] No town has chosen to do so. Furthermore, several offices, including the superintendent of highways and town clerk, remain elective offices in most towns.

Villages

Villages are municipal corporations and were chartered by the state legislature until voters ratified a constitutional amendment in 1874 forbidding the incorporation of villages by special acts. Subsequently, villages have been incorporated under the Village Law. This law was amended in 1897 to allow villages with special charters to reincorporate under the Village Law. Twelve villages decided not to reincorporate and now operate under their special charters. All other villages operate under the Village Law, which serves as a substitute charter whose provisions relating to government, property, and local affairs can be superseded by enactment of a local law.

The board of trustees, composed of the mayor as chair and four trustees, is the lawmaking body under the Village Law. A village, by local law subject to a mandatory referendum, may increase or decrease the number of trustees who are elected for a two-year term unless a local law provides for a different term.

The village board originally exercised executive and legislative powers, but revisions of the Village Law have converted the board into principally a legislative body. The mayor, elected for a two-year term, is the chief executive of a village unless the charter or a local law provides for a village manager or administrator who serves as the chief executive.

Counties

Counties originated as quasi-municipal corporations possessing only administrative powers, which acted as administrative arms of the state for convenience in administration. Today, counties are municipal corporations possessing legislative and executive powers.

There are fifty-seven organized county governments. New York City is a consolidated city-county government as the result of the enactment of a state law consolidating all local governments in a five-county area effective in 1898. Nineteen county governments operate under charters, but the Herkimer County charter is only a reapportionment plan for the governing body. The Schenectady County charter provides for a manager, and the Tompkins County charter provides for an appointed administrator. Although Genesee County voters rejected a proposed county manager charter, a local law providing for a county manager was enacted, and opponents did not seek to have the law rejected by means of a permissive referendum.

Historically, counties were governed by a board of supervisors composed of the supervisor of each town in the county and one supervisor from each ward of a city, if any, in the county. The U.S. Supreme Court's "one-person, one-vote" dictum was applied in 1968 to governing bodies of general purpose local governments and necessitated changes in the county governance system.[35]

A number of counties responded to the dictum by abandoning the board of supervisors system and replacing it with a county legislature (termed board of representatives or board of legislators in certain counties) elected by single-member districts. Sixteen of these counties have an elected county executive; Genesee and Schenectady Counties each also have a county legislature. The term of office is four years in eight counties and two years in the remaining counties. Counties that retained the board of supervisors use weighted voting; that is, each member casts a number of votes in proportion to the total percentage of the county's population represented by the member.

Noncharter counties are governed by the County Law, which does not provide for the separation of executive and legislative powers. The governing board, however, can delegate administrative authority to the chair to be exercised on behalf of the board. Furthermore, the governing board by local law may establish the office of county administrator to perform duties on behalf of the board.[36] State laws also authorize the board to create by local law the position of administrative assistant to the chair of the board or the position of executive assistant to the board.[37]

The district attorney, county clerk, coroner(s), and sheriff are elected officers in noncharter counties. Although the sheriff is a constitutional officer, the office has few law enforcement functions in a county with a police department. The treasurer is an elected officer unless this position has been eliminated by a charter provision or a local law approved by the voters.

Cities

Each of the sixty-two cities was chartered by a special act of the state legislature. Rye in 1942 was the last city to be incorporated. The state constitution contains no criteria for the incorporation of cities, and the largest village has a population greater than the population of forty-eight cities. Although the constitution adopted in 1894 provided for first-class, second-class, and third-class cities, a 1923 amendment abolished these classes.[38] Nevertheless, the state legislature continues to enact statutes applicable to first-class and second-class cities. The forms of city government are mayor-council, council-manager, and commission.

The most common form (forty-one cities) is the mayor-council form, which is the oldest type of city government and has a structural pattern similar to that of the state and national governments. The mayor is termed the chief executive of the city even though the mayor may not be in charge of the entire executive branch. This form typically is classified as strong or weak based upon whether the mayor possesses the veto, absolute appointment, and executive budget powers, and the entire executive branch is under the mayor's control. Most city charters contain both strong and weak elements.

Eighteen cities utilize the council-manager form, which is distinguished by a professional manager appointed by, and responsible to, the council. In theory, the council's function is to determine policy, and the manager's function is to execute policy. In practice, the manager typically is the leading policymaker since the council relies heavily upon the manager for advice on policy issues.

Three cities—Beacon, Mechanicville, and Saratoga Springs—use the commission form of city government. Each commission member is the head of one or more departments. In consequence, there is no separation of legislative and executive powers under this form. The mayor, who is chair of the commission, is elected at-large.

Special Districts

Special districts are limited to the performance of a single function, such as education or fire protection, and the governing bodies are elected by the voters. With the exception of school districts, relatively little media attention is devoted to the activities of special districts unless there is a major scandal.[39]

These special districts must be distinguished from special improvement districts in towns that are administered by the town board. The latter districts are service and tax areas and are not units of governments. Residents residing within a special water improvement district, for example, pay a real property tax to finance the service but do not elect a separate governing board.

THE EVOLVING LOCAL GOVERNMENT SYSTEM

This chapter traces the broadening of the discretionary powers of general purpose local governments that resulted when the *ultra vires* rule was reduced in importance as a restraint by constitutional provisions establishing an *imperium in imperio* and directing the state legislature to devolve political powers upon these political subdivisions. These grants of power, as noted, have been offset to an extent by the imposition of state mandates and restraints. Furthermore, there has been a severe erosion of local government powers as the result of extensive use of congressional powers of partial and total preemption since 1965.[40]

Federal mandates and restraints also have imposed significant costs upon local governments; available evidence suggests that the Congress will continue to use its powers of preemption to force these governments to implement national policies. Although it is impossible to quantify precisely the costs of the mandates and restraints, it is apparent that the costs are major ones.[41] By directing that local governments undertake a specific activity, such as filtering surface drinking water, or forbidding the units to take a specified action, such as dumping sewage sludge in the ocean, it is apparent that the Congress is reducing significantly the discretionary authority of local governments. Furthermore, the resources devoted to complying with the mandates and restraints reduce the resources that are available for policies and programs that may be initiated by local governments under their discretionary powers. In essence, many important governmental decisions are removed from the local arena and transferred to the national arena in Washington DC, where citizens have less influence and powerful interest groups have more influence.

Complex constitutional and statutory provisions make it difficult for municipal officials to determine the extent of their discretionary powers; hence they tend to be reluctant to exercise certain powers. Their reluctance is reinforced by typically conservative municipal attorneys who interpret the scope of municipal powers. In consequence, municipal chief executives and governing bodies seldom implement innovative solutions to longstanding problems in the absence of a special authorizing act enacted by the state legislature.

Opposition to the council-manager plan by most partisan politicians leads to the conclusion that few general purpose local governments will adopt the plan in the foreseeable future. Party leaders oppose the plan in part because there would be less job patronage, insurance patronage, contract patronage, and bank deposit patronage.

The strength of the prevailing political cultures make it improbable that many towns will adopt a charter providing for separation of powers with a strong chief executive. Counties have been more willing to adopt charters, yet a majority of counties operate without a charter providing for separation of powers.

The Lilliputian size of many general purpose local governments has raised the question of their viability. Many governmental reformers since the last decade of the nineteenth century have advocated the consolidation of local governments to achieve economies of scale and greater efficiency. A Blue Ribbon Commission on Consolidation of Local Governments appointed by Governor Mario Cuomo, for example, recommended in 1993 state legislation "to allow local governments the option to reorganize through merger."[42] The governor noted a year later that "significant reluctance by local politicians to any substantive move toward the consolidation of local government or shared services" was a key barrier to action on this recommendation by the state legislature.[43]

Competing evidence that smaller units may be more efficient than larger units should also be noted. In fact, one study concluded that smaller police departments are more efficient than larger ones.[44]

Darwinism does not pervade the New York local government system; very few of the "weaker" units fail to survive, and political realities suggest that a comprehensive structural reorganization of the system is improbable in the foreseeable future. Although local government boundaries may be anachronistic, they have not prevented the development of mechanisms to facilitate the resolution of pressing local and regional problems. Intergovernmental service agreements are common and produce economies and efficiencies in the provision of services.[45] Several larger cities, including Albany and Rochester, have transferred responsibility for a facility or service to the county, which broadens the base of tax support. County governing bodies have established service and tax districts for areas encompassing two or more cities or towns, and the state legislature transferred responsibility for most welfare functions to counties.[46]

The state legislature in 1981 initiated an innovative approach to ensure the provision of an essential service. If a city, town, or village declines responsibility for enforcing the state uniform fire prevention and building code, responsibility automatically is transferred to the county.[47] Should the county refuse to accept enforcement responsibility, it is shifted to the Department of State. New York City is exempted from the code.

A number of state agencies and departments provide services to local governments at their request. Approximately fifty towns and villages do not have police departments and receive police services from state police officers stationed in the towns and villages. The Division of State Police never has charged a town or village for its services but expects the units to provide facilities and supplies.

The complexity of local government problems and the impact of intergovernmental programs and requirements strain part-time citizen government in rural areas and raise the question of the need for professional management. Small municipalities possess the authority to appoint professional administrators or managers but are limited in their ability to do so by the lack of funds.

A possible solution is the sharing of a professional administrator by two or more small municipalities. The precedent for such an approach dates to the nineteenth century, when small school districts formed a superintendency union that hired a superintendent of schools who served as the professional administrator for each district.[48]

"Keeping things local" in New York can be expected to be increasingly difficult in the future. In today's complex society, power sharing is essential; many important governmental decisions will be made through negotiations among public, quasi-public, and private organizations. If New York's local governments are incapable of solving critical problems, especially environmental ones, pressures will mount in the state legislature to transfer responsibility for functions to regional bodies or the state government.

CHAPTER ELEVEN

The City of Greater New York, 1898– 1998: Balancing Organizational Capacity and Political Legitimacy

Robert W. Bailey

The institutional and territorial makeup of present-day New York City was established in the city's 1898 reincorporation, consolidation, and new charter. Although there have been important amendments to the charter during the intervening century, the essential institutional structure and geography of New York City have remained in place for nearly a century.[1]

The consolidation of 1898 and the establishment of a regional government for the greater City of New York was a response to the political problems of late nineteenth-century economic change and a daring attempt to propel New York into the status of a world-class city. Its inadequate political structure was viewed as an impediment to New York's rise. When present at all, planning was parochial. Conflicting jurisdictions led to inefficiencies and duplication. Managerial ineptness and simple corruption were commonplace. The Democratic party machine, the only social organization that could cut across the disparate domains of urban governance, was dishonest and too weak to direct the burgeoning public sector. Although the energy of the party organization was drawn from the alignment of ethnic groups, and it served as a vehicle to manage the tensions among different identities and economic interests in the city, the machine's structure was too informal to project New York to the heights sought by its business and professional classes, too informal to be competitive with London or to be dominant over Boston and Philadelphia.

Deeper still were the increasing class and ethnic conflicts that accompanied industrialization and immigration in the second half of the nineteenth century. Like many other American cities, the political sociology of New

York had become a matrix of conflicting class, ethnic, religious, and racial groupings. Poor Irish, Italians, Eastern European Jews, and American-born Africans lived close to the docks, or factories, or warehouses. Urban space had been organized to meet the most important test of urban arrangements at that time: efficiency in industrial production.[2] To escape the grit and danger of an industrial New York, many in the middle classes had moved to new neighborhoods in Brooklyn Heights, the new East Side of Manhattan, or further north to Harlem. Unlike in mercantile New York, where the classes lived and worked in close proximity, ethnic and class identity became associated with different urban spaces.[3] Crime, public health problems, and social dislocation were now concentrated as never before.

Reformers of the 1890s saw government reorganization and a revitalization of Protestant values as the major solution to New York's problems. Based among the professional middle classes, religious groups, and Republicans, both in New York City and elsewhere in New York state, reformers were spurred on by the new science of public administration, a sense of compassion for the poor, and a new vision for a world-class New York all filtered through an older class perspective. Their common enemy was Tammany Hall—the seat of the New York County Democratic party. The new government was framed around the ideals of rational and scientifically based management, urban governance proceeding from a regional perspective, the dispersion of machine-grounded political power, and a public works program and planning process that would provide for both public amenities and economic development. This new New York, to be merged with the City of Brooklyn and serving as the center of American finance and business, would dominate the economy of the United States well into the twentieth century. It would be capable of competing on a grand scale with the great cities of *fin de siècle* Europe,[4] and it would be governed through the firm establishment of a governing elite rooted less in capital or political acumen than on professional competence and élan. It would, indeed, be the nation's Empire City.

To create this new, regional metropolis, the designers of New York's governing institutions turned to models drawn from London and New York's own experience with a regional Metropolitan Police Force.[5] The framework created by the reformers of the 1890s remained as the central governing structure up to the 1990s: a federated system of government among five counties (boroughs, as in London) with a bicameral legislature and a modified strong mayor-council government.[6] These nineteenth-century reformers sought a professionalized and nonpartisan school system, a civil service system similar to Britain's, building and health codes protective of the poor, budgeting reforms and electoral reforms,[7] and a governmental framework to build some of the world's great public works. Ultimately, the reformers sought a rationalization of the New York region's governing structure.

Since those days of political innovation, New York's economic and social geography has far outgrown its legal jurisdiction. Once barely pushing past the confines of Manhattan, western Brooklyn, and Jersey City across the Hudson, the New York regional economy now encompasses more than twenty-six counties in three states.[8] The regional government once set up for New York has been overshadowed by its own success. The region has outgrown the city. The expansion of New York's legal jurisdiction through annexation or merger is no longer an option,[9] and thus the relationship between the city and regional, state, and federal governments is more important for New York's government today. Within the city, the spatial reproduction of race and class patterning has become more acute.

With a 1995–96 operating budget of $36 billion, New York is the largest local operating government in the American public sector. It ranks among the largest organizations in the country, public or private. As the scale of New York's public sector has grown and as the diversity of its population has increased, New York's leaders have constantly tried to balance two themes in the city's governance: the need for increased organizational capacity and group demands for greater political participation.[10] Within the institutional framework set in the 1890s, these have been the major means of managing social and economic change in New York.

From the perspective of organizational theory, New York City's government has evolved even within this century. The tension between organizational capacity—that is, the ability to administer policy effectively—and a sense of political legitimacy among city residents is evident at many points. The challenge to create more effective government has led to enhanced powers for the mayor, a challenge to the informality of the party mechanisms that sometimes are corrupt, the professionalization of urban service delivery, and enhanced controls over the fiscal and financial position of New York.[11] The challenge of political legitimization has been an equally important, if more subtle, political trend. It concerns the sense of accountability among those governed. How are decisions made? Who gains and who loses in the governance of the city? What are the racial, ethnic, and gender impacts of economic change? How should government respond to demands for equity and access? While these tensions per se are not unique to New York, they may be unique in terms of scale. Five extended themes illuminate this tension between organizational capacity and political legitimacy in the present-day governance of New York.

CONFLICT BETWEEN STATE AND CITY

When New York was governed by its party machine, George Washington Plunkitt, Tammany leader and shoeshine-stand philosopher, referred to the rural politicians who dominated the legislature in Albany as "hayseeds"— unimpressive and unsophisticated men interested only in the parochial interests of their counties. Eighty years later, Ed Koch would refer to upstate New York as "dull."

The ongoing arrogance of city dwellers continues to be matched by suspicion of the metropolis among "upstaters." Industrialization and the rapid increase in New York City's population, as well as a historical reputation for fiscal mismanagement, led upstate regions to impose fiscal controls on the giant metropolis.[12] Fearful of downstate political and economic dominance, the state legislature laid the foundation for the two-pronged strategy it has pursued toward New York City throughout the century. The city's home rule and legal powers were allowed to increase in a formal fashion, while, more informally, regulations, mandates, and limitations on local policy control were placed on the city.[13]

Welfare is an example of this two-pronged strategy. New York City has always needed funds to deal with the social problems associated with industrialization, immigration, and the internal migration of African Americans and Puerto Ricans. But the city has never been granted full state funding for social services or full administrative control over welfare policy. Even before the New Deal's Aid to Families with Dependent Children (AFDC), New York City provided assistance to its needy population. In 1996, more than one million city dwellers were on welfare, but administrative control remains in state and federal guidelines. New York City must also finance up to 25 percent of the total costs of nearly all redistributive programs—those programs funded by broad taxes but used primarily by the poor, including AFDC and health care for the poor through Medicaid.[14] No other state requires such a heavy local contribution to redistributive programs.

In education, too, state-granted powers were matched by financing limitations and programmatic requirements. Thus, as the legislature and courts impose important programs on the city's semi-autonomous school district, the state legislature has refused to redress inequities in local fiscal capacities to deal with education realities.[15]

In spite of the decades-long resistance of the state to fund solutions for urban problems, these problems did not go away for New York City or for most of New York's other major urban areas. The growth in New York City's regional economy generated new resources for social policy and allowed the city to respond to some of its problems during much of the century. But the gap between needs and resources has always been keen in New York City. As the city's economic growth peaked in the 1960s, followed by a decline of the manufacturing sector and a narrowing of growth in the financial services sector, New York could not deal with its social problems to the extent it had done so in the past. The great periods of fiscal strain in New York City have been partly the result of revenue shortfalls associated with economic change. Compassion, even if motivated by prudence, has been expensive.

Other incentives for state intervention into New York City affairs have arisen during critical periods when the growth in New York's public sector exceeded its ability to manage that sector. The very size of government grew so much by 1967 that the budget for New York City was larger than that for any of the fifty states. This rapid growth served as a basis for part of the city's financial problems in the 1970s. It was not just the strain of expenses on revenues that set the stage for the city's near bankruptcy during its 1975 financial crisis but also the fact that managerial systems had not kept up with that growth. The imposition of state regulations had largely disconnected policymaking from fiscal decision making in the state and city.[16]

Today, the tension between city and state has intensified the tensions between the city and suburbs. The political and policy interests of suburban residents frequently overlap with rural interests. High suburban taxes for schools, roads, and police allow for little enthusiasm to increase state taxes for the resolution of social problems in New York City. In welfare funding, school finance, and capital expenditures for higher education, it is the suburbs that now offer the greatest resistance to assistance to New York City.

PARTY VERSUS PROFESSIONALISM

A second theme evident in New York City is the rise of professionals in government service delivery who have challenged the political base of government organization. The professionalization of public health, social work and welfare, the police force, budgeting and finance, and management in general was a major goal of reform and business groups at the turn of the century. The conflict between authority grounded on professional criteria and on political criteria was clearest in the schools.[17] Would continued political interference in the public schools increase their effectiveness or limit it? The introduction of normal academies, teacher preparation and certification, standardized curricula, and testing were all aimed at professionalizing the schools.

For the business community, the agenda was both political and economic. Government rationalization would put an end to corruption and perhaps stabilize tax rates. More important, the introduction of efficient service delivery and a rational planning process for infrastructure investment would help ensure New York's preeminence in the nation's economy. Politically, professionalization of service delivery and policymaking would confine the domain of the party apparatus to candidate nomination, judicial appointment, and management of election processes.

The social programs of the New Deal, administered in New York under the LaGuardia administration, and the emerging new power center of public authorities run by Robert Moses were largely organized around these new urban professions: social work, civil engineering, building trades (and thus codes), public health, "normalized" education, public administration, and urban planning.[18] The programs of the 1930s offered competition to the "machine" organization of urban influence in two ways: they provided institutional competitors with new resources,[19] and they established professional criteria as a standard for future resource allocation decisions. In both cases, the new urban professionals became challengers to the machine.

The competition between party and professionals was in balance through the 1940s and 1950s. It was not until the 1960s, with dramatic growth in the size of New York's public sector and unionization of municipal employees, that the power of the political parties really reached its limit. Theodore Lowi cited the 1961 mayoral election as a watershed. It was in 1961 when Mayor Robert F. Wagner (first put forward by the party organization in 1953) ran against the party using the political resources of the city's bureaucracies and organized employees as his new base.[20] John V. Lindsay, New York's version of the new activist mayors who were elected in the mid-1960s, may have been the first of the city's mayors to experience the power of unionized employees vividly. Within hours of Lindsay's taking office on 1 January 1966, the Transport Workers Union struck against the subway system. The union's leader, Michael Quinn, took a firm stand against city threats to obtain a court injunction against the strike. He announced that he would bargain from a prison cell if necessary. He even refused to pronounce the new mayor's name properly, insisting on "Lindsly" in an Irish accent more affected than real.

As the delivery of public services was increasingly professionalized, the tension between party and professionalism in policymaking had largely been resolved to the benefit of the new urban professions. The medical and health-care professionals came to dominate policymaking in the health arena, teachers came to dominate education policy, police came to dominate much of policing policy, and so on. Their skills, defined by professional associations and overlapping with collective bargaining units, provided them access to state officials, control over funding streams for programs, and the definition of quality. The party organizations were left with lower-level judicial appointments and jobs in some of the older bureaus as their arena of interest.

Ironically, by 1990, the groups in the city that initially supported the urban professionals, the business community, the reform movement, and the press had become ambivalent toward their old friends. The urban service bureaucracies, overlapping with unionized employees, were almost as unaccountable to community and minority interests as were the urban political machines fifty years earlier and as unresponsive to fiscal restraint. Whereas John Lindsay's power base proved an insufficient match to professional and union power in 1966, Ed Koch could demonize transit workers and their union fifteen years later. In the 1980 subway strike, Koch stood at the foot of the Brooklyn Bridge cheering New Yorkers on as they walked over—rather than rode under—the East River. He wrote of those weeks: "There was something in the atmosphere of strikebound New Yorkers that made people, and not just me, ebullient. Women in their Madison Avenue business suits strode along wearing their Uptown nylons and jogging sneakers. People pulled rusty bicycles out of basements. Everyone had an excuse for being a little late. On rainy days, New Yorkers looked as if they'd just stood under a downspout. Somehow, all those things made people feel better about themselves and their City."[21]

Koch, the reformer who twenty years before had defeated the last of the Manhattan "bosses," Carmine DeSapio, was now fighting against the real underlying organizational forces that had gradually replaced the machines as a center of power in New York. David Dinkins's 1989 election victory was seen as partly a victory of the non-uniformed municipal unions, especially the newer ones whose membership had grown dramatically since the 1960s: those associated with health care and social services. Even Rudolph Giuliani, opposed by most municipal unions except the police in his 1993 election effort, had found it necessary to deal gingerly with the power of the teachers' union during his first term.

THE MAYORALTY BECOMES THE CENTER OF GOVERNANCE

As the bureaucracies grew and the party organization declined, New York's mayor became ever more important. Chief executive and leading mediator of social conflict among New York's many groups and identities, principal salesperson for the city's economy, and chief lobbyist for the city in state and federal legislative circles, the mayor occupies a nearly thankless office. As chief executive officer of a multibillion-dollar-a-year corporation, the mayor is the focus of nearly all administrative powers held by the city. As executive authority centered on the mayor, the focus of legitimacy did also. Even with some enhanced powers given the city council in the revised 1990 charter, the political nature of the city has required the mayor to balance differing identities associated with ethnic background, value structures, gender, and so on. This increased focus on the mayoralty can be observed on both the managerial level and the political level.

On the managerial level, New York's mayor is at the center of an organization with over 250,000 employees and an annual operating budget of more than \$35 billion. The focus of the city budget and of the public sector productivity is on the mayor: how can revenues, services, and investment all be aligned so that the regional economy will generate jobs and keep service commitments made to the poor and middle classes by generations of New Yorkers?

The managerial challenge to the mayoralty became most acute in the mid-1970s, when two important commissions were created to look into city government: the Charter Revision Commission, dominated by appointees of Mayor John Lindsay and chaired by state senator Roy Goodman,[22] and the State Temporary Commission for the Study of New York City, dominated by appointees of Governor Nelson Rockefeller and focused on managerial change.[23] Neither commission, however, could deal with the urgent financial problems facing New York City.

Minor reforms were not sufficient to deal with the city's mounting fiscal problems. By 1975, New York could not meet either its short-term debts or its current operating responsibilities. Attempts to solve the fiscal crisis of New York City in the winter, spring, and summer of 1975 had their own lasting effects.[24] The political-managerial responses to the expansion of New York's public sector and its crash at the time of the financial crisis were increased hierarchical controls, the installation of new management technologies, and the establishment of several new fiscal, financial, and managerial oversight bodies.[25] Together, the accumulated changes had the effect of establishing the city's mayor symbolically and legally as a modern chief operating officer for an integrated local public sector. Cutting off alternative power centers in the bureaucracies and also restricting the power of the municipal employees redressed some of the political weakness of the mayor.

The increased organizational capacity established during the 1975 fiscal crisis and Mayor Koch's first term led to more predictable fiscal and service patterns and altered the terms of political discourse within the public sector. It also positioned the city for international competition in post-industrial commerce. But the decade-long attempt at financial reform exacerbated New York's other major problem: establishing effective links among individuals, groups, and emerging political forms to the city's political and managerial structures. The 1975–78 period undermined prior progress toward community participation by recentralizing managerial, financial, legal, and, thus, political resources to deal with the political and managerial problems presented by the crisis. The number of participants in the decision arenas had dropped sharply. The amount of funds susceptible to influence by local school boards, for example, shrank to less than 5 percent of community school board budgets. When capital construction was begun again after the 1975 crisis, most of the major programs were financed by public authorities. Local community service (and planning) boards had become less influential.[26]

On the political level, the mayoralty became increasingly important as attempts to establish new channels of community and political accountability grew stronger and as older channels—party and city council—grew weaker. Attempts to gain greater community influence over decision making moved onto newer tactics: from administrative decentralization to greater institutional responsiveness. Two major legal challenges to the city's apportionment in the council and the Board of Estimate were successful.[27] Three charter commissions tried to make city government more responsive by revitalizing community boards, instituting campaign finance reform, and expanding the number of seats on the council. The end result was a stronger city council.

The financial and managerial reforms of the 1970s actually allowed the mayor to operate as a modern chief executive but, at the same time, made the mayoralty the center of most political conflict. The politics surrounding the mayoralty became more technical and managerial but also more symbolic. The occupant of the mayor's office distributes approval and disapproval, symbols and opportunities, and, for some, even a sense of well-being. The emotional level of politics has gone far beyond the equivalent of service and jobs allocation of the machine or even of the period of professional service delivery. Today, it is steeped in identity politics.

The allocative and symbolic dimensions of mayoral politics are evident in the realignment of electoral coalitions in New York. Contrary poles were largely set among two coalitions that have dominated politics in New York City since the early 1980s. One coalition was led by Ed Koch and later by

Rudolph Giuliani. The other was led by different individuals but eventually, with success, by David Dinkins. These coalitions were defined in part by race and in part by economic, fiscal, and service issues.[28] Additionally, they were defined by the symbols and values of gender and identity politics associated with post-industrial urban governance.

The racial component of both poles is particularly important. In 1989, the combination of Jesse Jackson's two presidential bids—each of which had major voter enrollment drives in New York's African-American communities—and the possibility of electing the city's first black mayor boosted the African-American voter turnout to a rate even higher than among Jewish voters, typically the highest voting group.[29] The increasing strength of racial identity voting in New York is reflected in the differing voting patterns of African Americans and "outer-borough" white Catholic and Jewish voters, frequently leaving the city's growing and diversifying Latino populations as the swing electoral group.[30]

The 1989 and 1993 election results illustrate the presence of these voting blocks. Economic, racial, and identity issues (e.g., abortion rights, feminism, lesbian and gay rights, and environmental concerns) were evident in both elections. The group coalition that supported Dinkins in 1989 was the same as in 1993; the same was true for Giuliani (see figures 12, 13, and 14). Changes in turnout rates in 1993—higher on Staten Island due to a referendum on secession and lower among African Americans—accounted for the altered balance between the two electoral coalitions. By chipping away a few percentage points among those groups that had supported Dinkins in 1989, Giuliani won by a slight margin in 1993. A pro-business, managerial, and budget-reduction agenda was put in place. In consequence, much of Dinkins's "Glorious Mosaic" of multiracial and gender-based identity politics was replaced by themes of privatization, budget cuts, and crime prevention.

THE UNWALLED CITY AND REGIONAL PLANNING

A fifth theme influencing New York City is its open economy.[31] From its beginnings, the city's history was influenced by the competition of trade, as it was already part of an emerging world economy from the start. Founded by Dutch traders, New York City was seized by the British seeking both economic and strategic advantage. Its geographic position had destined it to be a point of economic linkage between North America and Europe.[32] The opening of the Erie Canal, linking New York harbor with the Great Lakes and the

Figure 12: Mayoral Votes for Dinkins and Giuliani by Group Coalition, 1989

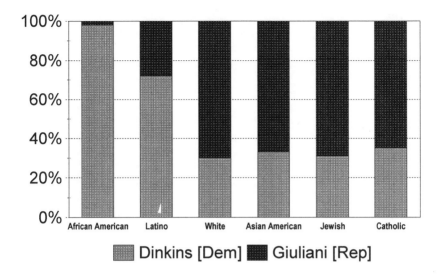

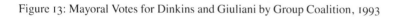

Source: WABC/*Daily News* 1989 Exit Poll.

Figure 13: Mayoral Votes for Dinkins and Giuliani by Group Coalition, 1993

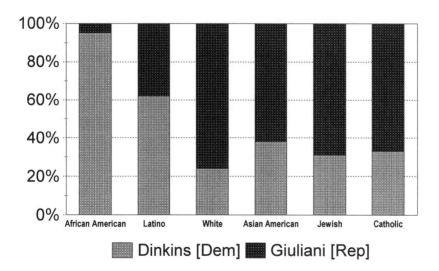

Source: NES 1993 NYC Exit Poll.

Figure 14: Mayoral Votes for Dinkins and Giuliani by Gender and Sexual Identity, 1993

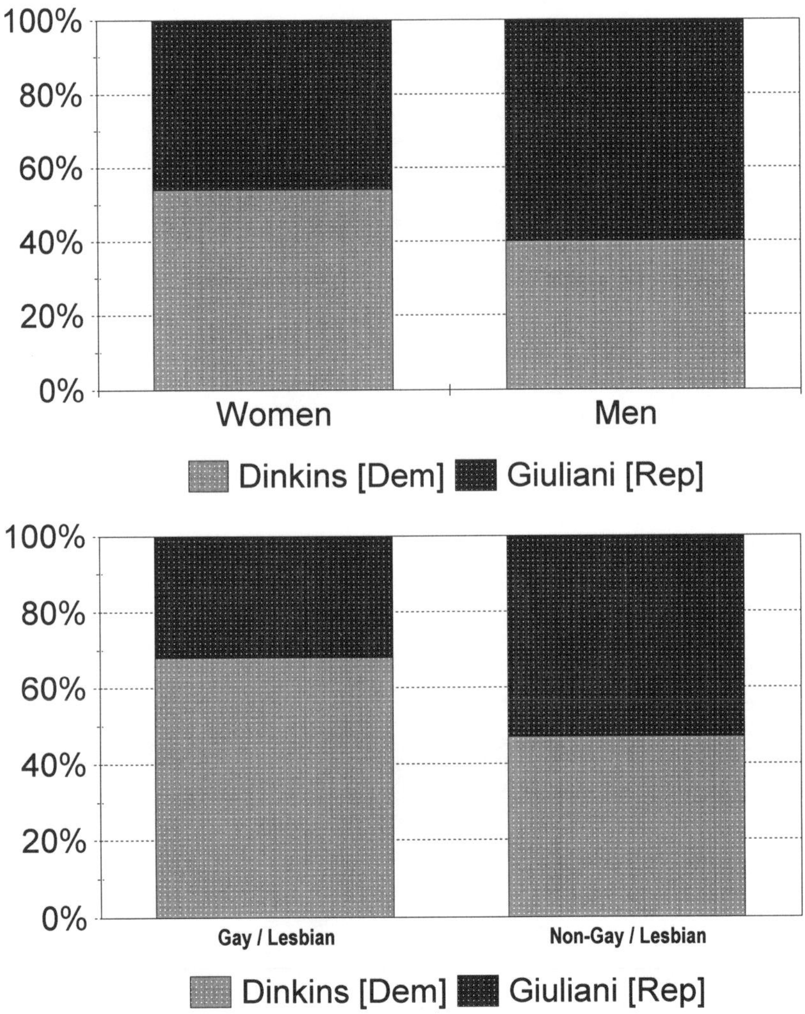

Source: NES 1993 NYC Exit Poll.

markets and resources of the Midwest, confirmed the city's preeminence over Boston and Philadelphia. Despite the effects of the Great Depression of the 1930s, the ambitions that the 1890s' reformers had for the city were fulfilled by the end of World War II. New York had begun replacing London as the center of the international economy.[33]

New York's economic standing rests on a mix of influences: the national (even international) trends outside the control of private and public leaders and those trends the city government could influence through tax and revenue policies, infrastructure investment, and regulation. Local policy could either take advantage of emerging economic trends or protect the city from the negative effects of those trends, but at a cost.

From 1960 on, a combination of local policies and larger economic trends had undermined the economic position of New York from its highpoint in the 1950s. The New York–New Jersey region was less competitive for the manufacture of goods than other areas of the country and the world. The most stark indication of this decline was industrial job loss. Between 1967 and 1975, the city lost more than five hundred thousand jobs, mostly in manufacturing.[34] The loss was related less to the burden of taxes and regulatory policies than to a decline in the relative advantage New York's economic concentration. There was a decline in the relative productivity of the city's skilled workforce, an overall increase in the cost of doing business in New York (including taxes and also electricity, cost of commercial space, etc.), and a general increase in the cost of living, which, in turn, pushed up the price of skilled white-collar labor. All of these developments made New York less attractive for the manufacture of most goods for national or worldwide consumption.[35]

The deterioration in New York's manufacturing sector was one part of a fundamental reorganization of New York's economic base. Between 1960 and 1990, New York City also become even more susceptible to influences from the world economy.[36] The sectors of the city's economy that have prospered most since 1977 have been linked to the national and international economy, particularly banking, finance, media and communications, and insurance. Activity in these sectors, along with an influx of highly skilled white-collar workers, placed upward pressure on Manhattan's real estate markets. The end result was an economy more focused on services than manufacturing, more focused on national and international economic domains than on local ones,[37] and more uneven than in the past.

Underlying the prosperity of the financial services sector in the 1980s were two negative trends. New York's economy was becoming less diverse, which had important implications for the stability of the city's public finances, and there was a growing set of mismatches within the emerging economy that exacerbated some of the city's social problems.

The first negative trend was an economy less diverse and more reliant on trends outside the control of both public and private decision makers.[38] As the financial sector grew and manufacturing continued to decline, New York became more vulnerable to uncertainties in the financial markets. The first real indication of this new vulnerability was the stock market shock of October 1987.[39] Hundreds of billions of dollars of paper assets were lost to the city's economy. In the next two years, the real estate industry suffered major losses as prices fell on residential property and vacancy rates in office towers grew. The banking and finance sector began a "downsizing" that continued into the 1990s. In 1995, city tax revenues were suffering because of slow activity in the municipal bond market.

The second negative trend was initially hidden by the growth of the mid-1980s. But underlying much of that growth was a series of new economic mismatches. One was the dramatic upward shift in the price of commercial and residential space. As a result, some low-cost residential and commercial spaces near the central business district were recycled for residential and retail use at significantly higher prices. This caused the displacement of many lower-income residents and small businesses. In addition, there has been a growing mismatch between the skills needed for employment in the new economy and the skills available in the local labor pool. New York City's public schools could not produce an adequate work force to meet the needs of a finance- and information-centered economy. The skills being generated in the schools found no market in the declining manufacturing sector. The result was that many of the jobs created by the new economy were in fact filled by new residents from outside New York City. These combined mismatches had racial as well as class ramifications that led to a fall in the labor participation rates among black males, an increase in employment of women in all racial categories, and a displacement of older workers.[40] In a sense, New York's economy was becoming less competitive and less compassionate at the same time.

The transformation of New York's economy was reflected in the reorganization of the city's politics.[41] In terms of New York's government institution, this change has pushed New York's current pro-growth political regime toward development policies, enhanced services through business development agencies, and, in some cases, direct subsidies to sustain the city's economic base. Tax policy and capital planning are geared toward potential new residents and investors, while more traditional facilities and amenities, such as parks and school buildings, remain undermaintained.

Economic growth has not been even. Regional growth has pushed New York as an economy far beyond the geographic bounds of New York as a city. Corporate headquarters and back-office operations had been moving to

Figure 15: Debt Issuance of New York City and Regional Authorities, 1960–1989

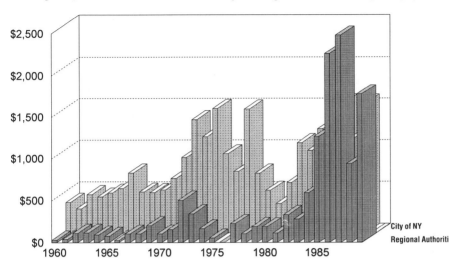

the suburban rings around the city since the late 1960s. In the 1980s, some advanced business services accompanied them, moving out of the inner-downtown areas of Manhattan and following their corporate clients to the Hudson Valley, Long Island, northern and central New Jersey, and south-western Connecticut.[42] Even in planning, the politics of economic development had moved outside the city. Investment for infrastructure now falls outside the city's traditional governing structure. Whereas before the 1960s there were only three major public authorities in the New York region—the Port Authority of New York and New Jersey, the New York City Housing Authority, and the Triborough Bridge and Tunnel Authority—by the 1990s there were almost forty. All together, these agencies accounted for more than 70 percent of regional debt issuance (see figure 15).

The new regional authorities that now oversee development have brought greater organizational capacity, technical sophistication, financial predictability, and a regional perspective that the older system dominated by the city's mayoralty and Board of Estimate could neither achieve nor implement. But the sector-specific base of organizations, such as the Port Authority of New York and New Jersey or the Health and Hospital Corporation, has distanced the capital planning system from popular accountability.[43] Viewed from the perspective of the 1990s, the 1898 attempt to create a regional government for planning eventually failed, not because of ambition, but because the region outgrew the government.

The economic reorganization of New York also defined a new set of conflicting political interests in the city. There is a clear division between those who are vested in and gain from the emerging world city of post-industrial New York and those whose interests are tied to older forms of social organization. Those who have gained from economic change include younger professionals, real estate interests, the financial community, and businesses tied to the entertainment, media, convention, and tourism industries. The losers include public employees and their unions, public sector clients (recipients of services), and those sectors of the middle class that are tied to traditional forms of interest mobilization (e.g., ethnic identities or older communities). The division between winners and losers in economic change is frequently reinforced by race, especially as quality education becomes even more critical to economic and social advancement. Neither the benefits nor the costs of economic transformation have been evenly distributed in New York City.

NEW YORK AS THE CENTURY CLOSES

The political tensions so apparent in New York City are largely the result of how social and economic forces influence—and are influenced by—the city's governing institutions. From the pre-Revolutionary town of merchants, shippers, and tradesmen, to an emergent hub for an industrial economy during the second half of the nineteenth century, to the present day, New York is constantly rebuilding itself.[44] Villages are replaced by towns, towns by an industrial city, and an industrial city by a modern post-industrial metropolis ringed by superhighways and dotted with high-rise buildings, airports, and satellite dishes. At each stage of economic transformation there was also a political transformation, a change in the core structure of New York's government.

As the year 2000 approaches, so too does the one-hundredth anniversary of the modern city of New York. The city of greater New York was established to make urban governance more efficient and less corrupt in servicing both business and the poor, more stable politically, and more scientific in its management. It was designed as a regional government in which the services and capital planning necessary to build a great industrial city sufficient to compete with the capitals of Europe would be assured. It was conceived by reformers and planners, entrepreneurs and businessmen, academics and journalists, to solve the problems of the corrupt and (more important) inept political machine. One hundred years later, many of these problems persist.

The search for greater organizational capacity in urban government—maybe the ultimate goal of the old reformers—has succeeded in part. But the very success has driven its polar challenge, especially in the polyglot New York City. Local government in the United States, and particularly in New York, is a service enterprise. Concentrating managerial power in a modern executive office concentrates political power as well. The enhanced power of the mayoralty, backed by enhanced fiscal and managerial structures, has been matched by only a half-hearted reaction, at best, to demands by communities and alienated groups for greater participation in city policymaking. The response to demands for inclusionary politics by New York's various groups and neighborhoods has been to alter the institutional arrangements of popular representation in the city through decentralization, neighborhood city halls, community planning boards, community school boards, and reapportionment of the city council. The success of these efforts has been mixed.[45]

Institutional rearrangements of city government will not resolve the enduring political cleavages. The mayoral elections in 1989 and 1993 reflect the new alliances that define postindustrial politics in much of urban America. On one side is a group that is conservative in its politics and values, fiscally restrained, pro-growth in development policy, and willing to invest in crime control but skeptical of all other urban expenditures. It is also disproportionately white. On the other side is an odd alliance between racial minorities and the remnants of some older traditions in urban politics, which still see city government as the distributor of services and jobs, now aligned with newer emerging groups—loose reflections of new social movements—that see city government as a distributor of symbols and affirmations. Racial politics, service politics, identity politics, and union politics are arranged in a new and common political front.

The most significant challenge to the legitimacy of local governance in New York, however, is no longer the barriers to participation or an insufficient distribution of policy victories so that each group can feel success at some point of the policy period. The most significant challenge is the very effectiveness of government itself. Parents and the business community are in perpetual revolt over the quality of education and the inability of teachers, a series of school superintendents, and mayors to meet the challenge of New York's new economy. AIDS activists protest the slowness and intransigence of health-care bureaucracies, and mothers put their lives on the line to patrol streets against drug dealers—a service for which they already pay through their taxes.

As present-day New York City ends its first century of governance, the tension between legitimacy and organizational capacity is palpable. Governmental effectiveness has become a cry of the frustrated regardless of class, race, or other identity. The minor reforms made to the region's governance since 1898 may be inadequate to attain that simple objective.

CHAPTER TWELVE

Compassion and Competition:
Public Finance and Public Policy

Sarah F. Liebschutz

The 1994 campaign for governor of New York focused mainly on spending choices and tax levels. Both Governor Mario M. Cuomo and his Republican opponent, state senator George E. Pataki—although their explanations differed—acknowledged three facts: state spending grew during Cuomo's three terms at a rate exceeding inflation (114 percent versus 41 percent);[1] state and local taxes were well above the national average (second only to Alaska); and private sector job growth during the prior decade was well below the national average.

Mario Cuomo, with 45 percent of the votes, failed to win a fourth term. He lost because voters held him, as chief executive, responsible for New York's job losses and high taxes.[2] Post-election surveys showed that voters negatively identified the governor with the problems that most concerned them. Pataki was supported by 76 percent of the voters who said taxes mattered most and 63 percent of those for whom government spending was most important.[3] Sixty percent of the voters said New York State was "on the wrong track."[4]

At its core, however, the 1994 election was about New York's self-image of competition and compassion. The election challenged basic assumptions about the coexistence of the individualistic and moralistic values that define the state's political culture. So, too, did the election challenge the appropriate role of government.

George Pataki, the victor, contended that the election signaled approval by New Yorkers of "less spending, lower taxes and more growth" and rejection of Mario Cuomo's "control and regulation and redistribution of wealth by governmental elites."[5] As part of his agenda for "smaller, more effective, more efficient government" to liberate individual entrepreneurialism,

Pataki called for a reduction in the state personal income tax rate of up to 25 percent over four years.[6]

Yet the evidence was not conclusive that collective benevolence had been rejected in 1994. Did Pataki's victory really mean, Joyce Purnick of the *New York Times* asked, that New Yorkers "would . . . refuse to admit an illegal immigrant to a public hospital or school? Would they put time limits on welfare benefits and shelter for the homeless? Would the more affluent be willing to do without publicly subsidized parks and beach clubs, or publicly financed busing to private schools?"[7]

Such questions exposed the delicacy of the balance between competition and compassion within the state's political culture. Pataki himself, six months after taking office, publicly recognized that tilting the public sector toward competitive entrepreneurialism and away from collective benevolence would meet with resistance. "No one knows better than I," he said in a Heritage Foundation speech, "that implementing conservative policy alternatives in a state where liberal policies were perpetuated for decades isn't done easily or overnight."[8] Just hours after that speech, Pataki met with Republican congressional leaders, warning "that he [would] fight a Sun Belt plan that would make 'Draconian cuts' in New York's share" of Medicaid and welfare funds.[9]

Past accommodations to the tensions between compassion and competition shaped the big state government against which George Pataki campaigned in 1994. All of New York's major political actors, individual and institutional, delineated in prior chapters, contributed to that outcome. They would also play significant roles in changing it.

THE SIZE OF GOVERNMENT

"New York has long been known for its large and expansionary public sector. The reputation continues to be well deserved."[10] In 1992, New York ranked second after Alaska in per capita state and local government expenditures (see table 10). State and local governments in New York employed more workers per 10,000 population than did forty-five states and ranked fourth in compensation for the average public sector worker. How did a state with a per capita income 20 percent above the national average, a state whose tax capacity was only slightly above the national average, manage to spend at a rate more than 35 percent above the national average? The answer is that New York state and local governments imposed a very high tax effort (second only to Alaska) and received a high level of federal aid (third in per

Table 10: Relative Fiscal Position of New York State and Local Governments

Variable	New York	United States	New York's Rank
Per Capita Expenditures (1992)	$5,670	$3,826	2
Per Capita Taxes (1992)	$3,534	$2,178	2
Taxes as Percentage of Income (1992)	24	19	4
Tax Effort Score (1991)	156	100	2
Tax Capacity Score (1991)	103	100	16
Per Capita Federal Aid (1994)	$1,235	$810	3
Employees per 10,000 Population (1992)	635	–	5
Average Employee Annual Compensation (1992)	$37,752	–	4

Sources: Data for per capita expenditures, per capita taxes, and taxes as percentage of income from Advisory Commission on Intergovernmental Relations, *Significant Features of Fiscal Federalism* (Washington DC, 1994). Data for tax effort score and tax capacity score from Advisory Commission on Intergovernmental Relations, *RTS: State Revenue Capacity and Effort* (Washington DC, 1993). Data for per capita federal aid from U.S. Department of Commerce, Bureau of the Census, *Federal Expenditures by State for Fiscal Year 1995* (Washington DC, 1995). Data for number of employees and average annual compensation from "Ranking the 50 States," *Governing: The Magazine of States and Localities* 8 (February 1995).

– not available

capita terms in 1994). The consequence of these and other fiscal indicators was that when Pataki took office, New York State's general obligation bonds were rated lowest in the country by Standard & Poor's; a year later, they were still rated at the bottom, just above Louisiana.

New York's economic decline was evident during the early 1970s. While personal income for the United States increased by 2.3 percent between 1970 and 1975, it declined by 0.1 percent in New York. The nation's employment grew in the same period by 1.7 percent but declined by nearly 1 percent in New York.[11]

New York state and local governments did not trim their expenditure growth correspondingly. Real state and local government spending "grew as fast . . . as in the rest of the nation despite the fact that the economic growth to support [it] was not present in New York. By 1975, per capita expenditures of New York state and local governments were 51 percent above the national average and taxes had climbed to 15 cents per dollar of personal income—nearly 37 percent above the U.S. average."[12]

Exposure in 1975 of New York's profligate ways, most dramatically those of New York City, however, turned out not to be a "major turning point in the way New York governments view[ed] the role of the public sector." The 1980s were marked by government growth fueled by increases in both revenue-raising capacity and spending demands. Higher revenue yields were driven by three factors: growth in the underlying tax base, a tax burden that remained very high by comparison with the rest of the country (even with reductions in the state personal income tax rate in 1985, 1986, and 1987), and New York's success in garnering federal aid, particularly welfare-related aid.[13]

Spending increases reflected demands from diverse sources. For example, state and local government spending on education was accelerated in response to increasing numbers of poorer, disadvantaged students in the central cities. Rapid growth in medical and hospital costs led to greater health spending. Highway and public safety expenditures increased in tandem with increased traffic volume on the state's highways, a large rise in the prison population, and significant growth in compensation for highway, police, and fire employees. Finally, "New York continued to offer a much more generous package of services to its low-income residents than the average state."[14]

In effect, New York significantly expanded the scope of its collective benevolence during the 1980s. New York's trademark generosity for persons dependent on public services—the poor, the educationally disadvantaged, the disabled, the elderly, and children—was extended to two other large groups of claimants: government employees and service providers. Public sector employee unions, among the state's strongest lobbies, negotiated effectively to improve the real salary position of state and local government employees. Well-organized providers of services—hospitals, nursing homes, community-based foster care, training and employment, youth, and mental health agencies—successfully lobbied for increased spending on health, education, and welfare. At the end of the 1980s, New York's collective benevolence encompassed three distinct groups of claimants—those dependent on government for services, those dependent on government for employment, and those dependent on government for business.

Yet individual entrepreneurialism was not neglected in New York's public sector growth in the 1980s. After the 1975 fiscal crisis, the state government, under the leadership of Governors Hugh Carey and Mario Cuomo, initiated aggressive actions on three fronts to improve New York's business climate. State tax rates on both corporate and personal income were reduced; spending to improve bridges, highways, local roads, and mass transportation was accelerated; and state funding was targeted to stimulate technology-based industries.[15]

Even so, more than twenty years after New York City's fiscal crisis, the state was not viewed as hospitable to business. "For too long," Governor Pataki asserted shortly after taking office in 1995, the "entrepreneurial spirit has been crushed by New York State regulation and taxation." The governor proposed a combination of tax reforms and spending cuts to "set New York's economy on a path that leads to economic growth and job creation." Pataki singled out one program in particular for substantial spending reductions. Medicaid in New York, he said, had "grown far beyond its original intent as a provider of care for the needy."[16]

MEDICAID

No program better illustrates the conundrum of balancing competition and compassion in New York than Medicaid. At the same time, no program better illustrates how Medicaid's inter- and intragovernmental web make its reform so difficult.

The size and rate of growth of Medicaid make this intergovernmental health-insurance program a national problem. Enacted by the Congress in 1965 to meet the health-care needs of the poor, Medicaid was, thirty years later, four programs, "configured and operated somewhat differently in each of the 50 states and the District of Columbia: . . . a health insurance program with comprehensive benefits and little or no cost sharing [for] 16 million children and 7 million adults in low-income families; a long-term care program for home- and community-based services and the dominant source of financing for nursing home care [for] nearly 4 million low-income elderly people and 5 million low-income people with disabilities; a supplementary insurance program to Medicare paying Medicare's premiums and cost sharing and covering additional services; and a health insurance program for low-income disabled adults who do not have Medicare coverage."[17]

Medicaid, combining all four programs, has become particularly burdensome in New York, which leads the nation in both absolute and relative spending for Medicaid. New York spent $19.4 billion on 2.7 million recipients in 1994. In contrast, California, with twice as many recipients (5.32 million), spent $15.9 billion. In per capita terms, New York spent 2.5 times the average of the rest of the fifty states on Medicaid in 1994; overall Medicaid costs in New York increased by an average of 12 percent annually between 1989 and 1994.[18]

Medicaid spending in New York is shared by federal, state, and local governments. Federal aid to New York for Medicaid—more than $11 billion in 1995—accounts for the lion's share of all federal aid to New York and about 50 percent of the state's Medicaid spending. Unlike most states, where the state government alone bears the nonfederal share of Medicaid, Medicaid in New York has significant implications for local governments. Consistent with its extensive mandating practices, New York is one of only fifteen states that require its local governments to share the state's portion. This mandate is targeted at the fifty-seven counties and New York City, which are responsible under state law for administering health, welfare, and social services. The local share, at more than $3 billion in 1994, represented nearly 40 percent of the nonfederal share. Small wonder that the New York State Association of Counties and New York City Mayor Rudolph Giuliani enthusiastically endorsed the Pataki Medicaid reform initiatives described below, which would reduce their spending obligations.[19]

The High Costs of Medicaid in New York

Why are New York's Medicaid expenditures so high? The answer rests in objective facts and policy choices. New York has an expensive mix of Medicaid recipients, with above-average shares of the aged, the disabled, and persons with AIDS and drug-abuse problems that lead to costly long-term care and natal-care expenses.[20] In addition, New York's costs for health-care practitioners (except for physicians) and for compliance with state regulations are higher than those of most states. Within the state, there are substantial disparities in spending on inpatient and outpatient services, nursing, and home health care; in all of these categories, New York City's spending per recipient far exceeds that of all individual counties.[21]

New York State has also made policy choices that contribute to costs. Two interrelated objectives have historically governed these policy choices: satisfying the demands of diverse constituencies and maximizing federal dollars. The federal Medicaid statute stipulates a set of mandatory services that must be provided to "categorically needy" groups. The statute also allows for federal reimbursement of certain additional services at states' option; it permits states to extend coverage of both mandatory and optional services to groups defined by the states as "medically needy."

Medicaid services in New York are generous. They include more optional services and extend to more persons than in many states; Medicaid coverage, additionally, "is broader and more extensive than [selected] private insurance packages" in the state. In addition to hospitalization, family planning, and nursing-home services, all required under Medicaid, New York provides twenty-six of the thirty-one services categorized as optional. Thirty-six states provide some Medicaid coverage to the medically needy, that is, to those whose incomes exceed the "categorically needy" welfare threshold, but most set their limits far below New York's. The net result, in 1993, for example, was that spending on optional Medicaid services in New York was about "44 percent of the state's total Medicaid spending; spending on optional services for the medically needy was nearly equal to spending on the categorically needy," even though they numbered only about 40 percent of the categorically needy.[22]

The high cost of New York's Medicaid program is no accident. The state's extensive array of optional services and generous definition of eligibility have long been endorsed by service recipients, service providers, and the state's political leadership. Organizations of health-care providers, such as the Home Care Association of New York and the New York State Association of Homes and Services for the Aging, and a broad array of advocates for the poor, disabled, and elderly are quick to defend the largest categories of optional spending for the medically needy—intermediate-care facilities for the mentally retarded, mental hospital services for the aged, and home health services.[23] In fact, it has been argued that the use of federal Medicaid dollars for these services, as discussed below, saves New York money.

The majority parties in each chamber of the state legislature have played an important role in creating and sustaining New York's extensive Medicaid program. Assembly Democrats, historically more liberal and more responsive to lower-income, urban New Yorkers, endeavor to protect the benefits of Medicaid clients; senate Republicans typically support lower taxes to retain business and professional workers, but at the same time they identify with and protect the interests of hospitals and nursing homes.[24]

Medicaid in New York is big business; it provides substantial revenues to hospitals, nursing homes, and home health-care agencies, which, in turn, provide substantial employment to New Yorkers. Medicaid typically constitutes from 70 percent to more than 90 percent of revenues for the state's approximately three hundred not-for-profit and government-owned nursing homes. Inner-city hospitals rely heavily on Medicaid income, and so do the home health-care agencies that principally serve the elderly urban poor. The health-care service industry, which accounted for 730,000 jobs in mid-1995, is the state's largest private sector service employer.[25]

Leveraging Federal Dollars

New York has consistently tried to maximize federal dollars. Immediately after Medicaid was enacted by the Congress in 1965, Governor Nelson Rockefeller seized the opportunity for New York to participate. He viewed Medicaid as the vehicle with which both to expand health services for New Yorkers and to obtain larger amounts of federal aid than were available to New York under prior public health programs.[26] In addition, Medicaid spending in New York, particularly since the 1980s, "is the result of skillful and sophisticated use of federal rules to shift [the] costs . . . [for] services to people who are mentally ill, mentally retarded or developmentally disabled . . . from the state to the federal government."[27]

.Unlike California, which aimed at cost containment from the outset, New York has always "challenged the federal government to match the state to pay for the liberal eligibility requirements, numerous optional services, and highly regulated administrative practices of Medicaid as defined in Albany."[28]

Medicaid Reform: 1995

Governor George Pataki's multifaceted proposal to contain the cost of Medicaid in New York was not the first such initiative. After an overrun by 36 percent of the state government Medicaid appropriation during the first year (1965–66), cost-containment reforms were advanced on an annual basis. Governors Carey and Cuomo proposed, and the state legislature adopted, incremental changes directed at both clients and service providers; they involved adjustments to eligibility criteria and services offered and strengthened regulation of health-care provider management practices.[29]

But Pataki's 1995 initiative departed from past incremental reforms. He recommended a decrease by $1.2 billion (11 percent) in the state government's share of Medicaid for the 1995–96 fiscal year. Seventy percent of the $1.2 billion decrease (or $834 million) was to derive from savings through rate reductions to hospitals, nursing homes, and home health-care providers. The remaining savings to the state government were to be realized largely through mandatory managed-care enrollment for nearly all nonelderly Medicaid recipients. When multiplied by the local and federal shares, the total decrease in Medicaid spending would be $3.6 billion.

Health-care providers, particularly hospitals, were stunned. They "had prepared for a strategy that increased managed care . . . or, alternatively, a rate cut. What started as a quality review of Medicaid," said the president of the major association of the state's hospitals, the Healthcare Association of

New York State (HANYS), "degenerated into a slash, burn, and cut approach."[30] Representatives of New York's nursing home and home health-care industries echoed that sentiment.

New York is a state with powerful interest groups. The " 'Medicaid–industrial complex,' dependent on the program for continued employment, salary growth, and revenue,"[31] constituted a contentious and volatile mix on the governor's proposals. Organized opponents included health-care provider associations (hospitals, nursing homes, and home health-care agencies), for whom the cuts "could have cost literally billions of dollars in lost reimbursement," unionized employees at state developmental and psychiatric centers, and advocates for the poor and the elderly, who saw the Medicaid cuts as "nothing less than a war on the poor."[32] Supporters of the governor's proposals included the Business Council (an organization of about four thousand private businesses) and the anti-tax group CHANGE-NY, which wanted "to lighten the financial burden of the program on the state's taxpaying public,"[33] the New York State Association of Counties (NYSAC), which sought mandate relief, and Blue Cross and Blue Shield, which endorsed lower costs through managed care.

Opponents and supporters of reform both claimed victory when the legislature adopted the 1995–96 Medicaid budget. Health-care providers, "who worked vigorously on numerous fronts to fight the devastating cuts proposed by the governor," succeeded in persuading the senate Republican leadership to restore about 54 percent, or $450 million, of the proposed reductions. The Business Council and NYSAC claimed success as well; even after the restorations, "significant provider losses remain[ed], particularly when the local and federal shares of Medicaid were factored in."[34] The state legislature did not adopt a mandatory Medicaid managed-care program for New York to seek a statewide federal waiver. But managed-care proponents did not lose; the New York Department of Social Services (and its successor program administrator, the Department of Health) would continue to encourage individual counties to seek federal waivers to increase the number of mandatory Medicaid enrollment programs.

In summary, New York's collective benevolence to those dependent on government for salaries and for revenue was trimmed substantially in the Medicaid reforms of 1995. Whether that trimming continues, and how and to what degree it affects those dependent on government for services, may depend on New York's success in stimulating jobs and generating investment by the private sector.

ECONOMIC GROWTH

The New York state government has a long tradition of intervention to promote economic development. From its early days, the state government created "an institutional framework that was conducive to economic growth and private enterprise." Beyond "its development of law and the legislative and judicial interpretation of property rights, [which] created a predictable and stable legal-economic environment,"[35] New York engaged in activities such as construction of the Erie Canal in the early nineteenth century to directly stimulate the economy. After a century-long hiatus, economic development reemerged as an organized state government activity; the stimulus was "a concern with the problems of distressed industries during and immediately after the Depression and . . . a recognition of the structural change that would undoubtedly confront the economy after World War II." Manufacturing was, and continues to be, targeted—"both as a distressed industry and as the [state's] foremost 'engine of growth'"—for special tax and finance incentives. At the same time, the state has not "abandoned its attachment to agriculture, nor failed to seize opportunities for promoting tourism."[36] As the twentieth century drew to a close, the multifaceted initiatives of Governors Carey and Cuomo emphasized that New York "had returned to its early nineteenth century posture of economic activism."[37]

Yet such intervention yielded neither reelection for the incumbent governor in 1994 nor uniform improvement in the state's competitive posture. New York's business and economic climate vis-à-vis other states, as illustrated by the comparative evaluation rankings of the Corporation for Enterprise Development, a Washington DC economic development research group, is mixed. Based on seventy-eight factors that assess current and future state economic growth, New York scored very high in 1994 on the competitiveness of its existing businesses and entrepreneurial energy. But its economic performance overall was assessed as poor, with job opportunities among the nation's worst, and with high annual pay and pay growth being the nation's highest. Its development capacity was similarly mixed, with first-rate technology and financial resources, but with the nation's sixth worst high school graduation rate and infrastructure (bridges and sewage treatment facilities) in need of serious repair. Table 11 displays this report card, which in the aggregate earns New York about a C+.

The labyrinthine politics practiced in the Empire State are a natural outgrowth of two long-favored activities of New Yorkers: making money and energetically participating in politics. These traits form the framework

Table 11: New York's 1994 Report Card for Business and Economic Climate

Economic Performance	D
Employment	F
Earnings and Job Quality	A
Equity	D
Business Vitality	A
Business Competitiveness	B
Entrepreneurial Energy	B
Structural Diversity	C
Development Capacity	C
Human Resources	D
Technology Resources	A
Financial Resources	A
Infrastructure and Amenity Resources	D

Source: Committee for Enterprise Development, *The 1994 Development Report Card for the States* (Washington DC, 1994).

within which the tensions between the individualistic and moralistic strands of New York's political culture have been played out since colonial times.

The state's powerful governmental institutions—the governor and executive branch, judiciary, and legislature—together with strong parties and interest groups, reflect and reinforce competing claims for compassion and competition. The line between redistributive and distributive politics has been blurred. Collective benevolence, one of the two major tenets of New York's political culture since the middle of the nineteenth century, has been pragmatically redefined and practically enlarged. At the end of the twentieth century, it includes not only those dependent on government for income and services but also those most deeply dependent on government for employment and for business—most especially, social service–sector businesses and nonprofit organizations.

The spending and taxes to support such largesse and the long regulatory reach of the state government are blamed for New York's fall from comparative economic dominance. Yet many of the same critics who advocate reduced taxes, spending, and regulation also look to the state and its local governments to intervene with tax and finance incentives and direct public spending for infrastructure improvements, job training, and education in order to stimulate private investment and job creation. Both the critics of government reform in New York and its advocates share a common mind-set of big government and public sector activism. As New York enters the twenty-first century, the balance between compassion and competition will undoubtedly remain high on the agenda of the state's political actors and institutions.

CHAPTER THIRTEEN

Suggestions for Research on New York Politics

Sarah F. Liebschutz

There are many sources of information available for the study of New York state politics and government. This chapter lists a number of them, including bibliographies, themselves useful in discovering additional sources. Both published and electronic resources are contained in the following listings.

GENERAL RESOURCES

Libraries provide the best starting point for research. New York State has a large number of both public and university-based libraries that can be easily accessed. The New York State Library, founded in 1818 in Albany, holds the largest collection of official state documents and many other sources of information on state government and politics. The State Library also distributes copies of documents to approximately two hundred other libraries throughout the state and beyond.

An additional source of original documents is the New York State Archives, also in Albany. The State Archives has copies of many records and has published the *Guide to the New York State Archives* (1981) to assist those who wish to search for specific records.

Internet Resources

The State Library's document retrieval system on the Internet at <gopher://unix2.nysed.gov/> is an extremely useful resource. The gopher provides access to:

- the full texts of State Library publications, including bibliographies and education law excerpts

- the Checklist of New York State Documents—sorted by year for 1992 to the present
- the New York State Information Locator, with lists of state agencies and services and connections to other governmental Internet resources
- the full texts of state government publications, including reports of the comptroller, Public Service Commission, and the Department of Housing and Community Renewal

Through its link to other governmental Internet resources, the Information Locator provides access to current census information and materials about state and local government projects.

New York State also has a home page on the Internet at <http://www.state.ny.us>. It is designed to provide the public with information about the Empire State, including such topics as the governor, tourism, economic development, citizen's access to state government, associations, and a search index that allows users to search a large database of state information using a basic key-word query system. While the home page has some general use, the State Library's gopher system is more useful for documentation, transcripts, and archived records.

Newspapers and Journals

Newspapers can provide excellent information for research. The *New York Times* features regular coverage of state politics and is indexed by subject matter to make finding references easier. Many libraries will have this newspaper on microfilm. Several other large city newspapers such as the *Times Union* in Albany, *Buffalo News, Long Island Newsday, Daily News* in New York City, *Democrat and Chronicle* in Rochester, and *Post-Standard* and *Herald-Journal* in Syracuse provide information on state politics. These can be found at libraries as well, but usually on a more regional basis.

The principal journal dealing with New York politics and government is *Empire State Report*. Published monthly, it deals with current state policy issues, changes to laws, important political figures in the state, and other related topics. Magazines such as *New Yorker, New York*, and *George* are useful sources of information on cultural aspects of life, particularly in New York City.

Other Sources of Information

Basic data on the state can be found in the *New York Statistical Yearbook* (Albany: Rockefeller Institute of Government). It is published annually and contains current economic, population, election, and financial data for the state. The *New York Red Book* (Albany: New York Legal Publishing), published and updated biennially, is a guide to the organization of state government: its departments, personnel, and the basic duties carried out by each unit of the government. It includes biographies of state officeholders. The state university system and various state authorities and commissions are discussed as well. *The New York Gazetteer* (Wilmington DE: American Historical Publications, 1983) is a directory of basic reference data as well as a listing of places of historical interest in the state. It also includes a biographical index of important people in state history.

Research centers that deal with New York state politics and government include the Nelson A. Rockefeller Institute of Government of the State University of New York. Established in 1982, the Rockefeller Institute publishes newsletters, reports, and papers dealing with a variety of public policy issues and conducts conferences on topics related to state and local government. Further information can be obtained by contacting the institute at 411 State St., Albany NY 12203, (518) 443–5522. The Edwin F. Jaeckle Center for State and Local Government Law at the State University of New York at Buffalo focuses on the legal structure of state and local government, problems encountered in the administration of municipal laws, and efforts to reform state and local laws. The Jaeckle Center publishes papers and sponsors conferences for local government officials and lawyers. The center can be contacted at O'Brian Hall, Amherst Campus, Buffalo NY 14260, (716) 636–2052. The Center for Governmental Research is a nonpartisan corporation based in Rochester that compiles and analyzes statistics to evaluate state and local government programs. The center has published studies of various programs and their impact on local governments. Information can be obtained at 37 South Washington St., Rochester NY 14608, (716) 325–6360. The Center for the Study of Business and Government at the Bernard Baruch College of the City University of New York, 17 Lexington Ave., P.O. Box 348A, New York NY 10010, (212) 505–5902, was established in 1978 to analyze the relationship between business and government and the effects that government policies have on the business world. The center's studies focus on the effect of programs and policies on the business concerns of New York State and New York City.

Public opinion surveys are conducted in New York State by the Marist Institute for Public Opinion at Marist College in Poughkeepsie. The institute is an independent, nonprofit survey and research center focusing on studies of voting behavior and electoral research.

Election data are made available by the State Board of Elections. Established in 1974, the elections board is responsible for the administration and enforcement of election laws. It monitors campaign finances and practices, provides assistance to local election boards, and investigates complaints concerning election procedures. The Board of Elections can be contacted at P.O. Box 4, One Commerce Plaza, Albany NY 12260. The *New York Red Book* contains a listing of current board members as well as election results. Each county in the state has its own board of elections. Addresses and names of current chairs are listed in the *New York Red Book*.

STATE GOVERNMENT DOCUMENTS

The New York State Library has developed several excellent publications that can be used to locate documents concerning state politics and government. Two publications issued by the Cultural Education Center of the State Library, *New York State Documents: An Introductory Manual* (Albany, 1987) and *Official Publications of New York State: A Bibliographic Guide to Their Use* (Albany, 1981), provide extensive listings of available documents as well as suggestions to researchers for locating these documents. Another State Library publication, the *Checklist of Official Publications of the State of New York* (Albany: 1947–, vol. 1–) is issued monthly by the State Library and lists all publications by state agencies.

Several sources provide information on the legislative process. The *Journal of the Assembly of the State of New York* and the *Journal of the Senate of the State of New York* are compiled annually and provide daily records of activity for each body, including floor proceedings, amendments, confirmation hearings, and voting records. The *Manual for the Use of the Legislature of the State of New York* (Albany: Division of Information Services, Department of State, 1840–) is published biennially and contains information pertaining to the members of the legislature and their staffs, such as committee assignments, voting statistics, and party strength and leadership. The *Legislative Digest* (Albany: New York Legislative Bill Drafting Commission) is an account of all bills introduced and action taken on previous bills. An annual summary of the progress of all bills is also available. The *Majority Leader's Report* (Albany: New York State Assembly, Office of the Majority Leader) is an annual account of the activities of the legislature from the perspective of the majority leader.

The executive branch produces numerous documents as well. The governor's office issues *Messages to the Legislature* (Albany, 1777–) and *The Ex-*

ecutive Budget (Albany, 1928–). Reports issued by executive departments include those of the Office of the State Comptroller (for example, the annual *Comptroller's Special Report on Municipal Affairs* and the *Comptroller's Report on the Financial Condition of New York State*, 1996), the *Annual Report of the Attorney General* (Albany: Department of Law, 1890–), and the *Annual Report of the Secretary of State*, 1919–).

The *Local Government Handbook* (Albany: Department of State, 1975–) is the best single source for information on the structural and functional features of local governments in the state and their relations to the state government. The Division of Information Services of the Department of State has produced various newsletters such as *State and Local* (Albany, 1983–88), dealing with general topics concerning state government, and *Excelsior* (Albany, 1988–), presenting various viewpoints on specific state issues.

The body of New York state laws and judicial proceedings can be found in publications such as *McKinney's Laws of New York Annotated* (St. Paul MN: West Publishing, 1943–) and *West's New York Digest* (St. Paul MN: West Publishing), which are updated and supplemented as changes occur. Selected opinions of the Court of Appeals, Appellate Divisions, and lower courts of the first and second judicial departments are published in the *New York Law Journal* (1888–).

One of the best sources of information on the New York state government is an internship in the legislature or an executive branch agency. Semester-long assembly and senate internship programs provide superior firsthand experiences for undergraduate and graduate students. Contact points for the internships are (518) 455–4704 for the assembly and (518) 432–5470 for the senate. Comparable experiences in a wide variety of executive branch agencies are available through the Albany Semester Program at (518) 485–5964.

TOPICAL BIBLIOGRAPHY

Numerous sources, useful for future study of New York state government and politics, are cited in each chapter. Rather than repeat each listing, the following is a group of selected sources, arranged by topic area, beginning with general works.

General Works

Bahl, Roy, and William Duncombe. *Economic Growth and Fiscal Planning: New York in the 1990s*. New Brunswick NJ: Center for Urban Policy Research, 1991.

Caldwell, Lynton K. *The Government and Administration of New York*. New York: Thomas Y. Crowell, 1954.

Gallie, Peter J. *Ordered Liberty: A Constitutional History of New York*. New York: Fordham University Press, 1996.

League of Women Voters of New York State. *New York State: A Citizen's Handbook*. New York, 1979.

Moscow, Warren. *Politics in the Empire State*. New York: Alfred Knopf, 1948.

Munger, Frank J., and Ralph A. Straitz. *New York Politics*. New York: New York University Press, 1960.

Schick, Thomas. *The New York State Constitutional Convention of 1915 and the Modern State Government*. New York: National Municipal League, 1979.

State of New York, Management Resources Projects. *Governing the Empire State: An Insiders Guide*. Albany, 1988.

Stonecash, Jeffrey, John K. White, and Peter W. Colby. *Governing New York State*, 3d ed. Albany: State University of New York Press, 1994.

Zimmerman, Joseph. *The Government and Politics of New York State*. New York: New York University Press, 1981.

Federal Government Relations

Elazar, Daniel J. *American Federalism: A View from the States*, 3d ed. New York: Harper & Row, 1984.

Liebschutz, Sarah F. *Bargaining under Federalism: Contemporary New York*. Albany: State University of New York Press, 1991.

Liebschutz, Sarah F. *Federal Aid to Rochester*. Washington DC: Brookings Institution, 1984.

Liebschutz, Sarah F., and Irene Lurie. "New York," in *Reagan and the States*, edited by Richard P. Nathan. Princeton: Princeton University Press, 1987.

Moynihan, Daniel P. *Came the Revolution: Arguments in the Reagan Era*. New York: Harcourt Brace Jovanovich, 1988.

Peirce, Neal R. *The Megastates of America*. New York: W. W. Norton, 1972.

Schechter, Stephen L., ed. *The Reluctant Pillar: New York and the Adoption of the Federal Constitution*. Troy NY: Russell Sage College, 1985.

Schechter, Stephen L., and Richard B. Bernstein, eds. *New York and the Union*. Albany: New York State Commission on the Bicentennial of the United States Constitution, 1990.

History

Alexander, DeAlva Stanwood. *A Political History of the State of New York.* Port Washington NY: I. J. Friedman, 1969.

Caro, Robert. *The Power Broker.* New York: Alfred Knopf, 1974.

Ellis, David M. *New York: State and City.* Ithaca: Cornell University Press, 1979.

Ellis, David M., James A. Frost, Harold C. Syrett, and Harry J. Carman. *A Short History of New York State.* Ithaca: Cornell University Press, 1967.

Flick, Alexander C., ed. *History of the State of New York.* New York: Columbia University Press, 1933−37.

Tripp, Wendell. *Coming and Becoming: Pluralism in New York State History.* Cooperstown: New York State Historical Association, 1991.

Trover, Ellen Lloyd, ed. *New York: A Chronology and Documentary Handbook.* New York: Oceana Publications, 1978.

The Legislature

Berle, Peter A. *Does the Citizen Stand a Chance? The Politics of a State Legislature: New York.* Woodbury NY: Barron's Educational Series, 1974.

Calicehia, Marcia, and Ellen Sadowski. *The Lobbying Handbook: A Guide to Effective Lobbying in New York State.* Albany: New York State School of Industrial and Labor Relations, Cornell University, 1984.

Chamberlain, Lawrence H. *Loyalty and Legislative Action: A Survey of Activity by the New York State Legislature, 1919−1949.* Ithaca: Cornell University Press, 1951.

Hevesi, Alan G. *Legislative Politics in New York State: A Comparative Analysis.* New York: Praeger, 1975.

Ruchelman, Leonard I. *Political Careers; Recruitment through the Legislature.* Rutherford NJ: Fairleigh Dickinson University Press, 1970.

The Judicial System

Gibson, Ellen M. *New York Legal Research Guide.* Buffalo: W. S. Hein, 1988.

Klein, Fannie J. *Federal and State Court Systems; A Guide.* Cambridge MA: Ballinger, 1977.

MacCrate, Robert, James D. Hopkins, and Maurice Rosenberg. *Appellate Justice in New York.* Chicago: American Judicature Society, 1982.

The Executive

Bellush, Bernard. *Franklin D. Roosevelt as Governor of New York*. New York: AMS Press, 1968.

Chessman, G. Wallace. *Governor Theodore Roosevelt: The Albany Apprenticeship, 1898–1900*. Cambridge: Harvard University Press, 1965.

Cole, Donald B. *Martin Van Buren and the American Political System*. Princeton: Princeton University Press, 1984.

Connery, Robert H., and Gerald Benjamin. *Rockefeller of New York: Executive Power in the Statehouse*. Ithaca: Cornell University Press, 1979.

Cuomo, Mario M. *Diaries of Mario Cuomo: The Campaign for Governor*. New York: Random House, 1984.

Davis, Kenneth S. *FDR: The New York Years, 1928–1933*. New York: Random House, 1979.

Eldot, Paula. *Governor Alfred E. Smith: The Politician as Reformer*. New York: Garland, 1983.

Flick, Alexander C. *Samuel Jones Tilden: A Study in Political Sagacity*. Port Washington NY: Kennikat Press, 1939.

McElroy, Robert. *Grover Cleveland: The Man and the Statesman*. New York: Harper & Brothers, 1923.

McElvaine, Robert S. *Mario Cuomo: A Biography*. New York: Charles Scribner's Sons, 1988.

Mitchell, Stewart. *Horatio Seymour of New York*. New York: DaCapo Press, 1970.

Prescott, Frank W., and Joseph Zimmerman. *Politics of the Veto of Legislation in New York*. Washington DC: University Press of America, 1980.

Wesser, Robert F. *Charles Evans Hughes: Politics and Reform in New York, 1905–1910*. Ithaca: Cornell University Press, 1967.

Political Parties and Interest Groups

Benenson, Bob. "Wake Up Call: Politics Resurge Big and Bold across the State," *Congressional Quarterly Weekly Report* 50 (5 September 1992): 2638–46.

Kass, Alvin. *Politics in New York State, 1800–1830*. Syracuse: Syracuse University Press, 1965.

Scarrow, Howard A. *Parties, Elections, and Representation in the State of New York*. New York: New York University Press, 1983.

Zeller, Belle. *Pressure Politics in New York—A Study of Group Representation before the Legislature*. New York: Prentice-Hall, 1937.

New York City

Arian, Asher. *Changing New York City Politics*. New York: Routledge, 1991.

Auletta, Ken. *The Streets Were Paved with Gold*. New York: Random House, 1979.

Bailey, Robert W. *The Crisis Regime: The M.A.C., the E.F.C.B., and the Political Impact of the New York City Financial Crisis*. Albany: State University of New York Press, 1984.

Benjamin, Gerald, and Charles Brecher, eds. *The Two New Yorks: State–City Relations in the Changing Federal System*. New York: Russell Sage Foundation, 1988.

Brecher, Charles, and Raymond D. Horton. *Power Failure: New York City Politics and Policy since 1960*. New York: Oxford University Press, 1993.

Brecher, Charles, and Raymond D. Horton, eds. *Setting Municipal Priorities: American Cities and the New York Experience*. New York: New York University Press, 1984.

Fuchs, Ester. *Mayors and Money: Fiscal Policy in New York and Chicago*. Chicago: University of Chicago Press, 1993.

Mauro, Frank, and Gerald Benjamin. *Reconstructing the New York City Government: The Reemergence of Municipal Reform*. New York: Academy of Political Science, 1989.

Mollenkopf, John H., and Manuel Castells, eds. *Dual City: Restructuring New York*. New York: Russell Sage Foundation, 1991.

Riordan, William. *Plunkitt of Tammany Hall*. New York: Dutton, 1963.

Sayre, Wallace S., and Herbert Kaufman. *Governing New York City*. New York: Russell Sage Foundation, 1960.

Sassen, Saskia. *Global City: New York, London, Tokyo*. Princeton: Princeton University Press, 1991.

Local Government

Frederickson, H. George. *Power, Public Opinion, and Policy in a Metropolitan Community; A Case Study of Syracuse, New York*. New York: Praeger, 1973.

Kennedy, William. *O Albany!* New York: Viking, 1983.

Miller, Robert H. *Politics Is People*. New York: James H. Heineman, 1962.

New York State Department of State, Division of Information Services. *An Introduction to Local Government in New York State*. Albany, 1985.

Notes

CHAPTER ONE

1 David M. Ellis, *New York: State and City* (Ithaca: Cornell University Press, 1979), p. 200.

2 Wendell Tripp, *Coming and Becoming: Pluralism in New York State History* (Cooperstown NY: New York State Historical Association, 1991), p. 79.

3 Emma Lazarus, "The New Colossus," in Ann Sanford, ed., *The Women Poets in English* (New York: McGraw-Hill, 1972), p. 141.

4 Richard D. Alba and Katherine Trent, "Population," in Jeryl L. Mumpower and Warren F. Ilchman, *New York State in the Year 2000* (Albany: State University of New York Press, 1988), p. 37.

5 David N. Dinkins, *Inauguration Message*, 1 January 1990.

6 Nathan Glazer and Daniel Patrick Moynihan, *Beyond the Melting Pot: The Negroes, Puerto Ricans, Jews, Italians, and Irish of New York City* (Cambridge: M.I.T. Press, 1963).

7 See Alba and Trent, "Population," pp. 89–91.

8 Sam Roberts, "New York Exports Its Talent as a Migration Tide Turns," *New York Times*, 6 March 1994, p. 36A.

9 Ellis, *New York: State and City*, p. 49.

10 Nonwhite includes black, American Indian, Inuit, Aleut, Asian, Pacific Islander, nonwhite Hispanic, and other races.

11 The New York City suburban ring counties are Nassau, Suffolk, Rockland, Putnam, and Westchester.

12 Heather Miller, "Al D'Amato: New York's Political Culture," in Jonathan Bernstein, Adrienne Jamieson, and Christine Trost, eds., *Campaigning for Congress: Politicians at Home and in Washington* (Berkeley CA: Institute of Governmental Studies, 1995), p. 51.

13 With few exceptions, New York's metropolitan areas are defined as Metropolitan Statistical Areas, i.e., containing a total MSA population of 100,000 or more and at least one city with 50,000 or more inhabitants, or a Census Bureau–defined "urbanized area" of at least 50,000 inhabitants. The exceptions are New York City, Poughkeepsie (Dutchess County), Nassau-Suffolk, and Newburgh, which are Primary Metropolitan Statistical Areas. A PMSA must contain a large urbanized county (or cluster of counties that demonstrate very strong economic and social links) and must have close ties to other portions of the larger area, i.e., the Consolidated Metropolitan Statistical Area. A CMSA contains more than 1.0 million population and two or more PMSAS.

14 Harold W. Thompson, *New York State Folktales, Legends, and Ballads* (New York: Dover, 1967), p. 286.

15 Washington Irving, *Tales of a Traveler* (New York: Maynard, Merrill, 1895).

16 Thompson, *New York State Folktales*, p. 26.

17 James Fenimore Cooper, *The Leatherstocking Saga* (New York: Pantheon Books, 1954).

18 Arthur G. Adams, ed., *The Hudson River in Literature: An Anthology* (Albany: State University of New York Press, 1980), p. 65.

19 Thompson, *New York State Folktales*, pp. 102–4.

20 English mercantilism, as practiced during the seventeenth and eighteenth centuries, was predicated on the assumption that England's national power and wealth depended upon its development as a strong maritime and commercial nation; thus, England constantly sought to increase its exports so as to achieve a favorable balance of trade. The role of the colonies was to "supplement, rather than compete with, the economy of the mother state." See Michael Kammen, *Empire and Interest: The American Colonies and the Politics of Mercantilism* (New York: Cornell University Press, 1970), p. 18. As elaborated by Kammen, the system worked to the advantage of both England and the colonies until the 1740s.

21 David M. Ellis, James A. Frost, and William B. Fink, *New York: The Empire State*, 3d ed. (Englewood Cliffs NJ: Prentice-Hall, 1969), p. 438.

22 Ellis, *New York: State and City*, p. 75.

23 Miller, "Al D'Amato," p. 50.

24 Miller, "Al D'Amato," p. 49.

25 Edward I. Koch, *Mayor: An Autobiography* (New York: Warner Books, 1985), p. 348.

26 Carl Carmer quoted in Ellis, *New York: State and City*, p. 24.

27 Frederick Jackson Turner quoted in Ellis, *New York: State and City*, p. 50.

28 Ellis, *New York: State and City*, p. 50.

29 Ellis, *New York: State and City*, p. 5.

30 Ellis, *New York: State and City*, p. 3.

31 Daniel J. Elazar, *The American Mosaic: The Impact of Space, Time, and Culture on American Politics* (Boulder CO: Westview Press, 1994), p. 55.

32 Elazar, *American Mosaic*, p. 56.

33 Daniel J. Elazar, *American Federalism: A View from the States* (New York: Harper & Row, 1984), p. 123.

34 Elazar, *American Federalism*, p. 126.

35 Elazar, *American Mosaic*, p. 57.

36 Ellis, *New York: State and City*, p. 118.

37 Ellis, *New York: State and City*, p. 118.

38 Ellis, *New York: State and City*, p. 117.

39 Peter D. McClelland and Alan L. Magdovitz, *Crisis in the Making: The Political Economy of New York since 1945* (New York: Cambridge University Press, 1981), p. 15.

40 McClelland and Magdovitz, *Crisis in the Making*, p. 15.

41 Glen Yago et al., "Economic Structure," in Mumpower and Ilchman, *New York State*, p. 210.

42 Matthew P. Drennan, "The Economy," in Gerald Benjamin and Charles Brecher, eds., *The Two New Yorks: State–City Relations in the Changing Federal System* (New York: Russell Sage Foundation, 1989), pp. 55–56.

43 Drennan, "The Economy," p. 57.

44 Mario M. Cuomo, *State of New York Annual Budget Message, 1990–1991* (Albany: State of New York, 1989), p. M8.

45 Mario M. Cuomo, *Message to the Legislature, 1994* (Albany: Office of the Governor, 5 January 1994), p. 2.

46 George E. Pataki, *Message to the Legislature, 1995* (Albany: Office of the Governor, 4 January 1995), p. 13.

47 Pataki, *Message to the Legislature, 1995*, p. 1.

48 David M. Ellis, James A. Frost, Harold C. Syrett, and Harry J. Carman, *A Short History of New York State* (Ithaca: Cornell University Press, 1957), p. 199.

49 One hundred forty-six women, mainly girls, were killed in that fire "either from being burned or from jumping from high windows. The chief cause of the heavy mortality, in addition to fright, was discovered to be locked doors." Recommendations of the Factory Investigation Commission led to "not only a new set of labor laws, but the creation of the State Industrial Commission with broad powers." See New York State Historical Association, *History of the State of New York*, vol. 10 (New York: Columbia University Press, 1937), p. 77. For elaboration of the growth of labor legislation in New York, see pp. 73–93.

50 Ellis et al., *Short History of New York State*, p. 477, 483.

51 See Sarah F. Liebschutz, *Bargaining under Federalism: Contemporary New York* (Albany: State University of New York Press, 1991), pp. 31–32.

52 See Lois Wilson and Joan Gavrilik, "Education Aid in New York State: Targeting Issues and Measures," *Publius* 19 (spring 1989): 95–112; and David R. Morgan and John P. Pelissero, "Interstate Variation in the Allocation of State Aid to Schools," *Publius* 19 (spring 1989): 113–26.

53 Sarah F. Liebschutz and Irene Lurie, "New York," in Richard P. Nathan and Fred C. Doolittle, eds., *Reagan and the States* (Princeton NJ: Princeton University Press, 1997), p. 207.

54 Elazar, *American Mosaic*, p. 220.

55 Elazar, *American Mosaic*, p. 233.

56 Elazar, *American Mosaic*, p. 232, 230.

57 Citizens Budget Commission, *New York State's Road to Fiscal Soundness* (New York, 1989), p. 10.

CHAPTER TWO

The author appreciates the research assistance of Mary Hussong-Kallen in the preparation of this chapter.

1 Ellis, *New York: State and City*, p. 204.

2 Milton M. Klein, "Shaping the American Tradition: The Microcosm of Colonial New York," in Tripp, *Coming and Becoming*, p. 23.

3 Klein, "Shaping the American Tradition," p. 23 (emphasis added).

4 Ellis, *New York: State and City*, p. 182.

5 Ellis, *New York: State and City*, pp. 59–60.

6 Ellis, *New York: State and City*, p. 60.

7 David Ellis, *New York State: Gateway to America* (Northridge CA: Windsor, 1988), pp. 71–72.

8 Ellis, *New York State: Gateway*, p. 75.

9 Glazer and Moynihan, *Beyond the Melting Pot*, p. 222.

10 Glazer and Moynihan, *Beyond the Melting Pot*, pp. 226–27.

11 Glazer and Moynihan, *Beyond the Melting Pot*, p. 227.

12 Mary Beth Norton et al., *A People and a Nation: A History of the United States*, 3d ed., vol. 1 (Boston: Houghton Mifflin, 1990), p. 343, 342.

13 Norton et al., *People and a Nation*, pp. 343–44.

14 Norton et al., *People and a Nation*, pp. 344–45.

15 Nancy Hewitt, *Women's Activism and Social Change: Rochester, New York, 1822–1872* (Ithaca: Cornell University Press, 1984), p. 19.

16 Hewitt, *Women's Activism*, pp. 17, 40, 252, 256.

17 Hewitt, *Women's Activism*, p. 160.

18 Ellis et al., *Short History of New York State*, p. 309.

19 Ellis et al., *Short History of New York State*, p. 312.

20 Warren Moscow, *Politics in the Empire State* (New York: Alfred Knopf, 1948), p. 132.

21 David L. Cingranelli, "New York: Powerful Groups and Powerful Parties," in Ronald J. Hrebenar and Clive S. Thomas, eds., *Interest Group Politics in the Northeastern States* (University Park: Pennsylvania State University Press, 1993), p. 255.

22 Paul A. Smith, "E Pluribus Unum," in Alan Rosenthal and Maureen Moakley, eds., *The Political Life of the American States* (New York: Praeger, 1984), p. 258.

23 Moscow, *Politics in the Empire State*, p. 203.

24 Cingranelli, "New York," p. 254.

25 New York Temporary State Commission on Lobbying, *1993 Annual Report to the Governor and Legislature* (Albany, December 1993).

26 James Dao, "Philip Morris Tops List of Bid Lobbying Spenders," *New York Times*, 24 March 1994, p. B12.

27 James Dao, "Once Again, Record Levels of Lobbying," *New York Times*, 16 March 1995, p. B8.

28 Clifford J. Levy, "Huge Rise in Spending on State Lobbying," *New York Times*, 14 March 1996, p. B1.

29 Cingranelli, "New York," pp. 265, 266, 268.

30 New York's interest group system is categorized as "complementary," i.e., "where groups tend to have to work in conjunction with or are constrained by other aspects of the political system," such as parties. See Clive S. Thomas, "The Changing Nature of Interest-Group Activity in the Northeast," in Hrebenar and Thomas, *Interest Group Politics*, pp. 383–84.

31 Cingranelli, "New York," p. 271.

CHAPTER THREE

1 Peter J. Galie, *Ordered Liberty: A Constitutional History of New York* (New York: Fordham University Press, 1996), p. 2.

2 Galie, *Ordered Liberty*, p. 9.

3 Galie, *Ordered Liberty*, p. 5.

4 Galie, *Ordered Liberty*, p. 175.

5 See Galie, *Ordered Liberty*, passim, for elaboration of these points.

6 Galie, *Ordered Liberty*, p. 263.

7 For details on the Council of Revision, see Frank W. Prescott and Joseph F. Zimmerman, *The Politics of the Veto of Legislation in New York State*, vol. 1 (Washington DC: University Press of America, 1980), pp. 19–72. See also J. M. Gitterman, "The Council of Appointment in New York," *Political Science Quarterly* 7 (March 1892): 80–115.

8 The constitution of 1894 principally incorporated the 1846 constitution and its amendments in a new document.

9 Constitution of New York, art. 7, § 11.

10 Constitution of New York, art. 7, §§ 14, 18–19.

11 Constitution of New York, art. 7, §§ 1–6.

12 *Baker v. Carr*, 369 U.S. 186 (1962), and *Reynolds v. Sims*, 377 U.S. 533 (1964).

13 Galie, *Ordered Liberty*, p. 332.

14 Constitution of New York, art. 8, §§ 2.

15 Constitution of New York, art. 10, §§ 1.

16 Joseph F. Zimmerman, *State-Local Relations: A Partnership Approach*, 2d ed. (Westport CT: Praeger, 1995).

17 Galie, *Ordered Liberty*, p. 350.

18 Temporary New York State Commission on Constitutional Revision, *Effective Government Now for the New Century* (Albany: Rockefeller Institute of Government, 1995), p. 11.

19 Temporary Commission, *Effective Government*, p. 22.

20 "Pataki on the Issues," *Empire State Report* 20 (August 1994): 38.

21 Galie, *Ordered Liberty*, p. 352.

22 Galie, *Ordered Liberty*, p. 352.

23 Galie, *Ordered Liberty*, p. 351.

24 *Model State Constitution*, 6th ed. (New York: National Municipal League, 1962). The league has been renamed the National Civic League and moved its offices to Denver.

25 Joseph F. Zimmerman, *Participatory Democracy: Populism Revived* (New York: Praeger, 1986).

26 Constitution of New York, art. 4, § 6. A casting vote is a vote to break a tie.

27 Constitution of New York, art. 4, § 5.

28 Constitution of New York, art. 6, § 24.

29 Jonathan Salant, "Tug-of-War Begins on Betting," *Times Union* (Albany), 18 January 1984, p. A-1.

30 Constitution of New York, art. 5, § 1.

31 Constitution of New York, art. 4, § 1.

32 Constitution of New York, art. 11, § 2, and art. 5, § 4.

33 State of New York, Executive Order no. 77, 23 June 1973. The order is published in the *Public Papers of Nelson A. Rockefeller*, 1973 (Albany: State of New York, n.d.), pp. 996–97.

34 Karen Nelis, "Critics Say Politics Is Clouding the Effectiveness of the Regents," *Times Union* (Albany), 4 April 1993, p. A-8.

35 "Pataki on the Issues," p. 38.

CHAPTER FOUR

1 Stanley Elkins and Eric McKitrick, *The Age of Federalism: The Early American Republic, 1788–1800* (New York: Oxford University Press, 1993), p. 188.

2 Stephen Schechter, ed., *The Reluctant Pillar: New York and the Adoption of the Federal Constitution* (Albany: New York State Commission on the Bicentennial of the United States Constitution, 1987) p. 117.

3 Robert S. McElvaine, *Mario Cuomo: A Biography* (New York: Charles Scribner's Sons, 1988), p. 3.

4 McClelland and Magdovitz, *Crisis in the Making*, p. 15.

5 Alan Rosenthal, *Governors and Legislatures: Contending Powers* (Washington DC: CQ Press), p. 25.

6 Archibald Cox, *The Court and the Constitution* (Boston: Houghton Mifflin, 1987), p. 87.

7 Cox, *Court and the Constitution*, p. 87.

8 198 U.S. 45.

9 198 U.S. 62.

10 Cox, *Court and the Constitution*, p. 131.

11 403 U.S. 713.

12 Cox, *Court and the Constitution*, p. 226.

13 Cox, *Court and the Constitution*, p. 227.

14 403 U.S. 715.

15 Cox, *Court and the Constitution*, p. 226.

16 505 U.S. 144.

17 David M. O'Brien, "The Rehnquist Court and Federal Preemption: In Search of a Theory," *Publius* 23 (fall 1993): 20.

18 505 U.S. 162.

19 O'Brien, "Rehnquist Court and Federal Preemption," p. 19.

20 Robert C. Byrd, *The Senate, 1789–1989: Addresses on the History of the United States Senate*, vol. 1 (Washington DC: U.S. Government Printing Office, 1988), p. 473. Senator Byrd served as both majority leader (1977–80, 1987–88) and minority leader (1980–86) of the U.S. Senate.

21 Byrd, *Senate*, p. 474.

22 Byrd, *Senate*, pp. 473–74.

23 William H. Riker, *The Art of Political Manipulation* (New Haven: Yale University Press, 1986), p. 11.

24 Riker, *Art of Political Manipulation*, pp. 12–13.

25 Senator Javits served as ranking Republican on the Senate Foreign Affairs Committee.

26 Heather Miller, "Al D'Amato: New York Political Culture," in Jonathan Bernstein, Adrienne Jamieson, and Christine Trost, *Campaigning for Congress: Politicians at Home and in Washington* (Berkeley CA: Institute of Governmental Studies Press, 1995), p. 59.

27 Miller, "Al D'Amato," p. 58; Sidney Blumenthal, "To the Pennsylvania Station," *New Yorker*, 14 March 1994, 70.

28 Among the issues where Senator Moynihan's effectiveness as advocate for New York has been prominently demonstrated are the retention of deductibility of state and local taxes from federal taxation in 1986, the retroactive reimbursement of New York Thruway construction expenditures in 1991 with federal transportation funds, and the transformation of New York City's historic post office into the new Pennsylvania Station replacing the one razed in 1963. For analyses of these issues, see, respectively, Liebschutz, *Bargaining*, chap. 3; Daniel Patrick Moynihan, "History Will Judge New York City by Its Airport Rail Link," *New York Times*, 6 June 1995, p. A28; and Blumenthal, "To the Pennsylvania Station," pp. 70–73.

29 Miller, "Al D'Amato," pp. 54, 60, 63.

30 Lloyd Grove, "D'Amato's Pork Barrel Polka," *Washington Post*, 19 October 1992, p. B1.

31 Philip Weiss, "The Senator Cannot Help Being Himself," *New York Times Magazine*, 3 March 1996, cover.

32 See Kirk Johnson, "Moynihan and D'Amato: A Collegial Couple," *New York Times*, 15 March 1993, p. B1.

33 Clay Richards and Carol Richards, "New York's Helpless Giant on the Hill," *Empire State Report* 1 (April 1975): 149.

34 See Sarah F. Liebschutz, "Assessing New York's D.C. Power," *Empire State Report* 19 (August 1993): 41–44, for an analysis of New York's status in the 103rd Congress.

35 Liebschutz, *Bargaining under Federalism*, p. 59.

36 See Liebschutz, "Assessing New York's D.C. Power," pp. 41–44.

37 Timothy J. Conlon, James D. Riggle, and Donna E. Schwartz, "Deregulating Federalism? The Politics of Mandate Reform in the 104th Congress," *Publius* 25 (summer 1995): 23.

38 See Conlon, Riggle, and Schwartz, "Deregulating Federalism," pp. 23–39.

39 In general, liberal Democrats "proved to be the most consistent supporters of efforts to weaken the mandate-reform bill—a response that is unsurprising given the origins of many of the environmental, health, and safety laws that could be weakened by the new law." See Conlon, Riggle, and Schwartz, "Deregulating Federalism," p. 35.

40 Liebschutz, *Bargaining under Federalism*, p. 67.

41 This case is presented in detail in Liebschutz, *Bargaining under Federalism*, chap. 5.

42 Liebschutz, *Bargaining under Federalism*, p. 86.

43 Liebschutz, *Bargaining under Federalism*, p. 65.

44 Liebschutz, *Bargaining under Federalism*, p. 66.

45 This case is presented in detail in Liebschutz, *Bargaining under Federalism*, chap. 6.

46 See Liebschutz, *Bargaining under Federalism*, for elaboration of all of these points.

47 John Kincaid, "From Cooperation to Coercion in American Federalism: Housing, Fragmentation and Preemption, 1790–1992," *Journal of Law and Politics* 9 (winter 1993): 333–430.

48 Kincaid, "From Cooperation to Coercion," p. 421.

49 See U.S. Advisory Commission on Intergovernmental Relations, *Regulatory Federalism: Process, Impact and Reform* (Washington DC: ACIR, 1984), and *Federal Regulation of State and Local Governments: Regulatory Federalism—A Decade Later* (Washington DC: ACIR, 1992).

50 See Timothy J. Conlon and David R. Beam, "Federal Mandates: The Record of Reform and Future Prospects," *Intergovernmental Perspective* 18 (fall 1992): 7–11, 15.

51 See Liebschutz, *Bargaining under Federalism*, for case studies of responses to these federal mandates.

52 Jeff Jones, "A Soluble Solution," *Empire State Report* 21 (May 1995): 50.

53 Andrew C. Revkin, "Chasing a Deal on Water with a Few Pitchers of Beer," *New York Times*, 5 November 1995, p. I44.

54 Jones, "Soluble Solution," p. 43.

55 "At Last, a Watershed Agreement," *New York Times*, 3 November 1995, p. A28.

56 Revkin, "Chasing a Deal," p. 44.

57 Andrew C. Revkin, "Agreement on Watershed Plan Is Praised," *New York Times*, 11 September 1996, p. B3.

58 Jeff Plungis, "From the Schoolhouse," *Empire State Report* 21 (November 1995): 24. See also Senator Moynihan's annual reports, *New York State and the Federal Fisc*, published since 1977.

CHAPTER FIVE

1 Robert J. Spitzer, "Third Parties in New York," in Jeffrey M. Stonecash, John K. White, and Peter W. Colby, eds., *Governing New York State* (Albany: State University of New York Press, 1994), p. 107.

2 Chao-Chi Shan, "The Decline of Electoral Competition in New York State Senate Elections, 1950–88" (Ph.D. diss., Dept. of Political Science, Syracuse University, 1991), p. 45.

3 Jeffrey M. Stonecash, "An Eroding Base: The GOP's Upstate Foundation Is Showing Some Cracks," *Empire State Report* 12 (May 1986): 53–58.

4 The data were compiled by Gerald Wright, University of Indiana, and Robert Brown, University of Mississippi. I greatly appreciate their willingness to share their data with me.

5 Low Income was defined in the *New York Times* polls as less than $12,500. High income was defined as above $50,000. Robert D. Brown, "Party Cleavages and Policy Outputs in the American States" (paper presented at the annual meeting of the American Political Science Association, Chicago, 3–6 September 1992).

6 Other analyses report similar findings. See John K. White, "New York's Selective Majority," in Maureen Moakley, ed., *Party Realignment and State Politics* (Columbus: Ohio State University Press, 1992), p. 217; and Jeffrey M. Stonecash, "Political Parties and Partisan Conflict," in Stonecash, White, and Colby, *Governing New York State*, p. 89.

7 Ellis, "Upstate vs. Downstate," *New York: State and City*, 180–99.

8 Stuart Rice, *Quantitative Methods in Politics* (New York: Alfred Knopf, 1928).

9 Jeffrey M. Stonecash, " 'Split' Constituencies and the Impact of Party Control," *Social Science History* 16, no. 3 (fall 1992): 455–77.

10 Ralph Straetz and Frank Munger, *New York Politics* (New York: New York University Press, 1960).

11 Jeffrey M. Stonecash, "New York," in Leroy Hardy, Alan Heslop, and George S. Blair, eds., *Redistricting in the 1980s* (Claremont CA: Rose Institute of State and Local Government, 1993), pp. 185–90.

12 For an analysis of differences in the 1960s and 1970s, see Alan G. Hevesi, *Legislative Politics in New York* (New York: Praeger, 1975).

13 Public Policy Institute, *The Comeback State* (Albany: Business Council, 1994).

14 Diana Dwyre, Mark O'Gorman, Jeffrey M. Stonecash, and Rosalie Young, "Disorganized Politics and the Have-Nots: Politics and Taxes in New York and California," *Polity* 27, no. 1 (fall 1994): 25–47.

15 Stonecash, "Political Parties and Partisan Conflict," p. 90.

16 Ken Auletta, "Profiles: Governor Mario Cuomo, Part II," *New Yorker*, 16 April 1984, pp. 1–23.

17 See also Gerald Benjamin, "The Political Relationship," in Benjamin and Brecher, *Two New Yorks*.

18 Judith Stein, "The Birth of Liberal Republicanism in New York State, 1932–1938" (Ph.D. diss., Yale University, 1968); Jeffrey M. Stonecash, "Political Cleavage in Gubernatorial and Legislative Elections: Party Competition in New York, 1970–82," *Western Political Quarterly* 42, no. 1 (March 1989): 69–81; Stonecash, " 'Split' Constituencies," pp. 455–77; and White, "New York's Selective Majority," pp. 210–24.

19 Lee M. Miringoff and Barbara L. Varvalho, *The Cuomo Factor* (Poughkeepsie: Marist Institute for Public Opinion, 1986).

20 James Traub, "Dollface," *New Yorker*, 15 January 1996, p. 34.

21 A 1985 statewide survey conducted at the Maxwell School, Syracuse University, showed this same pattern across the state. That survey differed in that people were asked to indicate the party with which they identify. The *Herald-American* survey relied on the enrollment chosen when registering. Since identification may differ from enrollment, the study using enrollment figures is used here.

22 The ideal way to assess the existence of split-ticket voting would be to have data on the individual level across years, which indicates the proportion of voters who choose opposing party candidates. Such data do not exist. It is possible to achieve a somewhat equivalent analysis by using counties as the unit of analysis. Legislative results have been reported in *The Legislative Manual of New York* since 1900. The results are presented by legislative district and then by county within districts. It is possible to construct a county-by-county analysis of partisan voting for assembly and senate races. This approach is limited in that some counties represent only a part of a district whereas others represent combinations of several or numerous districts (particularly in New York City and other large urban areas). Nonetheless, this is the only feasible way to undertake a historical analysis of party and split-ticket voting over any period of time. Using these data, it is possible to calculate for each county the extent to which the partisan vote for each house is the same by subtracting the partisan vote for one house from the partisan vote for the other house. If the two are the same, the difference will be zero. If the difference is zero across all counties, then it indicates that the electorate is voting essentially a straight party ticket. (The aggregate data may conceal some ticket splitting, but this approach provides a reasonably good estimate.) If the difference between assembly and senate votes is high in a county, it suggests a great deal of ticket splitting. If the difference is high across all counties, then it suggests that ticket splitting is a widespread practice in state legislative elections.

Those calculations were made for assembly and senate races from 1900 to 1990 for each county. The differences were expressed in terms of absolute scores (a difference of –12.5 percent becomes a difference of 12.5 and +12.5 becomes 12.5) to allow a calculation of average differences across the state. Once the difference was determined for each county, the average of the scores across all counties was calculated. The results give an indication of the divergence of assembly and senate results over the years.

23 Chao-Chi Shan and Jeffrey M. Stonecash, "Legislative Resources and Electoral Margins: The New York State Senate, 1950–1990," *Legislative Studies Quarterly* 19, no. 1 (February 1994): 79–93.

24 Roy V. Peel, *The Political Clubs of New York City* (New York: G. P. Putnam's, 1935); Norman M. Adler and Blanche Davis Blank, *Political Clubs in New York* (New York: Praeger, 1975); and Jerome Krase, *Ethnicity and Machine Politics* (Lanham MD: University Press of America, 1991).

25 Robert H. Connery and Gerald Benjamin, *Rockefeller of New York: Executive Power in the Statehouse* (Ithaca: Cornell University Press, 1979); and Hevesi, *Legislative Politics in New York.*

26 David R. Mayhew, *Placing Parties in American Politics* (Princeton: Princeton University Press, 1986).

27 Jeffrey M. Stonecash, "Working at the Margins: Campaign Finance and Party Strategy in New York Assembly Elections," *Legislative Studies Quarterly* 13, no. 4 (November 1988): 477–93; Jeffrey M. Stonecash, "Campaign Finance in New York Senate Elections," *Legislative Studies Quarterly* 15, no. 2 (May 1990): 247–62; and Jeffrey M. Stonecash, "Where's the Party: Changing State Party Organizations," *American Politics Quarterly* 20, no. 3 (July 1992): 326–44.

28 Jeffrey M. Stonecash and Sara E. Keith, "Maintaining a Political Party: Providing and Withdrawing Campaign Funds," *Party Politics* 2, no. 3 (1996): 313–28.

29 Cornelius P. Cotter, James L. Gibson, John F. Bibby, and Robert J. Huckshorn, *Party Organizations in American Politics* (New York: Praeger, 1984), pp. 51–56.

30 Daniel M. Shea, "The Myth of Party Adaptation: Linkages between Legislative Campaign Committees and Party" (paper presented at the annual meeting of the New York State Political Science Association, New York City, 1991.

CHAPTER SIX

1 Interview with Robert Herman, in Gerald Benjamin and Robert T. Nakamura, *The Modern New York State Legislature: Redressing the Balance* (Albany: Rockefeller Institute, 1991), pp. 239–44.

2 Based on interviews and discussions with legislators in the mid-1980s when this author, Jeffrey M. Stonecash, began working in the legislature and on stories appearing in the *New York Times* during this period.

3 Richard Lehne, *Legislating Reapportionment in New York* (New York: National Municipal League, 1971), p. 24.

4 Kwang S. Shin and John S. Jackson III, "Membership Turnover in U.S. State Legislatures: 1931–1976," *Legislative Studies Quarterly* 4, no. 1 (February 1979): 95–104.

5 Jeffrey M. Stonecash, "The Legislature: The Emergence of an Equal Branch," in Stonecash, White, and Colby, *Governing New York State*, p. 154.

6 Jeffrey M. Stonecash, "The Pursuit and Retention of Legislative Office in New York, 1870–1990: Reconsidering Sources of Change," *Polity* 26, no. 2 (winter 1993): 301–15.

7 If there were five new sessions during a decade, then there would be five times in which an assessment would be made as to how many legislators were starting with no prior experience. For example, with five sessions in the assembly there would be (5 × 150) 750 beginnings within the decade; the percentage of first-time legislators would be based on those 750 beginnings.

8 The average length of stay for the last decade is low because most of the legislators elected during the 1980s are still there, so they have not yet completed their length of stay. Some related evidence is presented in Benjamin and Nakamura, *Modern New York State Legislature*, pp. xv, xvi.

9 The ages when first elected are calculated by using information from the *New York Red Book* (Albany: New York Legal Publishing, published bienially), which lists the years in which legislators were elected. Most legislators indicate their birth date in their individual biography, so it is possible to calculate their age when first elected.

10 Benjamin and Nakamura, *Modern New York State Legislature*, p. xviii.

11 Jeffrey M. Stonecash and Rebecca Lo-Belky, "The Decline of Private Sector Experience among New York Senators, 1890–1990," *Comparative State Politics* 16, no. 4 (August 1995): 14–24. The published biographies of each senator were reviewed to determine if the senator listed any private or public sector job.

12 Interview with Warren Anderson, temporary president of the senate, 1972–88, p. 69, and interview with Stanley Fink, Speaker of the assembly, 1979–86, p. 119, in Benjamin and Nakamura, *Modern New York State Legislature*.

13 Stuart Witt, "Modernization of the Legislature," in Robert Connery and Gerald Benjamin, *Governing New York State: The Rockefeller Years* (New York: Academy of Political Science, 1974); and Alan G. Hevesi, "The Renewed Legislature," in John K. White and Peter Colby, eds., *New York State Today*, 2d ed. (Albany: State University of New York Press, 1989), pp. 167–68.

14 Anderson interview, p. 60; interview with Perry Duryea, Speaker of the assembly, 1969–74; and Fink interview, pp. 115–18; all interviews appear in Benjamin and Nakamura, *Modern New York State Legislature*.

15 Perry Duryea, "Toward a More Effective Legislature" (speech delivered to New York State Assembly, Albany, 14 December 1973).

16 New York State Bar Association, *Toward a More Effective Legislature* (Albany, 1975).

17 Inflationary adjustments are made by dividing expenditure figures by the Consumer Price Index, using 1967 as the base year. This means that the price level in that year = 100. Because the time series involved runs from 1900 to 1995, the CPI was adjusted so 1995 would be the base year. This puts past budgets in terms of current prices and makes a comparison with the past easier.

18 Jeffrey M. Stonecash, "The Pursuit and Retention of Legislative Office," in New York, 1870–1990: Reconsidering Sources of Change," *Polity* 26, no. 2 (winter 1993), pp. 301–15.

19 Alan P. Balutis, "Legislative Staffing: A View from the States," in James J. Heaphy and Alan P. Balutis, *Legislative Staffing* (New York: Wiley, 1975), pp. 106–37; and Alan P. Balutis, "The Budgetary Process in New York State: The Role of the Legislative Staff," in Alan P. Balutis, ed., *The Political Pursestrings: The Role of the Legislature in the Budgetary Process* (Beverly Hills CA: Sage, 1975), pp. 139–72.

20 Arthur J. Kremer, "The Resurgent Legislature in New York," *National Civic Review*, April 1978; and Hevesi, "Renewed Legislature," p. 168.

21 Robert P. Weber, "The Speaker of the Assembly: Party Leadership in New York" (Ph.D. diss., University of Rochester, 1975); Hevesi, *Legislative Politics in New York*; and John J. Pitney Jr. "Leaders and Rules in the New York State Senate," *Legislative Studies Quarterly* 7, no. 4 (November 1982): 491–506.

22 These conclusions are based on the conversations of this author, Jeffrey M. Stonecash, with legislators over the last several years while serving as professor-in-residence in the assembly.

23 Jeffrey M. Stonecash, *The Proposal and Disposal of Legislation in the New York Legislature* (Albany: Assembly Intern Program, 1989).

24 *New York Times*, 1 July 1985, sec. 2, p. 2, col. 5.

25 Stonecash, "Working at the Margins," pp. 477–93; Stonecash, "Campaign Finance," pp. 247–62; and Stonecash, "Where's the Party," pp. 326–44.

26 Stonecash and Keith, "Maintaining a Political Party."

27 Anderson interview, in Benjamin and Nakamura, *Modern New York State Legislature*, p. 60.

28 Gerald Benjamin, "Budget Battles between the Governor and Legislature: A Perennial New York Conflict," *Comparative State Politics Newsletter* 7, no. 4 (August 1986): 13–16.

29 Stephanie A. Miner, "The Roots of Budgetary Evil in New York" (Department of Political Science, Syracuse University, unpublished paper, January 1992).

30 Dwyre et al., "Disorganized Politics and the Have-Nots," pp. 25–47.

31 Roman Hedges, "Legislative Staff as Institutional Partisans: The Case of Tax Reform in New York," *Journal of Management Science and Policy Analysis* 7, no. 1 (fall 1989): 34–52.

32 Jeffrey M. Stonecash, "Political Development and Political Dialogue: The New York State Legislature" (paper delivered at the annual meeting of the New York State Political Science Association, Albany, April 1986); and Jeffrey M. Stonecash, "Why Rush to Reform," *Empire State Report* 14 (April 1988): 43–44.

CHAPTER SEVEN

1 Nelson A. Rockefeller, *Public Papers of Nelson A. Rockefeller* (Albany: Office of the Governor, 1967), p. 209.

2 Joseph F. Zimmerman, *The Government and Politics of New York State* (New York: New York University Press, 1981), p. 186.

3 Gerald Benjamin, "The Governorship," in Colby and White, *New York State Today*, p. 145.

4 Benjamin, "Governorship," p. 145.

5 Benjamin, "Governorship," p. 145.

6 Benjamin, "Governorship," p. 145.

7 Appointments that do not require the consent of the senate are the director of the Division of the Budget, the counsel to the governor, and other key staff members who serve at the pleasure of the governor.

8 Linda Greenhouse, "Politics and Little More Stopped Mr. Schwartz," *New York Times*, 11 April 1976, sec. 4, p. 6.

9 The most notable recent instance of rejection by the New York State Senate was its rejection in 1976 of Herman Schwartz, Governor Hugh Carey's nominee for chair of the Commission of Correction; the senate's action reflected the opposition of county sheriffs, "powerful political figures in suburban and upstate [Republican] counties," and "a feeling among [majority] Senate Republicans that they had been far too cooperative with [Democrat] Governor Carey in an election year." Greenhouse, "Politics and Little More," sec. 4, p. 6.

10 Paula Eldot, *Governor Alfred E. Smith: The Politician as Reformer* (New York: Garland Press, 1983), p. 65.

11 State of New York, Division of the Budget, *The Executive Budget in New York State: A Half-Century Perspective* (Albany, 1981), p. 77.

12 State of New York, *Executive Budget*, p. 51.

13 Zimmerman, *Government and Politics*, p. 197.

14 See Prescott and Zimmerman, *Politics of the Veto*, table 31, pp. 1169–70; and Zimmerman, *Government and Politics*, table 8.2, p. 202.

15 Zimmerman, *Government and Politics*, p. 147.

16 Zimmerman, *Government and Politics*, p. 203.

17 Gerald Benjamin and T. Norman Hurd, eds., *Making Experience Count: Managing Modern New York in the Carey Era* (Albany: Rockefeller Institute of Government, 1985), p. 248.

18 David Morrison, "The Legislatures in 3 States: A Farewell to Ignominy," *New York Times*, 11 April 1976, sec. 4, p. 6.

19 James Dao, "Albany Overrides a Veto by Pataki on Pay for Police," *New York Times*, 13 February 1996, p. A1.

20 See State of New York, Management Resources Project, *Governing the Empire State* (Albany, 1988), chap. 2, for elaboration of these points about the governor's office.

21 Robert J. Morgado, "Legacy of the Carey Years: An Insider's Perspective" (speech delivered to the Capital District Chapter, American Society for Public Administration, Albany, 23 September 1992).

22 Under Governor Cuomo, the four substantive areas or subcabinets were Criminal Justice, Economic Development, Health and Human Services, and Energy and the Environment.

23 Barry K. Beyer, *Thomas E. Dewey, 1937–1947: A Study in Political Leadership* (New York: Garland, 1979), p. 159.

24 Gerald Benjamin, "Governor Thomas E. Dewey: A Model of Leadership," *Rockefeller Institute Bulletin* (1992), p. 53.

25 Author (Sarah F. Liebschutz) interview with T. Norman Hurd, who succeeded John E. Burton as director of the budget in the last years of the Dewey administration, 24 October 1989.

26 See Ellis, *New York: State and City*, chap. 33.

27 Gerald Benjamin, "Nelson Rockefeller and the New York Governorship," in Gerald Benjamin and T. Norman Hurd, eds., *Rockefeller in Retrospect: The Governor's New York Legacy* (Albany: Rockefeller Institute of Government, 1984), pp. 299, 261.

28 Malcolm Wilson, "The Man and the Public Servant," in Benjamin and Hurd, *Rockefeller in Retrospect*, p. 33.

29 Wilson, "Man and the Public Servant," p. 13.

30 Wilson, "Man and the Public Servant," p. 262.

31 Wilson, "Man and the Public Servant," p. 68.

32 Nelson A. Rockefeller, *Message to the Legislature, 1973* (Albany, 3 January 1973), p. 4.

33 Advisory Commission on Intergovernmental Relations, *Measuring State Fiscal Capacity (M-156)* (Washington DC, 1987).

34 "The Carey Years" (publication for Tenth Anniversary Dinner, Nelson A. Rockefeller Institute of Government, Albany, 4 June 1992), p. 4.

35 Hugh L. Carey, *Message to the Legislature*, 8 January 1975, p. 4.

36 Hugh L. Carey, "Hugh L. Carey: The Transition," in Benjamin and Hurd, *Making Experience Count*, pp. 11, 16.

37 Gerald Benjamin, "The Carey Governorship," in Benjamin and Hurd, *Making Experience Count*, p. 237.

38 Benjamin, "Carey Governorship," p. 236.

39 See Benjamin and Hurd, *Making Experience Count*, chaps. 4 and 7, for amplification of these accomplishments.

40 See Sarah F. Liebschutz, "Economic Development Policy in New York," in Colby and White, *New York State Today*.

41 Benjamin, "Carey Governorship," pp. 241, 246, 247.

42 See Sarah F. Liebschutz and Irene Lurie, "Evolution in Federalism: The Reagan Program and Legislative Appropriation of Federal Grants in New York," *Public Budgeting and Finance* 4 (summer 1984): 24–41.

43 Benjamin, "Carey Governorship," p. 249.

44 Roy Bahl and William Duncombe, *Economic Growth and Fiscal Planning: New York in the 1990s* (New Brunswick NJ: Center for Urban Policy Research, 1991), p. 112.

45 Benjamin, "Carey Governorship," p. 248.

46 Kevin Sack, "Cuomo Ends an Era with a Message," *New York Times*, 31 December 1994, sec. 1, p. 28.

47 See McElvain, *Mario Cuomo*, for a detailed account of Cuomo's early life.

48 For Cuomo's recollections of the 1982 campaign, see Mario M. Cuomo, *Diaries of Mario M. Cuomo: The Campaign for Governor* (New York: Random House, 1984).

49 Mario M. Cuomo, *More than Words: The Speeches of Mario Cuomo* (New York: St. Martin's Press, 1993), pp. 9, 12.

50 "Cuomo on the Record: Interview Excerpts with the Governor," *New York Times*, 26 September 1994, p. B4.

51 Lee M. Miringoff and Barbara L. Carvalho, *The Cuomo Factor: Assessing the Appeal of New York's Governor* (Poughkeepsie NY: Marist Institute for Public Opinion, 1986), p. 4.

52 Elizabeth Kolbert, "After 12 Years in Spotlight Cuomo Is Still an Enigma," *New York Times*, 27 December 1994, p. A1.

53 Elizabeth Kolbert, "Cuomo Vetoes Driven by Pique and Fiscal Concern," *New York Times*, 11 June 1991, p. B6.

54 Kolbert, "Cuomo Vetoes," p. B6.

55 Cuomo, *More than Words*, pp. 23–30.

56 "Assessing Cuomo: Five Views," *New York Times*, 27 December 1994, p. B2.

57 Kolbert, "After 12 Years," p. A1.

58 U.S. Census Bureau, *State Government Finances* (Washington DC, 1986 and 1992).

59 Center for Governmental Research (Rochester NY), "New York State Is #1 in Taxes," *Close-up* 3 (June/July 1994): 1.

60 "Cuomo on the Record," p. B4.

61 Warren Moscow, *Politics in the Empire State* (New York: Alfred Knopf, 1948), p. 186.

62 Benjamin and Hurd, *Rockefeller in Retrospect*, p. 10.

63 Rosenthal, *Governors and Legislatures*, p. 1.

64 Steven D. Gold, in "Fiscal Woes Likely to Persist," *New York GFOA Newsletter* 13 (May 1991), a publication of the Government Finance Officers Association, argued that the growth of the service sector, the trend away from high income tax rates, and the sharp fall of new entrants into the labor force would cause all state tax revenue bases to slow in the 1990s.

65 Benjamin, "Governorship," p. 153.

CHAPTER EIGHT

1 Alexander Hamilton, James Madison, and John Jay, *The Federalist Papers*, no. 70, ed. Clinton Rossiter (New York: Mentor, 1961) p. 423.

2 State of New York, Division of the Budget, *Executive Budget, 1992–1993* (Albany, 1992), p. iii.

3 State of New York, *Executive Budget, 1992–1993*, p. 275.

4 Benjamin and Hurd, *Rockefeller in Retrospect*, p. 1.

5 Benjamin and Hurd, *Making Experience Count*, p. 1.

6 Benjamin and Hurd, *Making Experience Count*, p. 9.

7 See Alex Storozynski, "The State's Fiscal Abyss," *Empire State Report* 18 (January 1992): 27–30.

8 See Management Resources Project, *Governing the Empire State: An Insider's Guide* (Albany, 1988), chap. 3, for more details about the budget process.

9 See Management Resources Project, *Governing the Empire State*, chap. 4.

10 See Management Resources Project, *Governing the Empire State*, chap. 6.

11 State of New York, Division of the Budget, *Executive Budget, 1996–1997* (Albany, 1996), pp. 14, 16.

12 State of New York, *Executive Budget, 1992–1993*, p. 209.

13 State of New York, *Executive Budget, 1992–1993*, p. 198.

14 Donald Axelrod, *Shadow Government: The Hidden World of Public Authorities and How They Control $1 Trillion of Your Money* (New York: John Wiley, 1992), pp. 15–16.

15 State of New York, Division of the Budget, *Executive Budget, 1995–1996* (Albany, 1995), p. 425.

16 Axelrod, *Shadow Government*, p. 4.

17 Axelrod, *Shadow Government*, pp. 4, 5.

18 Axelrod, *Shadow Government*, p. 95.

19 State of New York, *Executive Budget, 1992–1993*, p. 510.

20 Axelrod, *Shadow Government*, p. 96.

21 Axelrod, *Shadow Government*, p. 123.

22 Elizabeth Kolbert, "Albany's Budget-Balancing 'One-Shots' Will Reverberate for Years to Come," *New York Times*, 21 April 1991, sec. 4, p. 18.

23 See Frank Pizzuro, "The Environmental Facilities Corporation," *Empire State Report* 17 (November 1991).

CHAPTER NINE

The author appreciates the helpful comments of Justin L. Vigdor, Esquire, past president of the New York State Bar Association, and the research assistance of Jeffrey D. Cook in the preparation of this chapter.

1 Cuomo, *Message to the Legislature, 1994*, p. 71.

2 George E. Pataki, *Message to the Legislature, 1996* (Albany: Office of the Governor, 3 January 1996), p. 17.

3 Justice Research Institute and National Center for State Courts, *New York State Courts: A Management Review* (Albany: Court Management Study Committee, 19 February 1993), p. 1.

4 Mario M. Cuomo, *State of New York Executive Budget, 1992–1993: Agency Presentations* (Albany: Division of the Budget, 1992), p. 249.

5 Pamela Lemov, "Judith Kaye: The Jurors' Jurist," *Governing* 9 (January 1996): 60.

6 Justice Research Institute, *New York State Courts*, p. 5.

7 Tom Goldstein, "Voters to Decide on Appointment of Judges," *New York Times*, 20 October 1977, p. B3.

8 Justice Research Institute, *New York State Courts*, p. 17.

9 Justice Research Institute, *New York State Courts*, p. 15. It should be noted, however, that the committee commended the financial management operations, labor relations, alternative dispute resolution programs, and statewide information services of the Unified Court System.

10 Mario M. Cuomo, "Real Reform: It's Time for a People's State Constitutional Convention: Special Message" (Albany NY: Office of the Governor, 1993).

11 As of 1994, nearly twenty states used some form of the Missouri Plan. In its pure form, the plan involves presentation of a slate of candidates by a nominating commission appointed by the governor. The governor selects a judge from the list; the judge, after each term of service, needs a simple majority of votes in a retention election to remain in office.

12 Litigants in criminal and civil cases may have their appeals heard by the Court of Appeals after a "final" judgment in certain cases has been rendered by a lower trial court. In other instances, litigants have an automatic right of appeal to the court, as in civil cases involving a substantial question of constitutionality of either the U.S. or New York State Constitutions, and in civil cases where there have been two dissenting justices on a question of law at the Appellate Division. All other litigants must petition the Court of Appeals or one of the four Appellate Divisions of the State Supreme Court to have their cases heard by the Court of Appeals. *Court of Appeals: State of New York* (Albany, 1993).

13 Goldstein, "Voters to Decide," p. B3.

14 Zimmerman, *Government and Politics*, pp. 285–286. See also the New York State Constitution, art. 6, § 1; and Sarah Lyall, "Panel Says It Won't Speed Up List of Choices for Judgeship," *New York Times*, 11 November 1992, pp. A1, B8.

15 Richard Dollinger, member of the New York State Senate and of the Judicial Committee, interview with author (Sarah F. Liebschutz), 13 July 1994.

16 Natacha Dykman, member of the Commission on Judicial Nomination (1981–90), interview with Jeffrey D. Cook, 1 March 1993.

17 David Margolick, "Picking of Judges Assailed by Cuomo," *New York Times*, 15 August 1983, pp. A1, B8.

18 David Margolick, "Challenge for Cuomo: Picking Judges," *New York Times*, 7 December 1984, p. B3.

19 "Judge Kaye for Chief Judge," *New York Times*, 6 February 1993, p. A20.

20 John Kincaid and Robert F. Williams, "The States' Lead in Rights Protection," *Journal of State Government* 65 (April-June 1992): 51.

21 Vincent M. Bonventre, "State Constitutional Adjudication at the Court of Appeals, 1990 and 1991: Retrenchment Is the Rule," *Albany Law Review* 56 (1992): 119, 120, 122.

22 William J. Brennan Jr., "A Tribute to Chief Judge Charles S. Desmond," *Buffalo Law Review* 36 (1987): 1, 3.

23 The brilliant judicial career of Sol Wachtler came to an abrupt ending in 1993 with his resignation from the Court of Appeals. The last member of the court to have gained by partisan election in 1972 the position of associate judge, he was appointed Chief Judge by Governor Mario Cuomo in 1985. In a series of bizarre and highly publicized events, Judge Wachtler was arrested on 7 November 1992 on charges of extortion and mailing threatening letters to the daughter of his former lover. On 1 April 1993, Judge Wachtler pleaded guilty to threatening to kidnap the daughter; he was sentenced in September 1993 to a term of fifteen months in a federal penitentiary. See Sol Wachtler, *After the Madness* (New York: Random House, 1997).

24 *Arcara v. Cloud Books, Inc.*, 68 NY2d 553.

25 *Arcara v. Cloud Books, Inc.*, 478 US 697.

26 Bonventre, "State Constitutional Adjudication," pp. 121, 142.

27 Vincent Martin Bonventre and John Powell, "Changing Course on the High Court, *Empire State Report* 20 (March 1994): 55, 57, 62.

28 Thirty-one states in 1992–93 used elections for selection of judges. Eighteen of those states used nonpartisan elections, thirteen used partisan. Lawrence Baum, *American Courts* (Boston: Houghton Mifflin, 1994), pp. 117, 122.

29 Bruce A. Green, *Government Ethics Reforms for the 1990s* (New York: Fordham University Press, 1991), pp. 280–81.

30 New York State Commission on Government Integrity, *Restoring the Public Trust: A Blueprint for Government Integrity* (New York, 1990), p. 16.

31 M. L. Henry Jr., *Characteristics of Elected versus Merit-Selected New York City Judges, 1977–1992* (New York: Fund for Modern Courts, 1992), p. 16.

32 Henry, *Characteristics of Elected*, pp. 6–7.

33 Task Force on Judicial Diversity, *Report* (Albany, 1992), Appendix B.

34 Task Force on Judicial Diversity, *Report*, pp. 14–15.

35 Ronald Sullivan, "Suit Challenges Process for Electing State Judges," *New York Times*, 19 February 1992, p. B3.

36 Charles A. Kuffner Jr., "Letter to the Editor," *New York Times*, 2 October 1992, p. A30.

37 Department of Correctional Services, *State of New York Executive Budget, 1992–1993: Agency Presentations*, p. 249.

38 Department of Correctional Services, *State of New York Executive Budget, 1992–1993*, p. 249.

39 Department of Correctional Services, *State of New York Executive Budget, 1992–1993*, p. 249.

40 Benjamin and Hurd, *Rockefeller in Retrospect*, p. 253.

41 Andy Danzo, "Penal Overload," *Empire State Report* 14 (January 1988): 46–47.

42 Marie Simonetti Rosen, "Who Is New York Jailing?" *Empire State Report* 17 (August 1991): 35, 33. Nonwhites, less than one-fifth of the state's population, accounted for four-fifths of its prison inmates in 1988.

43 Rosen, "Who Is New York Jailing?" p. 35.

44 Mario M. Cuomo, *Message to the Legislature, 1993* (Albany: Office of the Governor, 6 January 1993), p. 72.

45 Department of Correctional Services, *State of New York Executive Budget, 1992–1993*, p. 249.

CHAPTER TEN

1 For fiscal years ending in 1994, data came from the Office of the State Comptroller, *Comptroller's Special Report on Municipal Affairs* (Albany, 1995), Appendix B, pp. 650–51; figures updated to 1 September 1996 by Joseph Holland of the Municipal Affairs staff.

2 Joseph F. Zimmerman, *Measuring Local Discretionary Authority* (Washington DC: United States Advisory Commission on Intergovernmental Relations, 1981), p. 59.

3 Leonard W. Labaree, *Royal Government in America: A Study of the English Colonial System before 1783* (New Haven: Yale University Press, 1930).

4 New York Constitution, art. 23 (1777).

5 New York Constitution, art. 4, § 10 (1822).

6 New York Constitution, art. 4, § 10 (1833), and art. 4, § 10 (1839).

7 New York Constitution, art. 3, § 18 (1874).

8 New York Constitution, art. 12, § 2 (1894).

9 New York Constitution, art. 12, §§ 1–2 (1923).

10 New York Laws of 1928, chap. 670.

11 *Adler v. Deegan*, 251 N.Y. 467 at 473, 167 N.E. 705 at 707 (1929).

12 *Adler v. Deegan*, 251 N.Y. 467 at 491, 167 N.E. 705 at 714 (1929).

13 New York Constitution, art. 3, § 26(2) (1935).

14 New York Constitution, art. 9, §§ 11–13 (1938).

15 New York Constitution, art. 9, § 16 (1938).

16 New York Constitution, art. 9, §§ 1–2, 16 (1958).

17 New York Constitution, art. 9 (1994). See also *New York Statute of Local Governments; McKinney's Laws of New York Annotated* (St. Paul MN: West Publishing, 1969).

18 New York Laws of 1962, chap. 1009, and New York Town Law, §§ 50–58a (McKinney 1987 and 1996 Supp.).

19 New York Laws of 1976, chap. 805, § 1, and New York Municipal Home Rule Law, § 10(d)(3) (McKinney 1969).

20 "Advisory Opinion to Canandaigua Corporation Counsel, 5 June 1980," *Opinions of the Attorney General: 1980* (Albany: State of New York, 1981), pp. 164–68.

21 Joseph F. Zimmerman, *State Mandating of Local Expenditures* (Washington DC: U.S. Advisory Commission on Intergovernmental Relations, 1978).

22 New York Civil Service Law, § 209 (McKinney 1983 and 1993 Supp.). See also Mary B. Hagerty, "The Taylor Law: The Political Roles of Firemen and Policemen" (Ph.D. diss., State University of New York at Albany, 1992).

23 New York Laws of 1991, chap. 305, New York State Administrative Procedure Act, § 202(3)(e) (McKinney 1996 Supp.), and New York Laws of 1991, chap. 413. The latter chapter is an omnibus statute amending several consolidated laws. See, for example, New York General Municipal Law, § 104-b (McKinney 1996 Supp.).

24 New York Constitution, art. 8, § 10. See also Jon A. Bear, "State Fiscal Control of Local Governments: New York State's Debt and Tax Limits" (Ph.D. diss., State University of New York at Albany, 1993).

25 New York Constitution, art. 8, §§ 4–7.

26 *Town of Lockport v. Citizens for Community Action at the Local Level, Incorporated*, 423 U.S. 808 (1977).

27 New York Village Law, § 8–800 (McKinney 1973 and 1993 Supp.) and 18 Op. N.Y. State Comptroller 454 (1962).

28 Joe Picchi, "Wanted: One Supervisor for Town of Berlin," *Times Union* (Albany), 13 October 1993, p. B-7.

29 New York Election Law, § 15–104 (McKinney 1978 and 1996 Supp.).

30 New York Election Law, § 14–116(b) (McKinney 1978 and 1996 Supp.).

31 New York Town Law, § 10 (McKinney 1987).

32 New York Town Law, § 29 (McKinney 1987 and 1996 Supp.).

33 New York Town Law, § 52 (1987).

34 New York Town Law, § 58 (1987).

35 *Avery v. Midland County, Texas et al.*, 590 U.S. 474 (1968).

36 New York Municipal Home Rule Law, § 10(1)(a)(1) (McKinney 1969).

37 New York Municipal Home Rule Law, § 10(1)(b)(4) (McKinney 1969 and 1996 Supp.), and New York County Law, § 204 (McKinney 1991).

38 New York Constitution, art. 12, (1923).

39 Axelrod, *Shadow Government*.

40 Joseph F. Zimmerman, *Federal Preemption: The Silent Revolution* (Ames: Iowa State University Press, 1991). See also Joseph F. Zimmerman and Sharon Lawrence, *Federal Statutory Preemption of State and Local Authority* (Washington DC: U.S. Advisory Commission on Intergovernmental Relations, 1992).

41 Joseph F. Zimmerman, "Federally Induced State and Local Governmental Costs" (paper presented at the annual meeting of the American Political Science Association, Washington DC, 29 August–1 September 1991).

42 Governor's Blue Ribbon Commission on Consolidation of Local Governments, *Action Agenda: Setting the Stage for Regionalization and Local Government Cooperation in New York State* (Albany, 1993), p. 38.

43 State of New York, *Executive Budget, 1994–1995: Message to the Legislature* (Albany: Executive Chamber, 1994), p. M21.

44 Eleanor Ostrom, Roger B. Parks, and Gordon P. Whitaker, "Do We Really Want to Consolidate Urban Police Forces? A Reappraisal of Some Old Assumptions," *Public Administration Review* 33 (September/October 1973): 423–32.

45 Joseph F. Zimmerman and Richard Guastello, *Intergovernmental Service Agreements in New York State* (Albany: New York Conference of Mayors and Municipal Officials, 1973).

46 New York Laws of 1972, chap. 28.

47 New York Laws of 1981, chap. 707.

48 The county management system in the Republic of Ireland is an administrative innovation meriting close examination by local government officials and citizens in areas where the need for professional management and greater coordination of the activities of local governments is apparent and the desire to maintain local identity and governing bodies is strong. With the exception of Ireland's five cities, the county manager is the manager of all other local governments within the county. Under this system, executive integration and professional management exist within each county, yet policymaking remains decentralized. See Joseph F. Zimmerman, "Council-Manager Government in Ireland," *Studies in Comparative Local Government* 6, no. 1 (summer 1972): 61–69.

CHAPTER ELEVEN

1 Joseph P. Viteritti, "The Tradition of Municipal Reform: Charter Revision in Historical Context," in Frank Mauro and Gerald Benjamin, eds., *Restructuring the New York City Government: The Reemergence of Municipal Reform* (New York: Academy of Political Science, 1989), pp. 16–30.

2 Edward K. Spann, *The New Metropolis: New York City 1840–1857* (New York: Columbia University Press, 1980); see also Timothy J. Gilfoyle, *City of Eros: New York City, Prostitution and the Commercialization of Sex, 1790–1920* (New York: W. W. Norton, 1992).

3 Ira Katznelson, in *City Trenches: Urban Politics and the Patterning of Class in the United States* (Chicago: University of Chicago Press, 1982), gives a profile of how the demographic space of one neighborhood in northern Manhattan changed with the city's economy and ethnic makeup and how the interests of these groups citywide were never fully aligned due to local divisions.

4 David C. Hammack, *Power and Society: Greater New York at the Turn of the Century* (New York: Russell Sage Foundation, 1982).

5 The Metropolitan Police Force was created by the state legislature among the police forces of the older cities of New York and Brooklyn in the 1850s to provide regional coordination of police, professionalization of the service, and a broader tax base. Not incidentally, it also took management of the police out of the control of local party and ethnic networks.

6 The boundaries of New York City had expanded several times before its final and current geography. The initial New York City was located at the lower end of Manhattan Island. By the Civil War, New York took in all of Manhattan Island and included older commercial centers of Harlem and Greenwich Village. In 1874, the western part of the Bronx became part of the city of New York, and eventually all of the Bronx was included (which explains why Manhattan and the Bronx are in one state court division and Queens and Brooklyn are in another). When New York was reincorporated as it is today, it was composed of five counties and several smaller urban centers besides New York and Brooklyn, including Long Island City, Flushing and Jamaica in Queens, and St. George on Staten Island.

7 The Citizens Union, founded in 1897, was one arena in which reformers, businessmen, and academics could come together to press for a "good government" platform in New York City. Among the early tasks of the Municipal Research Bureau, founded in 1907 to apply scientific methods to urban governance in New York, was to provide background research for an improved civil service system. One young analyst, Robert Moses, had studied the British civil service system for his Ph.D. thesis. See Jane S. Dahlberg, *The New York Bureau of Municipal Research: Pioneer in Government Administration* (New York: New York University Press, 1966), chaps. 1 and 2.

8 See Michael N. Danielson and Jameson W. Doig, *New York: The Politics of Urban Regional Development* (Princeton: Princeton University Press, 1982), for a review of the greater New York economic region and its governing structure.

9 The annexation solution to regional growth has been a central strategy pursued by cities whose growth had outstripped their legal borders and tax bases. The Unigov' solution of Indianapolis, which merged the city of Indianapolis with most of its surrounding urban county, and Houston's ongoing annexation of contiguous land have been two of the most pronounced examples of the past twenty years. In such cities as Chicago, Los Angeles, and Miami, the transference of responsibilities to their larger urban counties has dealt with some of the revenue and policy responsibilities created by the growing metropolitan areas. In New York's case, neither solution is possible. The only strategies left to the city are transference of responsibility to the state of New York or to regional authorities and public benefit/enterprise corporations.

10 Organizational capacity is a dynamic concept. As a factor in governance, it is constantly challenged by growth in the fiscal base, social responsibilities, and political complexities of urban government. Ironically, political legitimacy was challenged at different points by two groups frequently in contention: new and evolving groups and identities seeking influence over city policymaking, and the business community and professionals of the middle classes seeking stability, economic growth, and a refined version of the older reform movement. The first challenge was expressed through the community movement and advocacy activism; the second challenge came through the reform and later through the demands for a more fiscally responsibility government in the city.

11 See Joseph P. Viteritti and Robert W. Bailey, "Capacity Building and Big City Governance," in Beth Walter Honadle and Arnold Howitt, eds. *Perspectives on Management Capacity Building* (Albany: State University of New York Press, 1986).

12 In the 1933 Bankers Agreement (a debt-refinancing covenant that offered cash-flow assistance to New York during the worst years of the Great Depression), the state created new fiscal controls for New York City. Similar controls were imposed during the 1970s when New York City again faced severe cash-flow problems. But the most critical restrictions on New York City's finances are the tax and bonding limitations incorporated as section 8 of the New York State Constitution.

13 These restraints come through a combination of imposed statutory and constitutional regulations in general and intergovernmental fiscal requirements associated with specific programs.

14 Excluding the veterans system, New York continues to maintain the largest public hospital system in the country at considerable capital and operating costs. See the discussion of the state-mandated local share of Medicaid in chapter 12.

15 In *Levittown v. Nyquist*, the New York State Court of Appeals accepted the submission by plaintiffs that the net school aid formulas are inequitable prima facie and even more so when one considers the imbalances in types of service demands presented to cities and some suburban jurisdictions by their residents. The court did not offer a remedy, however, saying it was the legislature's responsibility to develop appropriate fiscal policies for schools.

16 In the end, to save its own financial position, the state moved in to relieve New York City's cash flow problems by creating the Municipal Assistance Corporation for New York and the Financial Control Board.

17 Paul Peterson, *The Politics of School Reform: 1870–1940* (Chicago: University of Chicago Press, 1985); David Tyack, *The One Best System* (Cambridge: Harvard University Press, 1974).

18 Robert Caro, *The Power Broker* (New York: Random House, 1972).

19 For a history of the LaGuardia years in the economic and social context, see August Heckscher, *When LaGuardia Was Mayor: New York's Legendary Years* (New York: W. W. Norton, 1978).

20 Theodore J. Lowi, *At the Pleasure of the Mayor* (Glencoe IL: Free Press, 1964).

21 Edward I. Koch, with William Rauch, *Mayor: An Autobiography* (New York: Simon and Schuster, 1984), p. 183.

22 State of New York, State Charter Revision Commission for New York City (Senator Roy Goodman, chair), *Summary of Preliminary Recommendations*, 1975.

23 The New York State Temporary Commission for the Study of New York City was chaired by businessman William Scott. Stephen Berger was executive director.

24 See Ester Fuchs, *Mayors and Money: Fiscal Policy in New York and Chicago* (Chicago: University of Chicago Press, 1993), for a rigorous historical analysis of fiscal structures and politics in Chicago and New York; Liebschutz, *Bargaining under Federalism*, chap. 5, for an examination of the numerous issues and actors at city, state, and national levels in the bargaining around the crisis; and Robert W. Bailey, *The Crisis Regime: The M.A.C. the E.F.C.B. and the Political Impact of the New York City Financial Crisis* (Albany: State University of New York Press, 1984), for a more specific review of the actual impact of the 1975 crisis on New York's policymaking process.

25 The Office of Special Deputy Controller, which reports to the state comptroller, was given additional analytical and legal staff and was granted the sole responsibility to audit accounts, assess projections, and provide performance audits and managerial recommendations over New York City. The (Emergency) Financial Control Board has direct legal powers over the city's assets during financial emergency (control) periods, can regulate labor policy, and oversees the city's financial planning process. In addition, the Shinn Commission, created by Mayor

Abraham Beame, and the Mayor's Management Plan and Reporting System were among the changes.

26 For a more detailed perspective, see Robert Pecorella, *Community Power in a Postreform City: Politics in New York City* (Armonk NY: M. E. Sharpe, 1993). His analysis indicates that community boards still had uneven influence over decision making in budgeting, land use, and service administration.

27 The underlying intent was the application of the standards from *Baker v. Carr* and *Reynolds v. Sims* to the institutional structure of New York City government. See articles by Diaz and Macchiarola, Dunne, Grofman, and Gartner and Guinier in *Redistricting in the 1990s: The New York Example*, a special edition of *Cardozo Law Review* 14, no. 1 (April 1993).

28 John Mollenkopf, *A Phoenix in the Ashes: The Rise and Fall of the Koch Coalition in New York City Politics* (Princeton: Princeton University Press, 1993).

29 The following table shows how voter turnout rates among African Americans in major Democratic primaries by assembly districts increased dramatically throughout the 1980s:

Assembly Districts Defined as	1985 Mayoral Primary (%)	1988 Democratic Presidential Party (%)	1989 Mayoral Primary (%)
Black	26.8	48.3	70.9
Mixed	30.6	39.8	60.3
Latino	31.6	39.4	56.7
Liberal	36.7	44.7	43.1
White Catholic	30.9	40.5	36.4
Jewish	37.4	49.7	48.7
Total	32.6	45.0	49.9

Source: John Mollenkopf and J. Philip Thompson, "The Shifting Electoral Bases of New York City Politics: The David Dinkins Coalition" (paper presented at the annual meeting of the American Political Science Association, Washington DC, 29 August–1 September 1991).

30 See Jerome S. Legge Jr., "The Persistence of Ethnic Voting: African-Americans and Jews in the 1989 New York Mayoral Campaign" (paper presented at the annual meeting of the American Political Science Association, Chicago, 3–6 September 1992).

31 Stephen Elkin, *City and Regime in the American Republic* (Chicago: University of Chicago Press, 1987).

32 Thomas J. Condon, *New York Beginnings: The Commercial Origins of New Netherlands* (New York: New York University Press, 1968).

33 Danielson and Doig, *New York*, sec. 2.

34 Raymond Horton, *The City in Transition: The Final Report of the Temporary Commission on City Finances* (New York: Arno Press, 1978).

35 Only high value-added products that need small spaces for production could be made in Manhattan competitively, e.g., diamonds and jewelry, surgical equipment, computer software, specialty apparel. See, as an example, the report issued by the Office of the Borough President of Manhattan, *The Diamond Industry in New York* (New York, 1992).

36 Saskia Sassen, *Global Cities: New York, London and Tokyo* (Princeton: Princeton University Press, 1991).

37 Economic Trends Division, Office of Economic and Policy Analysis, Port Authority of New York and New Jersey, *Regional Economy: Review, 1992; Outlook, 1993 for the New York–New Jersey Metropolitan Region* (New York, April 1993).

38 See the monthly economic and revenue reports of the Office of Management and Budget, City of New York, which are based on Wharton Economic Forecast Associates and D.R.I., Inc., data.

39 The economic projections associated with the FY 1994–98 Financial Plan for New York City specifically state the dependence of the city on its service and FIRE (financial, insurance, and real estate) sectors as the locomotive of the regional economy: "after nearly five years of decline, New York City appears to be on the verge of a broad-based recovery which will lift nearly all sectors of the local economy. Employment, and more specifically private sector employment, the most widely followed measure of economic activity, peaked in the City in December, 1987 and fell practically every month until mid-1992 when it stabilized at approximately 2.7 million, about a year after U.S. employment bottomed. Since then, with the U.S. recovery gaining momentum and the securities industry resurgent, the City's important service and FIRE sectors received significant boosts and are expected to carry the rest of the economy out of its deep recession." Office of Management and Budget, City of New York, *United States and New York City Economic Outlooks: 1996–1998* (2 February 1994), p. 5.

40 Walter Stafford, *Closed Labor Markets: Underrepresentation of Blacks, Hispanics, and Women in New York City's Core Industries and Jobs* (New York: Community Service Society, 1985).

41 See Mollenkopf, *Phoenix in the Ashes*, and Sassen, *Global Cities*.

42 See the Port Authority's annual *Regional Economy: Review 1992*, "Statistical Compendium."

43 Robert W. Bailey, "Neo-Institutionalism and the Allocation of Debt Bearing Capacity in New York: A Case of Institutional Transformation" (Occasional Paper in Public Policy, Graduate Program in Public Policy and Administration, School of International and Public Affairs, Columbia University, 1993).

44 Oliver A. Rink, *Holland on Hudson: An Economic and Social History of Dutch New York* (Ithaca: Cornell University Press, 1986); and Spann, *New Metropolis.*

45 Robert F. Pecorella, "Community Governance: A Decade of Experience," in Mauro and Benjamin, *Reconstructing the New York City Government.* For a discussion of the 1990 investigation by the New York City Districting Commission of the possibility of coterminality of service districts with council district lines, see Joseph P. Viteritti, "Community Government, the City Council and the Reform Agenda: The Case for Full Coterminality" (report prepared for the New York City Districting Commission, Center for Management, Robert F. Wagner School of Pubic Service, New York University, 10 May 1991). For New York City Public Schools, see Diane Ravitch, *The Great School Wars* (New York: Basic Books, 1974). The specific difficulties in implementing change in New York's schools during the 1960s is documented in David Rogers, *110 Livingston Street: Politics and Bureaucracy in New York City Schools* (New York: Random House, 1968). For an assessment of the decentralization adapted for New York, see David Rogers and Norman H. Chung, *110 Livingston Street Revisited* (New York: New York University Press, 1983).

CHAPTER TWELVE

1 State government expenditures from all sources were $28.5 billion in 1982–83, the start of Cuomo's first term, and $60.9 billion in 1994–95, his last year in office; see Office of the State Comptroller, *Comprehensive Annual Financial Report of the Comptroller.* The consumer price index (with 1960 as the base year) increased from 99.6 in 1983 to 140.3 in 1994; see *Statistical Abstract of the United States.*

2 This explanation is consistent with evidence that governors, as chief executives, were accountable for the health of their state economies in the 1980s and 1990s; see Lonna Rae Atkeson and Randall W. Partin, "Economic and Referendum Voting: A Comparison of Gubernatorial and Senatorial Elections," *American Political Science Review* 89 (March 1995): 99–107; and Robert M. Stein, "Economic Voting for Governor and U.S. Senator: The Electoral Consequences of Federalism," *Journal of Politics* 52 (1990): 29–53. John Chubb, in contrast, found that state politicians during his period of research (1940 to 1982) were largely isolated from such accountability; see Chubb, "Institutions, the Economy and the Dynamics of State Elections," *American Political Science Review* 82 (March 1988): 133–54. See also Kevin M. Leyden and Stephen A. Borrelli, "The Effect of State Economic Conditions on Gubernatorial Elections: Does Unified Government Make a Difference?" *Political Research Quarterly* 48 (June 1995): 275–90.

3 James A. Barnes, "States' Evidence," *National Journal* 26 (12 November 1994): 2673.

4 Barnes, "States' Evidence," p. 2673.

5 George E. Pataki, "Remarks to the Heritage Foundation: July 12, 1995" (Albany: Executive Chamber, 1995), p. 3.

6 Pataki, *Message to the Legislature, 1995*, p. 1.

7 Joyce Purnick, "Core of Tax Cut Debate: New York's Self-Image," *New York Times*, 3 October 1994, p. B6.

8 Pataki, "Remarks to the Heritage Foundation," p. 3.

9 John Machacek, "Pataki Fights Plan to Cut New York's Federal Aid," *Democrat and Chronicle* (Rochester), 13 July 1995, p. B4.

10 Bahl and Duncombe, *Economic Growth*, p. 108.

11 Bahl and Duncombe, *Economic Growth*, p. 109.

12 Bahl and Duncombe, *Economic Growth*, p. 108.

13 Bahl and Duncombe, *Economic Growth*, pp. 112, 182–83.

14 Bahl and Duncombe, *Economic Growth*, p. 183.

15 See Mumpower and Ilchman, *New York State*, p. 310.

16 Pataki, *Message to the Legislature*, 1995, pp. 13, 7.

17 Diane Rowland, "Medicaid at 30: New Challenges for the Nation's Health Safety Net," *Journal of American Medical Association* 274 (19 July 1995): 271.

18 Steve Cole, "Winners and Losers: States Could Suffer as Congress Divides the Medicaid Pie," *Health Systems Review* 28 (May/June 1995): 18.

19 Bruce Bryant-Friedland, "Medicaid Makeover," *Empire State Report* 21 (March 1995): 39.

20 See Jane Sneddon Little, "Why State Medicaid Costs Vary: A First Look" (Federal Reserve Bank of Boston, working paper series, August 1991), pp. 29–30; and Sarah F. Liebschutz, "Political Conflict and Intergovernmental Relations: The Federal-State Dimension," in Stonecash, White, and Colby, *Governing New York State*.

21 Kent Gardner and Bethany St. Dennis, *Medicaid Cost Containment for New York* (Rochester: Center for Governmental Research, 1995).

22 Gardner and St. Dennis, *Medicaid Cost Containment*, pp. 16, 7.

23 Gardner and St. Dennis, *Medicaid Cost Containment*, p. 7.

24 Bryant-Friedland, "Medicaid Makeover," p. 47.

25 State of New York, Department of Labor, Division of Research and Statistics, *Employment in New York State* (Albany, July 1995).

26 Mark Lawton, "Three Case Studies in Budgeting," *Empire State Report* 5 (June/July 1979).

27 James E. Fossett, "The Complex Puzzle That Is Medicaid," *Times Union* (Albany), 18 December 1994, p. E6. See also James E. Fossett, "Medicaid and Health Reform: The Case of New York," *Health Affairs* (fall 1993).

28 Liebschutz, "Political Conflict," p. 58.

29 See Lawton, "Three Case Studies"; and New York State Division of the Budget, *The Executive Budget in New York State: A Half Century Perspective* (Albany: Division of the Budget, 1981) for elaboration of these reform efforts.

30 Bryant-Friedland, "Medicaid Makeover," p. 40.

31 Fossett, "Medicaid and Health Reform," p. 90.

32 Health Care Association of New York State (HANYS), "Memo on Final State Budget" (Albany, 12 June 1995), p. 1.

33 Business Council of New York, Health Committee, "Newsletter" (Albany, June 1995).

34 HANYS, "Memo," p. 1.

35 Paul Brace, *State Government and Economic Performance* (Baltimore: Johns Hopkins University Press, 1994), p. 60.

36 Frank J. Mauro and Glenn Yago, "State Government Targeting in Economic Development: The New York Experience," *Publius* 19 (spring 1989): 65, 66.

37 Brace, *State Government and Economic Performance*, p. 64.

CHAPTER THIRTEEN

The author appreciates the research assistance of Kathleen A. Frank and Sean Rickert in the preparation of this chapter.

About the Authors

Sarah F. Liebschutz is distinguished service professor emeritus of political science at the State University of New York, College at Brockport, where she was a member of the faculty from 1970 to 1997. A specialist in intergovernmental relations, she is the author of several monographs on New York State. She also wrote *Bargaining under Federalism* (1991) and *Federal Aid to Rochester* (1984).

Robert W. Bailey is assistant professor, Graduate Faculty of Public Policy and Administration, Rutgers University. His primary research interests are in urban politics and public management. He served on the graduate public policy faculty of Columbia University from 1985 to 1993.

Jeffrey M. Stonecash is professor of political science, the Maxwell School, Syracuse University. His research focuses on state political parties, their electoral bases, and their roles in shaping state policy debates about state–local relations and state assumption of fiscal responsibilities.

Jane Shapiro Zacek is director of Foundation and Government Support and adjunct professor of political science, Union College. She spent eleven years in New York state government, in the Division of Management/Confidential Affairs, Governor's Office of Employee Relations, and as senior project director, Rockefeller Institute of Government, State University of New York.

Joseph F. Zimmerman is a professor of political science at the Graduate School of Public Affairs, State University of New York at Albany. His most recent books include *Interstate Relations: The Neglected Dimension of Federalism* (1996) and *State–Local Relations: A Partnership Approach* (2d ed., 1995).

Index

taxation: high rate of New York, 169–
70; legacy of Rockefeller administration's high, 102; ratio of personal
income to revenues of, 101; reform
of New York, 90–91; under Cuomo
governorship, 107
Tax Reform Act of 1986, 57, 90–91
Taylor Law, 115
temperance movement, 27–28
Temporary Commission on Constitu-
tional Revision, 40–41
Temporary State Commission on Regu-
lation of Lobbying, 30
Tese, Vincent, 116
third political parties, 63–64
Thruway Transit Authority, 119
Tilden, Samuel J., 26, 48
Times Union (newspaper), 180
Town Court, 125
town governance system, 144–45
Town Law, 139, 140, 145
Transport Workers Union strike (1966),
156
Trial of Impeachment, 43
Triangle Shirt Waist Factory fire (1910),
19, 51–52, 191 n.49
Tweed, William March, 26

ultra vires rule (Dillon's Rule), 40, 136,
137–38, 148
Unfunded Mandates Reform Act of
1995, 54–55
unions, right to organize, 33
United States v. New York, 49, 50–51
United States v. New York Times Co.,
49, 50
upstate New York, 14–15
Urban Development Corporation
(UDC), 113, 116, 120, 121

urban-industrial frontier, 16
U.S. Advisory Commission on Intergovernmental Relations (ACIR), 57
U.S. Congress: New York House delegation to, 53–55; New York senators in, 51–53
U.S. Supreme Court, 49–51, 132–33,
142, 146

Van Amsterdam, Volckert Jan Pietersen
("Baas") [fictional character], 13
Van Buren, Martin, 24, 48
Varvalho, Barbara, 72
veto power, 96–97
Village Court, 125
village governance system, 145–46
Village Law, 140, 142, 145–46
voters: bases of partisan groups of, 66;
low turnout of New York, 73; NYC
ethnic blocks of, 160, 216 n.29 n.30;
political party enrollment of, 199
n.21; rise of independent, 74–75;
split-ticket, 75–76, 199 n.22; supporting Dinkins/Giuliani coalitions, 161–
62; turnout of African American, 216
n.29. *See also* political parties
Voting Rights Act, 132

Wachtler, Sol, 130, 131, 209 n.23
Wagner, Robert F., 51–52, 156
Wagner Act, 52
Walker, James J. "Jimmy," 29
Watergate scandal, 65
Weed, Thurlow, 24
Weprin, Saul, 89
West's New York Digest, 183
Whig party, 24. *See also* Republican
party
Willowbrook Developmental Center,
117